The
TYRANT
and the
TEEN

In 1968, an Australian teenager narrowly escaped the clutches of Philippines dictator Ferdinand Marcos. She lived to tell the tale ... for those who didn't.

Stephanie McCarthy

Mechanicsburg, PA USA

Published by Sunbury Press, Inc.
Mechanicsburg, PA USA

www.sunburypress.com

Copyright © 2026 by Stephanie McCarthy.
Cover Copyright © 2026 by Sunbury Press, Inc.

Sunbury Press supports copyright. Copyright fuels creativity, encourages diverse voices, promotes free speech, and creates a vibrant culture. Thank you for buying an authorized edition of this book and for complying with copyright laws. Except for the quotation of short passages for the purpose of criticism and review, no part of this publication may be reproduced, scanned, or distributed in any form without permission. You are supporting writers and allowing Sunbury Press to continue to publish books for every reader. For information contact Sunbury Press, Inc., Subsidiary Rights Dept., PO Box 548, Boiling Springs, PA 17007 USA or legal@sunburypress.com.

For information about special discounts for bulk purchases, please contact Sunbury Press Orders Dept. at (855) 338-8359 or orders@sunburypress.com.

To request one of our authors for speaking engagements or book signings, please contact Sunbury Press Publicity Dept. at publicity@sunburypress.com.

FIRST SUNBURY PRESS EDITION: January 2026

Set in Adobe Garamond | Interior design by Crystal Devine | Cover by Maurice Linehan and Lawrence Knorr | Edited by Abigail Bunner.

Publisher's Cataloging-in-Publication Data
Names: McCarthy, Stephanie, author.
Title: The tyrant and the teen : in 1968, an Australian teenager narrowly escaped the clutches of Philippines dictator Ferdinand Marcos. She lived to tell the tale . . . for those who didn't.
Description: First trade paperback edition. | Mechanicsburg, PA : Sunbury Press, 2026.
Summary: A dangerous political environment underpins this extraordinary story whereby a Western Exchange student found herself in the clutches of the charming, lecherous, murderous Philippines president—Ferdinand Marcos. The traumatised teenager found a way to escape, but in the ensuing battle for freedom many brave Filipinos died. In exposing the tyrant, this book honours them.
Identifiers: ISBN : 979-8-88819-369-3 (softcover).
Subjects: BIOGRAPHY & AUTOBIOGRAPHY / Asian & Asian American | BIOGRAPHY & AUTOBIOGRAPHY / Political | BIOGRAPHY & AUTOBIOGRAPHY / Historical.

Designed in the USA
0 1 1 2 3 5 8 13 21 34 55

For the Love of Books!

Author's royalties from the sale of this book will be donated to the Bantayog ng mga Bayani Foundation, a "Monument of Heroes" created to honour all those who died fighting for freedom during the Ferdinand Marcos dictatorship. It serves to remind us and future generations to never again take our democracy for granted.

Prologue

Almost sixty years further on I look down a tunnel into the past to see a young version of myself, a stranger, sitting far away in a pool of light. The teenager perches stiffly on the edge of the four-poster bed, hands clasped tight in her lap, breathing deeply to overcome her fear.

She is only vaguely aware that the coverlet is vast and white, and the posts are elegant and intricately carved. But one thing is certain—this bedroom is fit for a king.

Not far from the bed stands a wooden table. On its polished surface gleams a bottle of whisky and two crystal tumblers. This is a table for two. She glances at the door to the adjoining bathroom. The day has been hot and humid. She longs for a shower. But to undertake that would be too risky. She knows the moment she steps naked under the shower he will arrive. Besides, her instincts tell her it is imperative that her suitcase remains unopened. There must be no indication that she has accepted being a guest in one of his private houses. *His guest*! Beads of sweat break out on her forehead.

She recalls a discussion between two Filipinos only days after her arrival in Manila. The friends were discussing how Ferdinand Marcos as a teenager had murdered his father's political opponent in cold blood. Then the topic switched to his keeping of mistresses in Forbes Park, nicknamed "Millionaires' Row." One man claimed that the president was clever and could get away with murder. The other agreed, adding there was one crime the president could not commit in this Catholic country—getting caught! They had brayed with mirth, and she had chuckled with them.

She wasn't laughing anymore. How could the mature age President Marcos have regarded the seventeen-year-old exchange student as a potential mistress when he had invited her to "be his guest and see some of the beautiful island of Luzon"? Didn't he realize that his "guest" would assume she would be staying with the first man and his family at

Malacañang Palace? It dawns on her now that the president may never have heard of Rotary Exchange. As for her age, she knew from the moment she arrived in his country that most Filipinos saw her to be at least twenty. Why should Marcos be any different?

An escape strategy begins forming in her mind, but whether she will succeed depends upon several unknowns. First and foremost—can she persuade Marcos that it won't be good for his reputation to have even one night unaccounted for? Both she and the president will need to tell the same story, so she determines to repeat the mantra "for your reputation as well as mine." She will assure him that she can convince her Filipino friends that she had been in fantasy land in presuming that the president had invited her to the palace—from the beginning he had always meant to put her up at the Manila Hotel. She will pretend that she requested to forgo the hotel and stay instead with her original host family in Manila.

The second unknown is whether Marcos will eventually force himself upon her. The bedroom has no windows, but she knows it must be pitch-black outside. An hour ago, hearing the crunch of gravel on the driveway she had run out to the hallway expecting to meet the president and begin her strategy before it got any later. Instead, Colonel Fabian Ver—the rugged Marcos strongman—had towered over her in the doorway with apologies from his "boss" who was unavoidably delayed. After listening gravely to her proposition he replied, "Only the president can say ma'am. You must wait until the president comes." And with that he had walked out, leaving her alone as before. And very, very frightened.

An idea! The telephone. She springs to her feet, hurries from the bedroom to the lounge and dials the number of her host family. Puzzled, she hangs up and dials again. But there is no mistaking that silence. The line is dead.

Back in the bedroom, she fights a rising panic. It must be 11 p.m.! Please let him arrive soon. When he does, she knows she has only one chance to convince the most powerful man in the Philippines to let her spend the next twelve nights at her host's house. She must not babble. She must sound reasonable, so mature in fact that for a moment she might possess power equal to his. She must make him understand that while many people know of her being in Manila as his guest, she is also capable of keeping this meeting and his private house secret. If anyone discovers the truth, an international incident is likely. A public scandal with a teenage Westerner would tip Marcos out of office in a blink. She has no doubt the president will do anything to avoid that happening.

Anything at all.

January, February, March 1968
Location: South Australia

It was a typical summer afternoon in the Adelaide Hills—stinging hot and tinder dry. The heat didn't worry me at all, and I swung my racquet hard and joined in the laughter whenever I missed the ball. My friends may have been wearing Volley tennis shoes, but my feet were bare and liking the feel of the grass as I played. Dad had lovingly kept the court green and flat as a billiard table, but I didn't fully appreciate the work he'd put into it. The world was about me, wasn't it? Life was one big buzz. I had recently turned seventeen, on the same day I left school forever. I had stacks of loyal friends both male and female, and although I wasn't centrefold material, I knew that I was attractive to the opposite sex. Steve (SJ) and I had fallen seriously for each other, my parents were funny and loving and interesting, and I had just received a letter signed from Prime Minister Gorton that I had won a Commonwealth University Scholarship. And the cherry on the cake? The scholarship would be held over for a year because, as an exchange student, I would soon be headed for Zamboanga in the Philippines. Zamboanga! How romantic! How exotic! And dubbed, City of Flowers! Oh yes, the world was my oyster, and I was its pearl.

One of us whacked the ball too high, and we watched it arc up and over the wire fence. That was when we saw the smoke drifting up from the canopies of gumtrees and feral olives in the valley below. Laughter stopped. We sniffed the air, on full alert, uncomfortably aware of the density of foliage as far as the eye could see. My brother Steve and our two friends raced to the horse shed to grab some hessian feed sacks and fill buckets while I sprinted up to the house to ring the fire brigade. My mind was racing. Both Mum and Dad had gone out, so we teenagers would have to deal with the situation ourselves. My family had owned this lovely old home for less than two years, and the thought of it going up in smoke, along with the venerable olive tree gracing its side, did not bear thinking about. And Mum's beloved horse—in the paddock! For one selfish second I also envisaged my year in the Philippines going up in smoke.

Armed with buckets and the wet sacks, high on adrenalin, the four of us sprinted up the road until we could see flames fanning upwards towards the houses overlooking the valley. With each blow of our heavy bags we sweated, gasping out a word or two only when needed. By the time we heard the fire sirens, we'd already done a creditable job in preventing the flames from reaching the first house in the firing line.

The fire was conquered. Our house was saved, and so was my trip of a lifetime!

The departure date was early March when I'd fly from Adelaide to Manila via Sydney. The idea was that for the first week I'd be staying in Manila in the house owned by the mother of the president of the Zamboanga Rotary Club, (pronounced "Zambwunga"), before flying south to the old city and staying approximately one month with a different Rotarian family. There were so many things to prepare and so many friends to farewell right up to D-day. As for taking leave of those I truly loved, including my boyfriend SJ, I couldn't imagine how I would survive the pain of not seeing them for eleven months. Should the homesickness become unbearable, I harboured a "last resort" hope of contacting them by phone, but it was common knowledge that telecommunications between all countries was fearfully expensive, and that conversations between Australia and Asia would sound scratchy, almost inaudible. The next best form of communication would be by tape recorder—that way at least I could hear their voices, even though the events they'd be describing would already be weeks or months old.

There'd be letters back and forth. Looking back, it was more than a hundred in total, and all those received by my family would be stored safely for future reference. Not only would I need to respond to each of my friends, but to my family and the members of the Rotary Club who

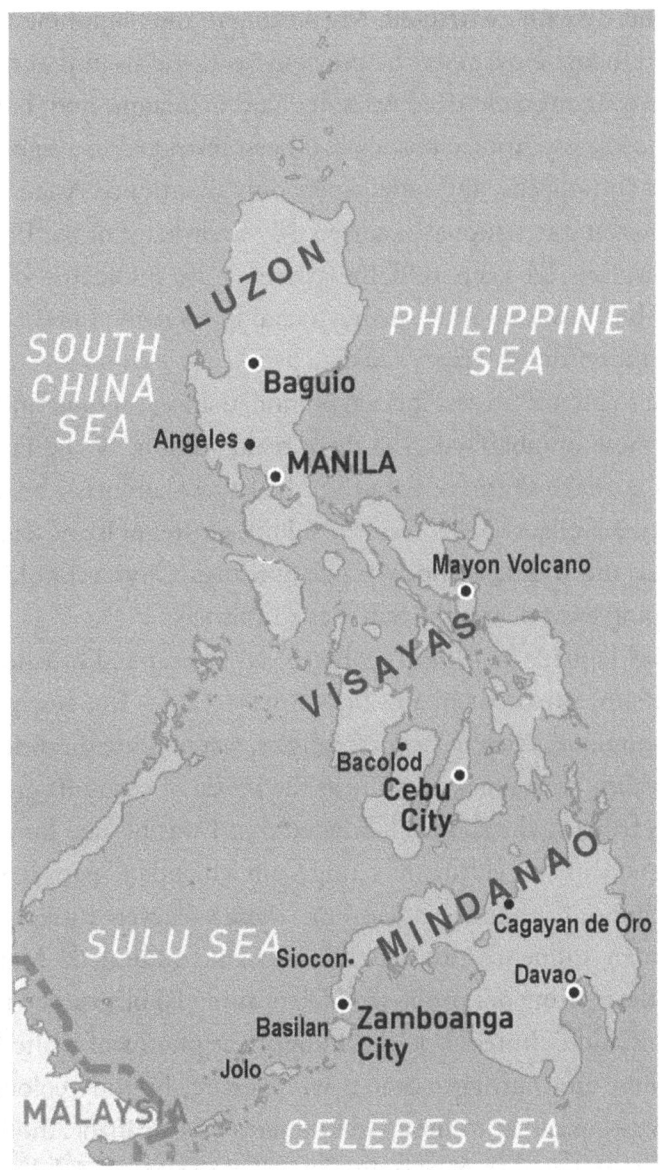

Map of Philippines highlighting relevant places.

expected monthly reports on my progress. Some of my school mates headed off to other more Western countries with similar lifestyles to Australia, and they were not asked to write such reports. The Philippines, on the other hand, was virtually unknown to Australians in 1968. Not once in my seventeen years had any of my family or friends met a Filipino.

I felt heady with excitement. My posting to the Philippines had been formalised in late November the previous year, and from that moment I had pored over our table-sized Atlas. It's hard to imagine now, but Google was unknown, my history lessons had been restricted to English battles and kings and queens, and newspapers only mentioned Asian countries when something sensational occurred. My knowledge of the Philippines was almost nil. I'd been told the name of its president—Ferdinand Marcos—but it was no more than a meaningless name I needed to hold in my memory for diplomacy's sake.

I tried to picture an archipelago of more than seven thousand islands, many of these uninhabited. The three main sections of the Philippines are, from north to south; one, Luzon, the largest landmass, boasting the capital city, Manila; two, Visayas, the middle cluster of islands; and three, Mindanao, the widest island, with Zamboanga City overlooking small isles stepping away across the Sulu Sea to Borneo.

By mid-January in 1968, I had received a letter and brochures from Charlie Reith, president of my host Rotary Club. The glossy pictures revealed mountains rich in tropical jungles, waterfalls and exotic flowers, and a coastline with sands as white as the inside of coconuts growing on the palms fringing the shores. It seemed that I was headed for a tropical paradise and a quaint culture resulting from a blend of Spanish, Chinese, native Filipino, Catholic and Muslim. There was even a touch of Swiss and German influence, as Charlie's surname indicated. Manila was dubbed "the melting pot of the world," meaning I'd be exposed to a great many races and cultures. I peered hungrily at photos of white beaches, coral islands, and outrigger canoes with square, brightly-coloured sails called vintas—peculiar to the southern part of Mindanao. Another oddity was an antiquated form of transport called a calesa, a high buggy with cart-sized wheels pulled by a small horse. Then there was Fort Pilar, built by the Spanish as an outpost in 1635 to guard the southern coastline. It might as well have been another planet, yet within a matter of weeks I'd be witnessing all these marvels with my own eyes.

At that crucial moment in my life, I felt I was poised on the edge of tomorrow, a tomorrow that shone and beckoned like the biggest brightest

Vintas and Nipa huts together on the sea.

star in the universe. My parents were fearful of letting me go alone to an Asian country they knew nothing about, suspecting from news items that all of Asia could be volatile. However, they became reassured by a more travelled person that Filipino girls traditionally were heavily chaperoned, courtesy of the all-pervading Spanish Catholic culture. By implication, I, as a teenager, would be too. Secretly, whenever the word "chaperone" was mentioned, my heart sank. After all, I was an Aussie girl born to liberal parents who had trusted me to conduct my own affairs. There had been dating rules of course, about my arriving home at a respectable time of the night, but because my parents had always set clear and reasonable boundaries; I strove to please them. My older brother Steve and I felt secure and loved. We were free to achieve whatever we could, and now that we understood childhood was over, responsibility for our own behaviour was expected. The possibility of being chaperoned at every step was chilling. Quietly I resolved to deal with that little problem when it arose, making sure that my mature side was displayed to every one of my Filipino host families in the hope that they would become increasingly complacent about my welfare.

No one had told me I should be careful what I wished for—with freedom would come a price, and that price would be danger in a variety of forms. But I was young, and therefore immortal, wasn't I?

One of my close friends had a mum who could sew, a skill unknown in my household. This wonderful woman decided she would make me a blouse and two dresses for my year in the tropics, and I can remember every detail of these garments. One dress was crisp white cotton, sleeveless, with a roll neck, and it curved to my figure which was my best asset. I had a small waist, a slim back, legs not quite long enough for a model, and big breasts. While I had cursed those bouncing breasts every Sports Day, I was now aware that these mammary items on a slim body tended to pique boys' interest, and so I chose to look on the bright side. The second dress also hugged my curves and was sleeveless, but this was a pale pink chiffon with a drape low on the back, more of an evening dress with a hemline just above the knees. Nevertheless, it was this one I chose to wear for the long plane ride all the way to the Philippines. A trip in a plane was a big deal, especially one flying into the vast unknown, and for this grand event one was expected to dress accordingly.

In the 60s I knew many people who had never been on a plane either big or small, and so I guess I was one of the lucky ones. When I was ten, I had been invited to ride in a Cessna, and although it felt as though I were inside a winged lawnmower, the bird's eye view of a farmhouse as we swooped low over the gum trees and hills was exhilarating. Then, during the first two years of my secondary schooling, I had experienced several DC3 flights between the fishing town of Port Lincoln where my family then lived, and the city of Adelaide where I was "incarcerated" within Woodlands Church of England Girls' boarding house. On those trips back and forth I wore my nurse-like uniform complete with suspenders and thick brown denier stockings, so there was no chance of feeling chic.

The poor old DC3 workhorses had a habit of shuddering, and when the shaking became particularly violent, I always comforted myself with the DC3's flawless safety record, which some kind soul had mentioned. Maybe they'd lied, but I chose to believe them.

When I was almost fourteen and still a boarder, Dad was studying ophthalmology and so needed to be based near the Eye Department of the Royal Adelaide Hospital. Sadly this meant a life-changing move from our beloved country town of Port Lincoln to Adelaide, my Mum doing all the packing up and driving behind the removal van for the 800 km to the big smoke. She wept silently as she drove, so greatly did she love Lincoln and the activities it offered. The upside of the move was that I would be freed from the "prison" at Woodlands to once more live with my family. Another great plus—our rented bungalow was a stone's throw from the Brighton jetty, so my studies were badly neglected as I seized every spare moment to be at the beach, on the jetty, or in the water. By contrast my poor father swatted every evening in his small den, with the eye sockets of his only companion (a genuine human skull) staring at him accusingly from where it sat on his desk.

Eventually, at the beginning of my sixteenth year, we moved from our rental by the sea to a house in the foothills on a large rambling property. Now we had room for our beloved dog Dash, several chickens, and a horse called Lochinvar. In that year I would meet SJ, my first serious boyfriend, and because he attended the same school as my brother, notes of great passion passed back and forth every day, with Steve acting as courier.

I was a virgin when I left for the Philippines, just so we're clear about that. In my thirteenth year I'd had my first kiss from a boy neighbour in Port Lincoln, but this lad made a big mistake in thinking that his tongue down my throat would suddenly render him wildly attractive. After that it took a while before I had the urge to kiss a boy. Also, I had been mildly assaulted (if there is such a thing as "mild assault") by an old male friend of my family, and that had rocked me to my core. But apart from that, and some very willing "pashing" with SJ, I had remained a virgin. In those days the fear of getting pregnant before marriage loomed large over every "decent" girl.

And so, at the start of 1968, life seemed like some magnificent dream. For this naïve, "decent" teenager, the cherry on the cake would be one huge adventure in a far-flung exotic land called the Philippines.

* * *

On 4 March 1968, I stood amongst a large group of friends and family in the Adelaide airport, which comprised a vast low shed with glass windows overlooking a paddock with a few runways. Compared to my previous experiences travelling by air, I felt like a glamourous jetsetter in my new pink dress, waiting in a confused clash of excitement and dread to board the plane to Sydney. Everyone was trying to smile and laugh, but there was tension too. Abruptly, it was time to go, and I whirled around in a flurry of hugs and tears and promises. I knew Mum was struggling not to cry, but over the last weeks I had steeled myself not to blubber at the last moment. After all, a swollen wet red face is not the last impression a girl wants to bequeath to anyone, especially her boyfriend.

With a huge effort at dignity I turned and walked out through the glass door, heading for the DC3. Clutching my handbag and my "cossie" case, I reached the foot of the gangway, turning to give a lingering, wistful wave. Then I stepped up towards the welcoming crew, their outlines blurring as I struggled to hold back a tsunami of tears, glad that I had armed myself with a hanky the size of a dishcloth. Ensconced in my seat, squinting through the cabin window, I yearned to catch one last glimpse of all those I loved. I had always treasured friends and family, but it was only now when my heart felt stabs of pain that I realized the excruciating extent of that love. The aircraft was positioned so that it cruelly blocked my line of sight to the building, but I waved to no one as the tears gushed forth and I saw nothing that made sense anymore.

By the time we touched down in Sydney my eyes must have dried, because in a letter written the following day, I admitted to feeling slightly scared in Sydney's bigger and more complex airport. Somehow I managed to get myself on the right plane, a Qantas aircraft, a juggernaut compared with the DC3s I had experienced. With the window seat all to myself, I became entranced as we flew over the iconic Harbor Bridge, then north towards lush green mountains and waterways that slowly gave way to the red drainage-patterned plain of outback Queensland and the town of Mt Isa. Over New Guinea it was frustratingly cloudy. An American businessman looked over his shoulder and began a conversation, eventually offering to look after me if my Filipino contact did not turn up.

The clouds lifted as we neared the numerous islands of the Philippines, and my first impressions were of a green and mountainous landscape with smoke rising from the top of every mountain and shimmering silver rice paddies on the plains. By late afternoon I was gazing down over Luzon Harbor to see a myriad of fishing nets and an army of cargo ships. Then I spied the Manila airport, a flat building on a flat plain. Hundreds of Filipinos had collected and were looking up, waving, and while I fantasised that they were all there to welcome me, my common sense told me to get real. Anyway, all I actually needed was the president of the Zamboanga Rotary Club to somehow identify himself and help me feel secure and safe in this alien country.

Seven months before meeting President Ferdinand Marcos
Location: Manila, Philippines
Host family — Reith

My first step down the gangway—I stopped as if I'd been slapped in the face. The smell! Multiple odours! In dry South Australia it never occurred to me that I had a sense of smell, except for that scary whiff of the bushfire smoke a fortnight earlier. But now I stood in the hot and heavy moisture-laden air of the tropics, a hearty mix of good and bad, sweet and sour, pungent as curry and sewage stew.

Charlie Reith, who while having a youthful appearance did not look *quite* as glamourous as his photo, was waiting in the reception area. He grinned from ear to ear and the smile was genuine. He tipped the porter as his driver stepped forward to take my luggage. Like most Aussies I felt uncomfortable with the idea of tipping, but because I was female and young and a guest in this country, I guessed I'd rarely be called to do so.

Sedately the driver drove a big red Dodge with Charlie alongside him. Seated in the back, I peered around avidly to catch every single image of suburban Manila, occasionally remembering to talk to Charlie. We were driving on the right side of the road—the wrong side!—weaving between gaudily painted jeepneys and psychedelic taxicabs along grubby streets lined with ramshackle wooden shops. A few Filipinos were walking alongside the ditches on the dusty verges. Some were dressed neatly in shirts or dresses, but many wore ragged clothes and had bare feet. Most footwear consisted of dusty rubber flip-flops.

Eventually we arrived at the walled city of San Lorenzo Village. The guards acknowledged the car, and the gates glided inwards. At a sedate pace we drove into a manicured haven of green palms and lawns glittering with purple and pink bougainvillea, the low houses typically rendered in white and every square inch sparkling clean. Even the smooth tarmac of each street sparkled! It was a small slice of paradise in the middle of a vastly grimier side of life, and I began to understand that within the Philippines there was an entrenched apartheid, not between skin colours, but between extreme wealth and extreme poverty.

Waiting to greet me inside the cool house was Charlie's mother, Mrs Reith. Petite and dark-haired, immaculately groomed and dressed, Susie Reith was wise and gracious with a wonderful smile. I immediately loved her. She looked about thirty-five, but I found out later she was actually forty-five. Her English was quite easy to understand, and charming because she placed emphasis on all the wrong syllables. Two maidservants were hovering by, but it was Mrs Reith who led me to my bedroom, a sweet space filled with sunlight and crisp white linen with green palms peeping through the window.

Then it was dinnertime. Mrs Reith excused herself—I came to understand that she ate sparingly and mostly in private. I was ushered by the head servant Augustine (pronounced "Owgoosteen") to a table where I sat between Charlie and his much younger brother, George. This tall, gangly youth with white pimply skin could easily have been mistaken for a Westerner—his features indicating he had collected more of his father's Swiss-German genes. Mrs Reith had divorced soon after George was born, and as I came to know her youngest child it was sadly obvious that he needed the guidance of a wise father. Instead, he constantly searched for that male mentor amongst his brothers who were not only much older but had been educated in Switzerland.

Impossibly gregarious and with a pronounced American accent, George immediately began describing his studies to become a medical student at Manila University. The quiet and ever-attentive Augustine kept filling up my glass of juice after I'd taken the slightest sip, and every now and again he'd vanish and then magically reappear with the next course, all of which came separately. First the vegetables, then the rice, and last of all—steak! In a letter I gloated about this to my family, because we rarely ate steak—it was way too expensive compared with lamb, which was delicious and relatively cheap in Australia. The juice tasted like fresh lemon with sugar and was incredibly refreshing in a climate with high temperature and humidity remaining high even after dark. This "lemonade" of the Philippines was squeezed from the calamansi, the only citrus fruit in Asia. Eventually, when Charlie managed to slip a word in, he mentioned the family's coconut plantation, Patalon, situated just out of Zamboanga. George piped up, "It's fifteen hundred acres Stephanie, all the palms grow right down to the beaches. They are purest white and there are horses. You like horses don't you? So you can gallop through all the plantation and swim as much as you want. Have you ever ridden a horse? Do you like swimming?" It became apparent George had not been told much about me, and he didn't care. I was a novelty; I had arrived, and that was that.

The boyish Charlie looked down at his apple strudel, smiling to himself. He had already examined the information about his Rotary Club's first exchange student and knew that my mother was a skilled rider and owned a horse. He was aware that I loved the ocean with a passion and could swim and ride horses. After all, I had been raised as a child in Port Lincoln, the fishing town abutting the Great Southern Ocean. Just before I left for the Philippines, the *Lincoln Times* got wind of me being awarded an exchange scholarship and published an article that made brief mention of me and where I was headed before devoting the remainder of the article to my parents. Dr Wicks, who had been a doctor in Port Lincoln for many years and who loved sailing, and Mrs Wicks, who was a champion horse woman on Eyre Peninsula, and who had taken on many lead acting roles in the Port Lincoln Players—all top gossip in a small country town.

The meal finished, and suddenly I was tired. I'd had little sleep since the eve of my departure from Australia. But when Charlie invited me to see *To Sir with Love*, all weariness vanished. What a novel experience this would be—to see a black person playing the lead role!

It was just Charlie and me in the Dodge, but this time the pace was not as sedate. Charlie fancied himself as a racing driver. While it was the norm for me to ride unrestrained in cars, I nevertheless attempted to avoid death by clutching the seat with one hand and a lock of my hair with the other. The Dodge swerved and ducked through narrow streets amidst a maze of jeepneys, bicycles, tricycles, and taxicabs. The barrage of noise—the beeping and honking and trilling of bells—assaulted my senses. Abruptly, we broke out into fast-moving traffic roaring along a boulevard flooded with light. At one stage, with three cars on either side of us, Charlie hit the accelerator once more and we began zipping in and out through the tiniest gaps between vehicles. That was, until we spotted a roadblock ahead and Charlie screeched to a halt, finishing up a hair's breadth away from armed guards who glanced at us and waved us on. As we hurtled off into the dance of death once again, I asked Charlie what the guards were looking for. "Bad types," he answered. I was perplexed. *What do "bad types" actually look like, and what might they do?*

Charlie slammed on the brakes in front of a shapeless monolith which proved to be a hotel. An undernourished, ragged urchin with windmilling arms guided us into a parking space before flinging open my door, his face serious as a judge. Charlie tipped him fifty centavos before we hailed a small taxicab painted in fluorescent multi-coloured swirls. Most of the time I squeezed my eyes shut for this mad drive into the heart of Manila. At last we came to a skidding halt in front of the cinema on a dark street. Poor people, mostly youths, clustered around in groups on the sidewalk. We entered the cinema, ascending an escalator to get to our seats. The national anthem started up and everyone stood and sang along with genuine fervour, a wondrous experience for an Aussie who had only ever heard "God Save the Queen" sung falteringly, even reluctantly. The film itself was riveting, Sidney Poiter giving a superb portrayal of the beleaguered teacher.

We arrived back at the car park amazingly in one piece, and after the urchin had ushered me into the Dodge and guided us back out, he was tipped again. We sped onto the boulevard, from where Charlie swung off and slowed in front of one of the many night clubs lining the highway. An armed guard ordered a youth to move another car out of the way so we could park more easily, and after tips all 'round we walked past a notice ordering patrons to "deposit firearms before entering." If Charlie had a gun, he didn't offload it, and we entered a pulsating world of hazy red, the ceiling so low it felt as though we were in a cave.

Never having come within cooee of a nightclub before, I was intrigued. The Filipino musicians with their electric guitars could only just be sighted through the red smoke, but they made their presence felt with a highly skilled performance of Spanish and English music that got your toes tapping. Charlie ordered a Scotch and water, and I ordered coffee. If my choice had been cyanide, Charlie could not have looked more shocked. I asked him what he thought I should order. "Leave it to me," said Charlie. A minute later we were clinking glasses, and I was sipping a clear liquid in a martini glass while dreamily watching an olive on a toothpick floating just under the surface. It was a gimlet—half gin and half lime. From now on I was a gimlet girl!

A group of Aussie blokes below us were singing "Waltzing Matilda," a painful experience because their lead singer was not only screamingly out of tune but out of his brain as well. A vendor offering white flower necklaces approached our table, and Charlie bought me one. "Sampaguita," he told me. "It's our national flower." As he placed it over my head I breathed in the exquisite fragrance, similar to the jasmine vine blossoms in our Aussie garden. Charlie and I had a couple of dances, and I surrendered to the music. By the time we returned to our table we were hysterical because Charlie claimed he could not understand one word of my weird accent. "Say milk," he ordered. "Merlk," said I, and he reeled with laughter. I smiled at some Filipinos looking at us from their table, and Charlie's grin vanished. He warned me to never smile at men in this country, because Filipinos would immediately assume I was making a play for them. I was taken aback. In Australia I could smile at strangers of both sexes whenever the occasion warranted, and the thought of not being able to be myself worried me. By now, too, I was so exhausted I could barely keep my eyes open.

After much tipping we left the nightclub and Charlie drove back by another route, less populated but convoluted, involving narrow lanes and dark alleyways. Even though it was the wee hours of the morning when the sentries let us back into San Lorenzo Village, Augustine magically greeted us at the door. I felt immediate sympathy for this man, thanking him profusely. Charlie, as he led me to my room and switched on the air-conditioner, cautioned me. "Don't thank servants too much, and never do anything yourself. Otherwise they will think they are not doing their job properly." All I could do was thank Charlie for a wonderful night, and to wish him sweet dreams. After I had peeled off my clothes and pulled on a cotton nightie, I fell into bed. Within seconds my head was lying on an embroidered linen pillowcase, the perfume from my sweet-smelling lei wafting me into deep and beautiful dreams.

* * *

Gradually I became conscious of dappled sunlight streaming through my window. It seemed surreal that I had left one country this time the day before and awoken in another. It was late morning, and I yearned for a shower. The bathroom adjoining my bedroom was used by both Charlie and his young brother George, so I peeped inside to make sure it was empty. The room was tiled from top to bottom with a step-down shower recess the size of a small pool. There was a bathroom sink, a mirror, and some cupboards. In the recess there was a tap, with no *H* or *C* to indicate whether hot or cold water would emerge, and a bucket underneath—that was it. Thinking perhaps the shower rose was magically hidden, I searched up and down to no avail. Finally, I half-filled the bucket, with cold water as it turned out, and tipped it over myself. Because of the warm ambient temperature, this was a surprisingly refreshing experience.

After dressing I wandered out into the dining room, and once again the wizard Augustine appeared and carefully enunciated, "Breakfast ma'am?"

"Just coffee please Augustine."

Looking baffled, the poor man turned on his heel and disappeared into what must have been the kitchen. Quickly he re-emerged carrying bread and jam. He vanished again. For a while I sat there looking at the dish of tinned strawberry jam and the small bread roll. Despairing of ever receiving coffee or butter, I spread the roll with the jam. Immediately Augustine appeared with a dish of butter.

"Egg?" he said, and I answered as clearly as I knew how, "No thank you Augustine, just coffee." Then he said "Zanges?" and as I was now the one looking baffled, he kept repeating this word until he finally remembered the English, "Orange?" I grinned and nodded, and he brought me a glass of orange juice. By now I had finished my roll, so I took the orange juice to my room and began writing a letter at my dresser.

Eventually I became aware that Augustine was peeping shyly through the door which I hadn't bothered to shut. As soon as I turned towards him he launched into a barrage of words. At last I recognized the word "close."

"You want the door closed? Go right ahead." Returning to my letter, in a few seconds I realised that he was still standing there, this time with a pained expression.

"Close," he stubbornly repeated, pointing to my dress and underwear draped on my bed. The penny dropped. "Clothes!" I gathered up my discarded items of clothing and handed them over. This language thing was getting quite tiring. Five minutes after Augustine had disappeared with my clothes, he reappeared with—a cup of very strong coffee!

I was still trying to finish my letter when George appeared. As he perched on the edge of my bed, I diplomatically mentioned the unusualness of my recent shower, and he explained with glee that I had just showered "Zambo style."

He then gave me a lecture on the thrills and realism of science fiction, getting even more animated when I didn't look convinced. We ended up swapping stamps, and that was when I learnt that Mrs Reith had two more sons, one married and living in Sydney, and Hans, who resided with his wife Rosie in Zamboanga. Owning almost more Aussie stamps than I did, George began showering me with Filipino stamps. To square up I was forced to offer him two of my precious First Day Covers. Drug companies had sent my doctor father these specially stamped envelopes for years, so I selected two of the best, and George beamed.

Mrs Reith firmly but sweetly took over from George, asking if I'd like to select a candy from a box she had just opened. Eagerly I agreed to be her taste-tester. With George trailing along she led me into the

Fern Room, a vast sunlit area featuring palms and ferns, decorations of fish and birds, and the tools of an artist's studio. From her canvases and tapestries it became clear that Mrs Reith was artistic. Out came the box of sweets. The first one, she told me, came from a spiked tropical fruit, then she added that if it "falls on your head from a tree, it will kill you." Later I discovered that what I was eating derived from a durian, which looks like a mace and is morbidly obese, each fruit weighing in around three kilos. But the most fascinating thing of all about durian is that the odour of the cut fruit resembles putrefied flesh.

Later during the year, some Filipino friends claimed that once you got past the smell, the taste became addictive. They challenged me to try a piece of durian flesh. Bravely I bit into it, and I can guarantee the taste was as putrid as its perfume!

I was beginning to peel the paper off the next candy when I saw George pop the long cube into his mouth without unwrapping it. "Mm," he mumbled, shooting me a wicked glance. With trepidation I followed suit, and to my surprise it melted on my tongue and the aftertaste was nutty and delicious. It was rice paper! The third candy on the menu looked like small blocks of petrified wood and tasted like frozen honey, very moreish, so I popped another one. And just when I began to feel disgustingly full, Augustine called us to lunch!

It was a more typical Filipino meal than the night before—tender chicken and pieces of pork, a bowl of beans, and rice salad, all followed by mango ice-cream that I couldn't resist. A young maidservant with a sponge was working in the bathroom when I entered to clean my teeth. She was painfully shy, so I asked her name, but her answer was a soft mumble. She could have been swearing at me for all I knew. Throwing her a radiant smile, I finished cleaning my teeth then slipped into my bedroom. The wave of relief from the poor girl was almost palpable.

As I was finishing a letter to my parents Augustine delivered my washing, all perfectly ironed, and proceeded to hang everything, even underwear, meticulously in the wardrobe. "Thank you, Augustine," I said warmly. The custom of the wealthy—not thanking the servants—went against my DNA.

When I sauntered into the lounge Charlie was reading a newspaper. The big television was switched on, but no one was paying it any attention. As soon as I asked where I could post my letter, he jumped to his feet and called for the family chauffeur. Perhaps this man slept in the garage because never once did I spy him in the house.

We cruised to the nearby Makati shopping centre, which was as sterile and charmless as all major shopping centres were back home. I posted my letter, bought aerograms and cashed some traveller's cheques. Then, instead of heading for home, Charlie directed the driver to take us to Forbes Park, an exclusive suburb nearby. The area between the shopping centre and Forbes Park was a vast, flat area unoccupied by either trees or man, and looking back on it I think this was deliberately designed to keep the riffraff from getting too close—somewhat like clearing land beyond the castle moat, to give an uninterrupted view of the enemy.

At the edge of no-man's-land we reached the grand entrance of Millionaires' Row, as the locals dubbed it, an exclusive gated district containing the Manila American Cemetery, the country's major golf and polo clubs for the elite, and the mansions of the mega-rich—impossibly lavish and set back behind high stone walls of tropical greenery.

Little did I know that Millionaires' Row, in seven months from that day, would become a place of great dread and fear for me.

Slowly we drove to a vast plateau crowned by the cemetery, parked atop the hill, and from there we gazed in awe at row upon row of white crosses stretching away as far as the eye could see. The white images on green lawn presented a simple but effective picture, and I tried to recall the few bits and pieces about World War II I had learnt at school. I did know that Imperial Japan had swept through Asia and the Pacific, crushing all who resisted, and that many Filipinos had fought valiantly to regain their country's freedom. Americans, of course, had fought alongside the Filipino soldiers, and most secondary students knew that when General MacArthur had been forced to retreat, he had promised to return. It had all sounded so glorious and heroic.

As an Australian teenager I was ignorant of the Bataan "death march." In April 1942 the victorious Japanese had forced sixty-six thousand Filipino and ten thousand American POWs to walk 106 kilometres, suffering the most heinous atrocities with many dying along the way.

A jet plane screamed overhead as if saluting us, and just as quickly it vanished. Suddenly Vietnam felt disturbingly close. Back in Australia the conflict had seemed distant and vague, but now, from where I stood in the Manila American Cemetery, I realized that some of the Australian defence forces may, at this very moment, be on shore leave not far away, perhaps mingling with the American navy at Subic Bay or air force personnel at Clark Air Base.

Charlie explained that most of the crosses represented American soldiers who had fallen in the Philippines in World War II, because from the time of the Korean (and now the Vietnam) War, America preferred to repatriate its war dead. I told Charlie that our former PM Robert Menzies had imposed upon Australian males the "Birthday Ballot." Depending upon the birth date of every boy turning twenty, that young adult had a one in three chance of winning the lottery—a free ticket to Vietnam. But—and I reassured myself avidly—right now nothing about the war impacted upon me personally, and more than two years would pass before my two Steves (boyfriend SJ and brother) turned twenty. Two years was an eternity away, and by then the war would be well and truly over, wouldn't it? Surely the communist "domino effect" would be stopped in its tracks, and the Vietnam War would be all over with us coming out the winners.

We returned to the Dodge. Charlie, who spoke with a hybrid accent, ordered his driver "You gor drarve to the porlo club, nor?" In a few minutes we were cruising through a grand entrance flanked with stonework and heading for the impressive club rooms fringed by tropical trees. We found a parking space, but instead of entering the building we wandered towards a grass field where a polo game was in progress. I had only ever seen photos of royalty swinging the mallet, never imagining polo to be so fast, tricky and dangerous. The sheer pizzazz of the game was thrilling. Charlie told me that the riders were practicing for a great tournament on Sunday, and that 90 percent of horses in these stables were from Australia! Most of the world champion players were American, and several were out on the field today, including an obese Texan who was remarkably agile given his wide girth. Talking of "girth," I felt sorry for his poor horse. As we watched, I tried to remember every detail so that I could describe the event accurately to my mother, the horse lover and champion show jumper.

A man began chatting to Charlie, then turned to me asking if I'd like to attend the big Sunday tournament. "Even the ex-president will be here," he said. Hoping that no one quizzed me too closely about who exactly was the former president of the Philippines, I told him I was flying to Zamboanga this Thursday. Charlie said, "Nor, we gor maybe Friday now." I stared at him—*when did the departure date change from Thursday to Friday, and why?*

After Charlie had dragged me away from the polo game, we headed for the stables filled with rows of stalls and Filipino boy grooms. "I need a good stallion for my coconut plantation," was all Charlie said, and we walked up and down the lines of stalls admiring the horseflesh until he found a man with whom he quietly discussed the deal. Eventually we left the polo club and made our way through ritzy Forbes Park back out into no-man's-land. All too soon we were once again amongst the noisy, confused traffic and the pungent smell that goes with an overcrowded tropical city.

That night Augustine served up lamb chops, cooked to perfection the Aussie way. Then I asked for a cup of tea. It would have been a fine cuppa, except for the milk. Tinned evaporated milk having turned my tea into a revolting beige beverage, I decided there and then that from now on coffee would be my hot drink of choice.

Charlie did indeed fly off to Zamboanga on Friday 8 March, and the reason I would not be going with him became apparent when Mrs Reith magically appeared and asked in her soft voice whether I would like to attend the Australian Ballet that night. I was confused. Didn't she mean the Philippines Ballet Company? But no, with a slight smile she explained that the Australian company was on tour and would be performing *Raymonda* at the Rizal Theatre.

It was incredible luck. I was crazy about ballet. When I turned seven my mother gave me two options—learning ballet, or the piano? It wasn't an easy decision. I had spent endless hours on my toy piano given to me one Christmas, and every time we visited a house with a real piano, I would head for it like a homing pigeon. But the lure of being a prima ballerina was irresistible. Also, my father had given me a double LP of *Swan Lake* after a trip to Adelaide, and I played Tchaikovsky until the vinyl was tested to its limit while I twirled, pirouetted, and arabesqued in our living room. In fact, from that fateful moment when I opted to outshine Anna Pavlova, my correspondence name suddenly transformed from the unexciting Stephanie Paula Wicks to the stellar Stefania Paulinova Wickstein. As I reached puberty, however, it became clear that while my neck and back were swan-like enough and my five-foot-six frame may have scraped in under the height limit, my breasts let me down. Instead of swelling just a fraction to pert, they ballooned to womanly proportions designed for a number twelve Berlei bra—not quite the look of a swan.

Hans and Rosie, who, like Charlie, had their main residence in Zamboanga, flew to Manila especially to see the Australian Ballet in action. While they stayed in their mother's house in Manila, they spent much time in the company of Rosie's sister who was a ballerina. Rosie herself was athletic and taught dance. It seemed that every member of the Philippines Ballet Company had been asked to accommodate at least one Australian dancer, and I was thrilled to meet Gailene Stock who was boarding with them. I learnt that at age eight Gailene had contracted polio and spent eighteen months in an iron frame. Inspirational!

I spent an hour getting dressed and applying makeup and piling my hair up high in curls which I thought looked terrific. As I dived into my cosmetic (cozzie) case, my fingers explored an outside pocket and found a piece of paper. It was a love note from SJ, and my heart leapt then sank. *How would I survive a year without him?* When Rosie's brother Jo arrived in a beautiful sports car to collect me, I felt much like Cinderella going to the ball.

In *Raymonda*, performed on 8 March 1968 at the prestigious Theatre Rizal, the handsome knight was danced by Garth Welch, and the countess Raymonda by Marilyn Jones. I was amazed that Marilyn had made it to the top despite having the most ordinary surname in the western world, but as I watched her dance it was obvious that the name was irrelevant—she was pure magic. Peering hard at the stage, I tried to detect Gailene amongst the Corp de Ballet, but every one of these gorgeous young women looked as if they'd been cloned—petite, slim and perfect. I wrote to my family saying that I never thought of myself as particularly patriotic, but after the performance I was so proud of Australia I thought I would burst. The choreography, by Rudolph Nureyev, was outstanding.

By 7 A.M. the next morning, I was up and dressed and ready to watch another type of show—George's swim carnival. The swim meet involved only two schools, but the talent was excellent. I would soon discover that very few Filipinos could swim. Given that they are an island nation this seemed strange. However, the swimmers I witnessed in Manila on this day were the sons and daughters of the wealthy elite, and most of them lived in mansions with pools and had rarely swum in the sea. Hans and I were thrilled when George came second in a race where the winner was an Olympic champion.

After a much-needed afternoon siesta Mrs Reith took me into her boudoir, sitting me at her dressing table and giving me advice on how to arrange my hair and apply make-up. From her gentle lessons it gradually dawned on me that I had a lot to learn about grooming, and that perhaps my piled-up curls of the night before had not flattered me at all! Although a manicurist and a pedicurist visited the house once a week, it was Mrs Reith's deft hands that applied her art and nail polish to my fingers and toes, and I felt as spoilt as a princess.

In the Fern Room, Mrs Reith began to describe Patalon as we sipped cups of coffee. Her coconut plantation, some way along the coast from Zamboanga, was where she had been raised as a child. I was just thinking how lucky she was when the tale turned grim. She had been in her late twenties when the Japanese overran the Philippines and all too soon turned up at the plantation. Her mother and father were dragged out of their house, lined up on the little white beach, and shot. She told me that while she and one of her sisters had been lucky enough to escape, all her other siblings had been killed by the Japanese.

A Google search reveals that a court case played out in 1948 whereby a Filipino traitor called "Captain" Moreno was sentenced to death for the killing of Susie's father and mother and extended family (including two servants). Moreno's justification had been that the Reiths had provided the freedom fighters with food supplies. Before Moreno was executed, he was fined a huge amount to be awarded to the surviving Reith family.

By the end of that afternoon, I was truly in love with Mrs Reith—I found her to be deeply spiritual yet practical, self-disciplined yet not extreme, reserved and soft yet with a powerful presence. In so many ways I found myself wanting to emulate Susie Reith.

Later that evening Hans and Rosie took me to see a farcical comedy crazily titled *Oh Dad, Poor Dad, Mamma's Hung You in the Closet and I'm Feelin' so Sad*. I laughed until I cried. It seemed that Hans and Rosie were determined to make the most of the arty life in the big smoke, because the following night they took me back to Theatre Rizal where this time the Australian Ballet were performing *The Display*. Named after the lyrebird's spectacular ritual courtship dance, it was a masterpiece. A far cry from the classical European fairytale stories such as *Giselle* and *The Nutcracker*, it depicted an Aussie bush picnic. It was the first time I had experienced a "modern" Australian ballet with a dark-edged story climaxing with a girl being seduced (or raped!) by a lyrebird. Spellbinding. And so risqué for 1968!

* * *

The following day was packed with several emotionally charged events. As soon as I'd finished breakfast, a friend came to visit Hans at the Reiths' house. He was a tall, swarthy man called Werner Garmsen, and there was a strength and presence about him that impressed me. His father was German. A man of few words, when Werner spoke everyone sat up and paid attention. Hans laughingly called him a "Moro," but Werner just stood easy, returning the jibe with the faintest of smiles. In an aside Hans explained that Moro was a term for a Filipino with Moorish (Muslim) ancestry, and because many of the Moros down south were pirates, amongst the Catholics the name was derogatory.

And this was when I heard Werner's shocking story, which didn't fit with my image of a "modern" western world. He and his family owned a small plantation island to the south of Zambo, where six months earlier pirates had collected in boats and held the island under siege for eight hours. The Garmsen family managed to hold them off with gunfire from behind sandbags, and when they were down to one hundred rounds of ammunition, the American navy turned up—the cavalry to the rescue. Presumably one of the US ships was patrolling the shores of Vietnam, and had been heading to the American naval base at Subic Bay when it received a plea for help over the radio. What happened to the baddies on that occasion I don't know, but Werner and his family were safe for the time being.

Hans told me they were going to see Werner's uncle, a prominent Congressman at Parliament House, and invited me to join them. Never one to miss out on an interesting experience, I accepted and off we went in someone's car. On the way to parliament house we slowed in a tangle of traffic, and I spotted a man with one eye limping amongst the cars. He made a beeline toward our car, his hand stretched out for us. I fumbled in my purse for a peso, winding down the window with the other hand. Quickly sensing what I was up to, Hans and Werner tried to stop me from giving my money to the beggar, but the poor wretch was already grabbing the note and mumbling thanks. The vehemence of my hosts took me aback. "Those so-called beggars," they informed me, "are a well-organised group who deliberately maim themselves to get money, and they're filthy rich!" I stared at them in disbelief, then replied, "Anyone who has to put their eye out and cut off their foot to earn money, can have some of mine."

This caused an unhappy silence for some time in the car before a welcome distraction occurred. We had pulled up in front of a small shopping complex, Werner hopping out to purchase something and leaving me in the car with Hans. It seemed that within seconds the car was surrounded with excited Filipinos of all ages, pointing at me and jabbering in Tagalog. Hans locked the car and wound up the windows, but just when I was feeling uneasy, he burst out laughing. "Hey, they think you're Gina Pareno!"

"Who's Gina Pareno?"

"A movie star," Hans replied. "They want your autograph."

Now I could see people in the crowd brandishing scraps of paper and pens. "I can't do that," I said. "I am not Gina Pareno!"

But Hans had found a way to be thoroughly entertained. "Go on," he urged, "make them happy, sign!"

I hesitated, then realized that if these fans believed I was Gina Pareno, becoming this lady for a few moments would give many people a thrill. So we wound down the windows, notepads were thrust through at me, and I signed again and again, smiling magnanimously as I imagined a good movie star should. The girls in the mob were jumping up and down and calling out to me, star of the screen! *Would I ever be so famous again?* By the time Werner strode back through the swelling throng, the excitement had reached fever-pitch. "Sigi na lang," laughed Hans, using a slang expression which I would use daily during my stay in Zamboanga. "Let's go!"

The legislative building was impressive, festooned with columns, a beautiful example of American colonial architecture. We met a congressman, and after Werner had talked privately with him, we all watched a session from the gallery, a very lame affair. Those few present lounged lifelessly in their chairs as a congressman droned on into a microphone out front. After watching the proceedings for a respectful amount of time, we filed back out and Werner drove us to another old building not far away—the Philippines General Hospital. I was puzzled. "Are we visiting someone?"

Werner looked stony. Hans whispered, "Werner's cousin."

Then the hour of horror began.

Two weeks earlier Werner's cousin, a twenty-year-old Filipina living on a little island south of Zamboanga near the Garmsen's coconut plantation, had been attacked by at least four men while she was home alone. She had been raped, then shot in the head and left for dead.

I had been in many Aussie hospitals before, both country and city, and all had qualities in common—gleaming linoleum flooring, a comforting smell of antiseptic wafting on fresh air, and patients tucked up safe and sound in crisp white linen. I wrote to SJ the day afterwards, the details sharp in my mind:

"I have never seen such a hospital. The smell was unpleasant . . . and as we walked down the huge open-air corridors, patients were lying on makeshift beds—patients with bloody bandages tied around their heads, their eyes covered—patients with deformed faces; noses as big as their head—patients moaning in corners with ragged-looking relatives standing around. That was bad enough. But that was nothing. Then we entered the room of Werner's cousin. Terribly tiny and dainty, she was lying on the bed with her face turned away. The neck muscles around her throat were quivering, and her eyes were covered by a bandage. She will never see again. There was a bullet hole in each side of her head. Werner said something to her, and she finally understood it was Werner. She tried unsuccessfully to talk and was in agony if anyone lightly touched her skin from her throat upwards. Or maybe the reaction was terror, I don't know."

Feeling sick to the pit of my stomach, I shrank back against the wall. Two women in sarongs also stood aside, and I guessed they were relatives. It was becoming obvious that in this hospital you needed to be wealthy to obtain basic medical care, and relatives were vital to provide proper food and tend to the personal needs of their loved ones. I glimpsed Werner's face as he leant over and whispered in his cousin's ear. I had never seen such pent-up fury.

From the time of the visit until halfway home in the car, I couldn't speak. I kept mopping up the tears that flowed in a constant stream from under the rim of my sunglasses, but at last I began to ask careful questions. "You will kill the men who did this to your cousin?"

"Yes."

"You will shoot them?"

"No."

At that moment I guessed that Werner and his family, when they found the perpetrators, did not intend to have a quiet talk with them and send them on their way. A minute later I found the courage to ask the question. "What will you do to them?" Werner didn't hesitate. It was almost as if he were relieved that someone had asked the question. "We will string them up by their thumbs, on my island."

I swear my heart stopped, and my voice broke. "Why would you do that? Be so cruel?"

I caught a glimpse of Werner's craggy face in the rearview mirror, studying me as though he were gauging how far he could push reality onto this ideological western teenager who had been cocooned from birth inside a safe, civil world. Finally, he spoke. "Some will last for three, maybe four days. People for miles around will hear them scream. They will never touch my family again."

It was the end of the conversation, and the shattering of my cocoon. With a silent scream I wrote the following to SJ:

"Werner is right! That's the trouble, he's right! The Christian principle of 'turn the other cheek' doesn't apply here, and I'm so utterly confused."

When Werner deposited Hans and me back in San Lorenzo Village, I threw myself on my bed and bawled my eyes out until Susie Reith appeared quietly by my side. Taking me by the hand, she led me to the Fern Room and dried my eyes. It was as if she understood that my faith in humankind had shattered, and the suffering I had witnessed was, for the moment at least, too great to bear. Then she began showing me photos of Patalon, and I became entranced at the green of the plantation grass and palms up against the snowy beach, the aqua blue of the sea, and the white cattle and bay horses feeding under the trees and palms.

* * *

The following morning, I overheard a conversation which seemed trivial, but in fact served to provide me with critical information which helped to save my life the following October.

Hans and his friend Johnny were talking about their president, and to my astonishment they seemed to be relating what they could remember about Marcos as a sixteen-year-old murdering his father's political opponent while he was cleaning his teeth!

"He was convicted in 1940," Hans said, "and he did time."

"Not for long," retorted Johnny. "He was a law student, studying all these legal books while he was sitting in jail, and he got himself off!"

"Cunning," mused Hans. "So . . . he literally got away with murder."

Johnny cut to Marcos's love life. "And he's got mistresses in Millionaires' Row."

"Looks like the president can get away with anything!" laughed Hans.

Images came flooding back of the walled suburb, Forbes Park, where I had been taken by Charlie only days before.

Johnny chuckled. "But there's one thing he can't get away with in this Catholic country."

"What's that?"

"Getting caught!"

The two of them chuckled. At that point I had no idea what President Marcos even looked like, nor did I care. But some conclusions stacked up in my mind. Ferdinand Marcos had been capable of cold-blooded murder. Because he was close to the end of his first term in office, 1968 was critical in his campaign to win a second term. No other Philippine president had ever won a second term, and nor might Marcos if the Catholic public ever suspected he kept mistresses in Forbes Park. It went without saying therefore, that Marcos would have no qualms about eliminating anyone who might publicly divulge his secret.

Only in recent years have I discovered that Marcos's father, Mariano, suspected of collaborating with the Japanese, had been executed by Philippine guerillas in 1943. Some say they beat him to death while others maintain he was "quartered" by tying him to carabaos (water buffalo) and watching as his body was literally ripped apart.[1] Perhaps Hans Reith also knew of the terrible death of his president's father. After all, Hans's own grandparents had been murdered by another Filipino traitor who had in turn been executed more formally at the end of the war.

Johnny must have assumed I was a very sporty girl, because for the rest of that day he took me swimming and diving in a massive pool somewhere, and I remember playing a game called Pelota with its origins from the Basque country, somewhat like open-air squash.

Because I became hot and sweaty as I leapt about with my racquet under the hot sun, Johnny returned me to the Reiths' to bathe and change. After, he swept me away to a nightclub called Nina's where I

---

1. Baguio Chronicle, accessed 2 September 2022, https://baguiochronicle.rappler.com

surrendered to my newfound love of gimlets. The band offered to grant me any request, so I ended up singing "Waltzing Matilda" and "Santa Lucia" without much inhibition and was thrilled when the crowd yelled "More! More!" The Filipinos' ready willingness to burst into song was infectious and gave me confidence, but I puzzled over the fact that, given much of Australia's ancestry included the Irish and the Welsh, why did Australians tend to cringe when it came to singing in public?

We were sitting chatting after my "performance" when a friend of Johnny's joined us at the table. He was a playwright, actor, and director, and as soon as he learned I was interested in drama he offered me a part in a movie, insisting it was a "good part." I felt hugely frustrated, knowing that I was leaving for Zamboanga the very next day, and there was no getting around that. Wryly I wrote to my family that "once again, due to circumstance, the world is deprived of talent."

Now, with hindsight and help from the Internet, I wonder whether the film in question was Maharlika. A movie purportedly funded by the CIA and keenly supported by President Marcos because the movie star Paul Burke would depict him as a gallant Second World War hero leading a group of guerillas called Maharlika ("Noble Warriors") against the Japanese.

But in March of 1968, in a nightclub in Manila chatting to a movie director, I did not have a crystal ball. And I can only blame gimlets for the fact I never did remember the handsome movie director's name.

* * *

Hans and Werner drove me to Manila airport where we waited for three hours. I would soon learn that long delays were quite the norm for flights within the Philippines.

My male friends wisely omitted to tell me that in July of the preceding year a Fokker Friendship aircraft, just like the one I was about to board, had crashed into a mountain in Mindanao, killing twenty-seven people.

Eventually I was flying southwards, destination Zamboanga. The hostess began a conversation with me, and we clicked. Within minutes of settling into the flight she led me into the cockpit where I was given royal treatment by the three pilots. I was offered a seat, the captain standing over me and laughing about our language gaffs. Then the hostess brought me a cup of coffee (and chewing gum!). The wide cockpit vista had the effect of feeling as if I were sitting on a moving raft in the sky, surrounded by a silvery haze streaked with red clouds. As we crossed over the northern part of Mindanao, I could see solid green mountains below, and as we approached the landing strip, I was still ensconced in the cockpit, treated to a view of white beaches, green sea and palms—it was the very paradise I had imagined for the last few months, and it was real!

14 March 1968
Location: Zamboanga, City of Flowers
Host family — Marasigan

First to disembark, I spotted Charlie with his big smile, grinning from ear to ear and surrounded by a crowd of Rotarians and their wives. Stepping forward he slipped a lei of sampaguita around my neck and apologized for not having brought out the red carpet. So many people were trying to talk to me, and I could barely make out a word. Eventually I was bundled into a white Kombi marked Brent Hospital. Driving the van was Dr Esteban Marasigan, and next to him was his wife, Mary. Instantly I liked them. Doc had a kind, wise aura about him, and Mary had the sweetest smile and soft brown eyes. Sitting beside me in the back seat was their twenty-two-year-old niece Linda, who told me she was studying nursing at the Brent Hospital which adjoined the Marasigan house.

With Charlie following behind we drove through the squalid hub of the city and out onto a wide boulevard which ran parallel to a sea dotted with the bright sails of Zamboanga's trademark sailing boats, the vintas. Further out but not far away were several green islands with glaringly white beaches. That's all I had time to take in. We parked near a solid two-story house adjacent to the Brent Hospital, also on two levels. Within the hour I had been introduced to the children, three little boy devils who played without supervision, brandishing the most horrifying toy weapons, but who nevertheless guaranteed to bring out the maternal instinct. Then the only girl—the tiniest, chubbiest, sweetest little thing I had ever seen. The air hostess had given me a swag of left-over sweets, and without a thought of ruining their appetites for supper I showered them with candies.

I soon learned there existed three classes in Catholic Filipino society—businessmen at the top level; doctors, dentists and teachers in the middle; and the working classes battling along on the lowest rung of the ladder. But even though the Marasigans were of that middle class, they still managed to employ two boys and two girls to help look after the kids and the household. Servants came cheap, but I always suspected that Esteban and Mary employed as many young people as they could afford to help them earn their livelihoods, meagre as they were.

Charlie, Linda, Mary, the Doc and I all sat down at the table to a great supper of lobster, pickles, some sort of corned beef, rice, and baked fish. No sooner had I finished my meal than Mary asked if I'd like to watch an operation—Doc Marasigan needed to operate on a man who'd been stabbed with a pointed stick. I jumped at the chance. The opportunity would never be offered to me at home unless I was training to become a nurse, which was never going to happen. Within the hour, Linda and I were standing in a soundproof room looking through a double-glazed window at Doc, who wore a surgical mask as he bent over the victim and began to cut. There was plenty of blood and guts on show, but that was when I realized it was only suffering that upset me, not the cutting into a patient who was mercifully unconscious. Intrigued and fascinated, I was imagining my own father operating on humans and even on animals, for specialists and vets were in short supply in Australian country towns in the 50s and 60s. It is a kind of courage which is hard to describe or quantify, but bravery it is, and at that moment I felt proud of my father and full of admiration for Dr Esteban Marasigan.

Linda and I used a tiny and very rudimentary bathroom attached to our upstairs bedroom, but for some reason water emerged from the tap only in the evenings, and it was cold. By the time I got up on my first morning Linda had already gone to the hospital, so I sat down to breakfast and watched with fascination what the kids were gobbling—boiled rice mixed with chocolate ground from the cacao bean and mixed with sugar. I found that with evaporated milk the mixture was quite bearable, tasting somewhat like chocolate rice pudding. It was obvious that the formal quiet breakfasts I had experienced with Augustine in Manila would no longer be happening. From now on it was delightful chaos with kids and maids and Mary and any visiting relatives. In her quaint accent Mary told me that in this provincial city most people went to bed at nine and rose about six. "That suits me!" I replied, then wrote to my mother, "Nightclubs might be fun, but you can have too much of them." I also observed there was no TV to entertain even the wealthiest in Zamboanga, because the city had no reception.

In a VW Beetle Mary drove me downtown so that I could have my first good look. It had evolved over hundreds of years, some of its narrow streets running over sewage ditches with pigs snuffling in them. Traffic consisted of an untidy assortment of cars, passenger trikes and jeepneys, all honking and beeping and jostling for position with seemingly no rules and few traffic lights. Taxis were rare, but unlike Manila, Zamboanga's public transport boasted calesas. When I saw these in real life I was horrified. Calesas are high wooden buggies pulled by small horses and driven by men wielding rope whips and crouching on a front platform, and it was the general condition of the horses that upset me. Some simply looked weary and dusty, but most were rubbed raw by stiff harnesses and scarred by the whip. It was rare to see one which was not pitifully bony and thin. I pictured my mother's horse Lochinvar with his flawless glossy coat and his health and energy, and my heart ached for the calesa horses. I felt furious and puzzled too. *Why would anyone, no matter how poor or uneducated, mistreat the source of their livelihood?*

Talking of equine activities, Mary took me to a small store to buy jeans for my visit to the Reiths' coconut plantation (Patalon) the following Saturday, where I hoped to ride horses kept in much better condition. After shopping we drove up a long road leading inland towards the jungle-clad mountains and a place I would come to know and love for the rest of my stay—a vast park created on top of the first hilly ridge, awash with bougainvillea and acres of grass between venerable trees. Central to this was a large mountain pool fed by waterfalls from higher up, and at the very top of the ridge, the road led around to a pretty bungalow house. "That belongs to the Mas family," Mary explained. "In one of your months here you will stay with them."

At noon Dr Marasigan drove me to the Zamboanga Hotel, a multi-level building in the middle of town. Its roof was flat, filled with bougainvillea and palms, used as one of the most beautiful venues for all sorts of events, including the Rotary Club's lunch meetings. As I entered, all the men clapped and cheered as I was ushered to the long narrow table at the front and placed at Charlie's right hand. He whispered to me that I should say a few words—my main speech would be next week. I scanned the merry Rotarians sitting at round tables, amazed to see them dressed in bright short sleeved shirts and light slacks. Throughout the four-course meal a man kept popping out from behind plants and taking my photo with a flash camera while Rotarians came up individually to shake my hand and introduce themselves. I came in for more claps and cheers when I stood for my "few words" and opened my speech with what was probably badly uttered Spanish. "Buenos Tardes con todos ustedes. Como estan?" ("Good afternoon to you all. How are you?")

As part of their good works, the Rotary Club had sponsored a band made up of blind guitarists. These proved to be top musicians, and soon different Rotarians began to step up to the microphone—to sing! The contrast between the Australian and Filipino Rotary meetings astonished and amused me. The Australians, well-intentioned men in suits and ties sitting in function rooms with linen-covered tables, cleared their throats into a microphone before delivering information in monotones. However, it seemed the Filipinos preferred an open-air venue filled with flowers and spontaneous singing!

* * *

After breakfast the following morning, I sat in my room writing to my family, every so often gazing down at the scene on the esplanade. The temperature was heating up, and the mountains far across the sea were becoming hazy with clouds. A freighter was hugging the pier on my left, and a small tugboat chugging by the low islands seemed quite close to the house. Gangs of youths, laughing and singing, strolled along the top of the wide wall protecting Cawa Cawa Boulevard from the sea. All in all, it was a sweet and dreamy scene. Yet, as I peered at the islands, I wondered how far away Werner's troubled island was, and whether his poor female cousin would ever see her home again.

I finished my letter with what I now realize was insensitive, even though I was half-joking, expressing my hope that "Werner sticks to his promise and takes me down to the Jolo Islands some time. I'll probably arrive in the midst of gunfire from the pirates, but with Werner around there will be nothing to fear. A man like that does not lie down and die easily. Besides, I don't think the pirates have given trouble since the American navy destroyed their siege." Two weeks later, a letter from my sweetheart SJ would warn me to be more careful what I wrote to my parents.

On 16 March 1968, as I wrote that letter in the Marasigan's house overlooking the dreamy Sulu Sea, a massacre which would have major repercussions years later was taking place not far to the west in South Vietnam. An American contingent began raping and murdering civilians in the hamlet of Mai Lai.

* * *

Jo-Jo was mostly Spanish with some American and Filipino thrown in. A great friend of the Reith family, he was in his late twenties, lived with his father, and drove a big black Chevrolet. He had graduated in commerce at some college but had no ambition which niggled at him. He seemed to have most days free and took it upon himself to drive me wherever he thought I might like to go. Knowing that I loved swimming, he would give me the choice of the beautiful white beach of Caragasan twelve miles down the coast, or the mountain pool of Pasonanca in the park overlooking the township.

Caragasan Beach was fringed with coconut palms along its length. To one side stood about seven huts on stilts in the sea, connected by a wooden jetty from which half-naked urchins jumped and splashed. The huts were strung together from loose wood planks, and the floors from bamboo. There was no furniture to speak of, and the inhabitants slept on frond matting. The people who inhabited these huts above the sea were broadly called Sea Gypsies, and it was said that some were born and lived and died on the water. The men wore loose trousers and filthy shirts, and those who made their living from the sea went barefoot, their toes splayed and soles tough as buffalo hide. Often, they perched on the side of the dusty coast road, trying to sell their fish. The women dressed themselves in pieces of Batik, cotton with a particular design, one piece slung around the waist, a skimpy blouse overlapping this, and a scarf to shield themselves from the sun. Like the men, they went mostly barefoot.

As for the mountain pool of Pasonanca, it was a natural cavity five hundred metres above sea level filled with greenish-brown water and fringed with jungle ferns and palms. As fresh rainwater trickled down to replenish the pool, the overflow formed a small creek leading down towards the town. The main pool was very deep towards the centre and featured a short tower with a solid diving platform at two levels. The local kids were fascinated by my diving, especially during the back dive or the handstand dive where I held the upside-down position on the board for as long as possible before knifing into the still water. Immediately the urchins would copy me, often with spectacular splashy results, but they'd always surface laughing, not a care in the world.

They didn't always surface happily, as I would discover a few months later.

Before the second Rotary lunch, Mary drove me to a small wooden shop opposite the town's university, Ateneo. Sometime in May I would be attending classes of history and Spanish somewhere within the old two-floor buildings positioned far back from the road. A path led across mown grass and through big trees to the place of learning. However, for now I was to receive a manicure from the girls working for Angie's House of Charm. Mary explained the situation to the owner, Mrs Ebby, paid her in advance, and advised me how to hail a calesa out the front to bring me home. Mrs Ebby had a strident voice but a big heart, and all the staff treated me and my nails as if I were a princess. I was offered an array of colours and designs, such as white stars on a bright pink background. Intrigued and delighted at the skill of these artisans, I enjoyed myself immensely. However, when all was finished and my nails looked better than they ever had, it was time to catch a calesa. Suddenly I felt insecure. Mary had warned me about the exact price to pay the driver, assuring me that he would know the location of the Brent Hospital on Cawa Cawa Boulevard. *But what if he didn't understand? And what if he demanded more pesos when we got to our destination?*

All went smoothly as I climbed up on the step and into the high passenger seat from where I overlooked the small horse. Although this one didn't have sores all over it, nevertheless it was disgracefully thin, and I pondered the inevitable conundrum of financially supporting unethical businesses. If I didn't use the calesa, the driver would have less to feed his family and his horse. If I used it, I would be aiding bad practice. As we set off, the little horse trotting, I felt like a memsahib from Queen Victoria's empire demanding that the natives exert their starving bodies to give me an easy ride from A to B. In this case it was the horse exerting itself, but it still felt wrong. When we reached Brent Hospital I climbed down and opened my purse to pay the driver. It was then that my nail polish, not quite dried, scratched. I smiled at the irony—a First World problem in a Third World country.

With my less than immaculate manicure I fronted up for my second Rotary Club lunch with some trepidation. It was time for my grand speech about Australia atop the Zamboanga Hotel. My oration was excruciatingly formal, the kind expected by the men in suits from any Australian Rotary Club of that era. A few minutes into my talk I became aware of the restlessness of my Filipino audience, and I tried to brighten up my style of delivery, not yet having the experience to switch to a livelier subject matter. Toeing the Rotary line and saying what was expected of me, I finally brought the dreary speech to an abrupt end and asked if there were any questions. A hand shot up, and I prayed that my political and geographical knowledge of Australia was up to scratch. "Yes?"

"Miss Wicks, would you be available this Saturday morning for a game of tennis?" Sporadic laughter broke out, but it wasn't unkind—everyone could see I was lost for words. Suddenly I knew what to say. "I will play tennis with you if my host father agrees." I smiled. "So you will need to be okayed by Doc Marasigan." The audience roared with delight while Doc sat quietly, his eyes shy and amused behind the thick lenses of his glasses. From that moment, I came to genuinely like most of them and we got on famously. Not taking their flirtatiousness too seriously was the key.

The next day, Linda being at work, I asked Mary if I could go for a stroll along Cawa Cawa Boulevard towards the town. It was a glorious morning, and, dressed in sandals and a cotton dress, I clutched my handbag and set off along the high concrete footpath, pausing at times to squint out at the various boats and to wonder whether I would ever set foot on those tempting isles dotted like stepping-stones across the Sulu Sea. On one of those islands Werner and his family lived precariously, never safe and always wary.

Three urchins emerged from nowhere and began following me, and as I reached the end of the boulevard and emerged onto a stone-paved square, the few kids had turned into a crowd of young and old. Everyone was silent, watching me not with malice but with awe. An unfamiliar sense of shyness began to overwhelm me. For the first time in my life I was in the minority, being singled out because of my colour. Even though the crowd showed nothing but fascination, I didn't like it one bit. I uttered a few clumsy phrases of greeting. Someone asked me if I was "Americana." "No!" I exclaimed, "Australiana!" Everyone looked baffled, and so, pointing to the south, I tried to explain in pigeon-Spanish that Australia was a "grande pais" (big country) far away across "el mar" (the sea). I knew that Americans were not always popular here, so I was keen to dissociate myself from them. Now the group had swelled to about fifty. When I tried to move on to where the calesa ponies and ungainly carts were lined up, they all followed in deathly silence. I felt increasingly hot and bothered and wished with all my heart that they would vanish and leave me alone. Although I would have liked to explore further, I couldn't bear being on show one moment longer, turning and hurrying back along the boulevard, back to the haven of the Marasigan's. That night I had a bout of homesickness, feeling light-years away from any of my previous support bases.

Next day, from dawn until midnight, we had no running water. Everyone in the household lugged buckets to the kitchen and bathrooms from an outside tap offering up only a reluctant trickle. I confessed that

I had always taken running water for granted. Mary informed me that power outages were common too, adding that most of the poorer populace didn't have any power at all.

One evening after I had swum at the mountain pool, Jo-Jo took me to supper at the Hotel Byot which had decking projecting out over the sea. At the Marasigan's house, every meal was concentrated around pork, so it was a real treat to have some barbequed chicken skewers or beef, and because Byot had its own generator it could make and store ice-cream without threat of power cuts. Ice-cream! With real mango or coconut in it! The only food missing from my perfect meal was a plain lamb chop.

We dined out on the very edge of the platform. To our left across a tree-filled park stood the grim walls of the Spanish-built Fort Pilar overlooking a breakwater that kept the sea at bay on one side. The lee side looked swampy, covered with perhaps one hundred huts belonging to the town's poorest Muslims. No luxuries like electricity there, I guessed! Rising in stunning contrast above the hovels loomed the dome of a mosque, attracting my gaze as it glinted fiercely in the setting sun. Vintas with their colourful square sails headed towards us, each with a barefoot boatman skillfully manipulating a sail or motor while an ancient female passenger would plead with us to buy shells or coral. I gave in once, but that quickly attracted more boats and desperate sellers. My guilt swelled to the point I no longer enjoyed my food. As the great red ball of sun sank into the sea, darkness fell and little lamps from the boats began to gleam on the water. Each pier with its electric illumination revealed two seriously big ships loading copra and hemp.

* * *

Charlie kept his word and one day drove Linda and me some thirty miles down the coast road to his coconut plantation. After passing the white beach of Caragasan, the huts became fewer and more hidden amongst the vines. Some were clustered into villages, and occasionally we saw a woman with a big bundle of washing on her head, or a bucket of water which she had collected from the communal well. When I spied pigs, chickens, and small boys running around amongst the huts and the jungle growth, I asked Charlie "But don't Muslims have some law against the eating of pigs?" Charlie grinned. "They sell them to us Christians!" His smile switched to a frown. "You never want your car to break down out here, or have an accident, especially at night. We're beyond help this far out of town."

It was as if Charlie had foreseen his own fate. In 2010, when he was seventy-two years old, he was kidnapped one night from his home at Patalon by a notorious Muslim gang.

About halfway to Patalon Charlie pointed to a compound some distance inland, surrounded by jungle—my first glimpse of San Ramon prison. Charlie told me the prisoners were a mix of Muslim and Christian males, all hardened criminals. If any one of them were daring enough to escape, their aim would be to disappear quickly into the mountains.

A few miles further we turned into a sandy driveway flanked by palms leading to the Patalon homestead. George and Mrs Reith had waxed lyrical about the plantation, yet I was unprepared for its beauty. Forests of coconut palms interspersed with deep-green coffee bushes as far as the eye could see, all the way to the lower slopes of the jungle-clad mountains. The two-story house sat just a stone's throw from a white beach, and immediately I loved it. Construction comprised gleaming woods, carved and varnished. The feeling of space and light was enchanting. A small chapel situated on a slope below the house was created entirely from various timbers, and as we exited the chapel into a pristine garden, we saw the white cross on a grassy mound where the bones of Charlie's grandparents had been buried after they had been murdered—in that exact spot. I stood there for some time, trying to imagine how such an atrocity could have taken place in that little piece of heaven.

Charlie's staff had set up a table and chairs on the lawns under the palms overlooking the beach, and there we dined in our swimsuits. One of the nearest coconut palms had a curved trunk, and after seeing one of the workers shinning up a straight one to pick us a fresh young coconut for dessert, I decided that it couldn't be too hard to conquer the bent trunk. I did quite well for the first few feet before it dawned on me that our trees at home had been easy to climb because they had branches

Linda and I dine al fresco at Patalon.

and toeholds, although memories persisted of me as a five-year-old being retrieved from the upper branches of an oak tree by my grandfather on a ladder. I retreated, and descending was even scarier. Eventually my bare feet touched grass, and soon Linda and I were splashing around in the cool green sea. We dried and dressed and wandered around to the back of the homestead where we watched laborers husking the coconuts with long razor-sharp knives. A jeep backed out of a vast shed, Charlie behind the wheel. "Get in girls," he said, and the next thing we knew we were bouncing along too fast on a precarious track through the plantation then up and around the side of a mountain. The track was so steep, the vegetation so thick, I was mystified as to how we didn't come to grief. But at the same time, I was exhilarated.

We never did get to ride the horses that day, Charlie mumbling something about not enough saddles and bridles. The only horse at Patalon I saw was almost as small as the calesa horses. It was being ridden bareback by one of the workers who steered using a rope halter.

* * *

My activities rarely allowed much chance to rest. For example, all in one day, Jo-Jo took Linda and me for a swim at Caragasan, then to Hans and Rosie's house for lunch, and afterwards he tried to teach me how to do the Boogie Woogie. I'd always had a mental block with rock and roll. At one stage I twirled in the wrong direction and crashed into Jo-Jo, then trustingly arched back when I should have twirled so that he very nearly dropped me on my head, and after an hour of this spectacular lack of coordination we were panting and laughing until the tears streamed down our faces, forced to accept that Boogie Woogie and I would never be friends.

Mary gave me a bolt of the strangest material I have ever seen. It was psychedelic, the fabric gleaming like sheet metal fired into swirls of deep greens and reds. I determined to put this gift to good use by designing a glorious dress for me to wear to the wedding anniversary of Hans and Rosie, which was to be celebrated at Jo-Jo's house the very next day. With no time to lose, I fronted up to a Filipina seamstress with the bolt of fabric and drawings of the dress, despite being aware that my artistic talents had not improved since the cradle. My design showed a bodice with slim straps over the shoulders, a V-line neck and the waist and hips hugged before the skirt hung elegantly to just above the knees (gathered so that it would flare out when I twirled). That was the picture in my head anyway. But I forgot to draw the person wearing the dress, so the seamstress had no idea of the dress's length. The next afternoon I picked up the dress, and when I got home, I wriggled into the completed article and looked in the mirror. To my dismay I found myself in a mini-skirted dress looking shiny, garish, and dare I say, tarty!

That evening when dressing for Hans and Rosie's party, I folded the bodice inwards and wore the whole as a skirt of decent length topped with a bright pink blouse. My hair was piled up with a blue rose in it, and so I guess the result was nothing if not colourful! Jo-Jo picked me up, and off we drove to a small castle that he and his father called home. The driveway snaked mysteriously through his ten-acre property and suddenly the so-called house appeared atop a slope. It wasn't a house; it was a castle! The ground level was vast, but the floors above shrank as the construction rose higher, creating a tower effect. I was fascinated.

We walked through the huge verandahs from which a vast kitchen could be glimpsed, and then Jo-Jo led me up circular stairs until we came to a room where Rosie's cook Sy was preparing a big table of food. A few weeks later Hans and Rosie would be my foster parents, so I would come to know and like Sy. He had studied to be a chef somewhere in Europe, and it was obvious the Reiths relied on him absolutely. Not only was his food delicious, but he had a cheeky sense of humour.

Jo-Jo led me up another circular staircase and out into an open space decorated by pink and yellow frangipani peeking between the turrets. Cushions were piled against the stone walls; dance music filtered from somewhere in the background; stars twinkled overhead. The air was balmy, and the night promised to come close to heaven. More iron stairs led to the top of the tower where the bar had been set up, and we ate and drank and danced, Jo-Jo wisely avoiding the Boogie Woogie. All in all, it was a magical evening and ended, as parties in the Philippines invariably did, in the wee hours of the morning.

* * *

It didn't take Aunt Mary long to realize I was an outdoor girl who relished adventure. Towards the end of March, she conscripted her sixteen-year-old brother Ronnie to accompany Linda and me on a bicycle ride down the coast. Linda and I wore huge sombreros, and our lunches and water were carried courtesy of the gallant Ronnie. Perhaps because of the extreme heat we had only ridden three miles or so when Linda felt dizzy and had to sit on the verge. By some miracle, a jeepney appeared with Health Services written on it, and soon Linda was being driven back to town while Ronnie and I waited with the bicycles. Soon the Beetle appeared, driven by Aunty Mary. Linda was also on board, and insisted she was okay and would like to continue. So off we pedaled, occasionally passing clusters of huts with ragged urchins always running for a while beside us, pointing at me and shouting "Peace Corps, Peace Corps!" As I had learnt to do, I would call back "No, Australiana!" The PC, funded by the American government, had its headquarters another twelve miles further down the coast, and so it was natural that the locals assumed I

Linda, me and Ronnie on Cawa Cawa Boulevard.

was one of them. Whether the kids understood me or not, we always waved at each other and shouted our goodbyes.

We passed Caragasan, the glistening white beach fringed with coconut palms, and after a few more miles we reached the Peace Corps base, a spacious wooden building with a bamboo floor quite bare of any furniture. It was also bare of inhabitants. We headed to the nearby pebbly beach where we found three PC boys and one girl, two relaxing on the pebbles and two swimming in the baby waves. Ronnie, Linda and I stripped off to our bathers and happily joined the swimmers to cool off. For hours we talked and swam before hopping aboard one of the outriggers, canoes so slim they were almost impossible for anyone but an expert to manage, especially as the current was fierce. In fact, so strong that we had to paddle like mad to stay in one position which we found hilarious. By now the tropical sun was scorching and I knew I was burnt when we eventually mounted our bikes and pedaled home.

* * *

One morning Mary packed a lunch box and two hefty boys, Eddie and Sierno, arrived to escort Linda and me. In the van Mary drove us up to Pasonanca Park. Where the track ended against the edge of the jungle,

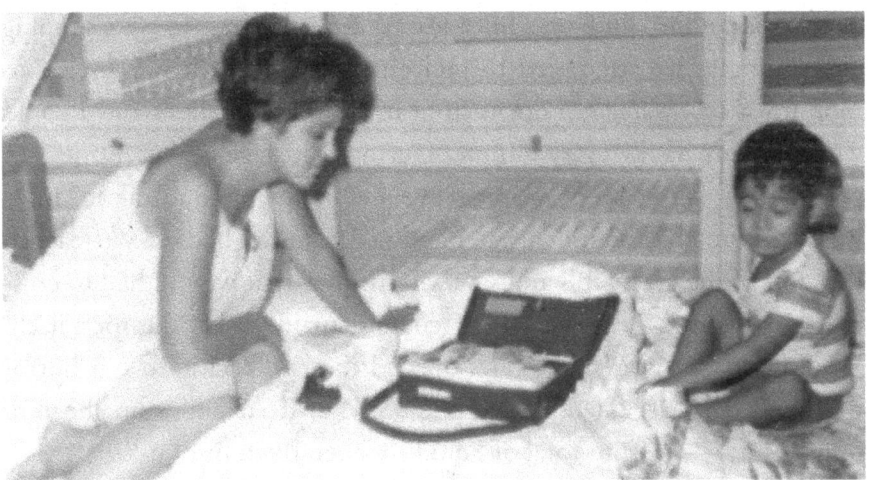
Me with Marasigan child, recording on tape to send home.

she dropped us off, and with a cheerful wave she left us gazing out over the valley. And there it was—Pulong Bato, Island of Rock, a monolith unlike most volcanic mountains, consisting of solid rock. Its dome rose straight up from the valley floor, and in most of its nooks and crannies it had hosted so many tropical plants it resembled a vast vertical garden. But in patches where the mountain's slippery stone was exposed, even the smallest plants couldn't get a grip, and from its crevices trickles of water oozed. Clouds of mist hovered over certain depressions, giving the whole mountain a mysterious and almost sinister look.

A dirt track wound its way through the jungle valley towards the rock. A host of birds sang all around us. We began the climb up a path spiraling around a hill that partly obscured Pulong Bato. I would have preferred to go straight up the face of the rock, but Eddie and Sierno had been instructed to take care of us girls, and I presumed they were playing safe. We stumbled around the hill and slipped and slid all the way down. At times the path was so narrow we had to cling to roots on each side and swing ourselves along. We came to a flat area, crossed a wide river on stepping-stones, clambered over a huge fallen tree, and suddenly found ourselves standing by a deserted hut near a river. We drank from the stream, but it would never be enough given what happened over the next few hours.

We began the climb on a hillside of sharp tall grass. We were slipping and sliding as we attempted to pull ourselves higher. It was useless to mop my face—water ran down from my hairline in rivers and I could wring out my hanky every minute. During that stage of the journey my perspiration simply seemed unladylike and annoying, but unknowingly we were losing far too much water and salt from our bodies. We reached the crest of the grassy hill and saw with dismay that we still had to cross the spur in front of us before we could actually tackle the rock itself. We flopped down, and the boys opened the backpacks. To our horror we found that Mary had packed one bottle of Coke and a small can of tomato juice—the sum total of liquid between the four of us!

If we'd been older and wiser we may have turned back, but after drinking the few sickly-sweet gulps of Coke we set off again. By this time my new sneakers had rubbed my heel raw, and blood was showing through. Linda and the boys sat me down, then bound up the foot with a hanky. With the pain dulled a little, we soldiered on until we came to the very base of Bato towering over us. We climbed hand over hand, grasping for tree roots and branches and finding toeholds with our feet. At last we hit a narrow pathway winding upwards through the densest jungle I had ever experienced, the vines tripping us at every step and cutting our hands and feet. Linda, who, like most Filipinas, lived a sheltered life, was finding it hard going, and inwardly I applauded her for never whining or giving up.

At long last we reached the summit, but before enjoying the view we ransacked the packs for the rest of the liquid. We divvied up the drinks so that I was given the small can of tomato juice while the other three finished off the Coke. And that's when we did something really dumb. We opened the pack of food and ate everything that Mary had prepared for us—a lunch that contained no fruits, just bread rolls and biscuits. We ate until our mouths were dry as paper. Without saying a word, and after a sweeping gaze at the green carpet far below us, we stood up and began to stumble down. But we could not remember precisely which way we had climbed up, and we reached a dead end on the edge of a cliff—too treacherous to attempt a descent. Retracing our steps to the summit, we tried again.

At this point I would have given forty pesos for a glass of water. The entire way down the Island of Rock we kept losing our footing, Eddie and Sierno shouldering the packs and managing to grab either Linda or me when we began to fall. At the base we trudged towards the gentler slopes of the grassy hill, eventually reaching its crest. Our mouths were too dry to talk much. We descended that hill with great difficulty, slipping and sliding and clutching at the razor-sharp grass. Blood began streaming down one of my hands, so Sierno held that hand so that I would not need to grab the grass again.

At the base of the hill we came to a more generous track through the jungle, and suddenly there it was—a fallen coconut! Our saviour! Eddie produced his machete, and with its tip gouged out a hole. Silently we

Me exhausted in the spikey grass after Pulong Batu climb #1.

stood in a circle, Sierno cradling the precious gift before offering it to me. I shook my head. Linda should go first. All three shook their heads. I was the guest in their country, and I must drink first. It was terrible trying to repress the urge to keep drinking until the milk was gone, but after two swallows I handed the coconut to Linda. She did likewise before handing it over to the boys. They did the same, and it was my turn again. By the weight of the coconut I knew that none of us could have the luxury of two more sips each, and so I took one mouthful before handing it to Linda. I had never liked coconut water, but right now it was up there with the best beverage in paradise. The last to take his share, Eddie probably got nothing, but he didn't complain and hacked up the nut and offered us a piece. If the coconut had been young, with soft translucent flesh, I would have accepted, but this was an old coconut, and I wasn't about to repeat the same mistake and dehydrate myself further.

A little further on we came to the clearing with the hut, the river swirling below us. We limped and stumbled to the bank and dived in, clothes and all, yelling as the water stung our cuts. Ignoring the possibility of pollution, we drank from that blessed river until we couldn't drink another drop, eventually dragging ourselves up and collapsing onto the grassy bank. Every now and again one of us would rise and go to swim—and drink!

Out of the blue two men appeared, both holding rifles. Instantly Eddie and Sierno jumped up and approached them. A garbled discussion ensued in a strange dialect between the four.

Within minutes the men were leading us Indian file along another track. They both wore sandals and seemed fascinated when I took off my shoes and traipsed happily over stones and through creeks much faster than I had in those agonizing sneakers. About 2 km from Pasonanca Park, which reared high above us, the men turned back and waved us goodbye. When we finally climbed that last hill to the park it was 5.30 P.M. We conferred with each other, finding that none of us had the money to hail a jeepney. Now Linda's feet were so chaffed that she, too, took off her shoes.

We trudged 12 km into the city, dirty, cut and bedraggled, humming the Filipino anthem "Land of the Morning" to revive our spirits and retrieving splinters of glass from our feet every hundred yards or so. Linda's feet were as burnt and painful as mine, but I was in no condition to help her. The four of us had walked a total of 30 kms over hilly jungle terrain. Dr Marasigan cleaned our cuts, and when he poured antiseptic on my wounded heel I hit the roof. That night, as I was dismembering lobster on the tea table, I cut my finger quite deeply with the knife and began to laugh hysterically. The little Marasigan boys scrutinized me with bewildered brown eyes as I gobbled down three servings of crayfish, two servings of sweet potato and beans, a bowl of soup, two pieces of fish, two bananas, and several glasses of my new favourite drink, *water*!

Six months before meeting President Ferdinand Marcos
Early April 1968
Location: Cagyan de Oro

A Rotary convention was held in Cagyan de Oro, a city in northern Mindanao. Several exchange students from other parts of Australia who were being hosted by other Filipino cities gathered there. Dr Marasigan and Charlie accompanied me on a Fokker Friendship aircraft, and we arrived the afternoon before the convention. At the home of the city's Rotary president I met with my three Australian female counterparts whom I liked immediately. We each grabbed a bed and hastily unpacked before an older man, presumably a Rotarian, arrived in his jeep to take us nightclubbing. It was a long night. Not only did our escort prove to be a crashing bore, but the other exchange students included a bighead called John who smoked, drank, and boasted. Not a good role model for my country. Because I was with a group I was unable to leave when I wanted to, and so it wasn't until 2.30 A.M. that the kindly Filipino bore delivered us back to the house. To our dismay we found that the high gates were locked and bolted. In the dark street we called out as loudly as we dared, but nobody stirred within. I eyed off the thick concrete wall topped with jagged glass before removing my sandals. While other guard dogs in the street were barking savagely, our host's property remained as quiet as the grave, so somehow I climbed that wall without cutting myself, fell down the other side, and rustled up a servant to open up. Like a Trojan horse the jeep moved silently through the gateway.

Creeping inside we found our beds, and oddly enough we never did find out why our hosts had locked us out. I was tired, especially knowing I must be up at 6 A.M. to play in a tennis tournament, one of the activities on offer that I had opted for. The other two girls had chosen more wisely—a sightseeing tour of some sort. In my defence no one had informed me that all the other participants in the tournament would be men. To make matters worse I had forgotten that courts in the Philippines were not of cool green grass, but of unforgiving concrete that absorbed the tropical sun.

By 7.30 A.M., after a small breakfast, I was partnered up with someone who proved to be about my standard. However, our opponents were classed as A-grade which did nothing for my confidence. Thinking we had no way in hell of winning, I relaxed. My partner and I forged ahead, winning the first set. But then, as the sun rose higher and heatwaves began shimmering over the court, the gash in my heel (a legacy from Pulong Bato) reopened. Once again blood oozed through my canvas sneaker, and the pain began to bother me. I kicked off my shoes and began to play barefoot on that steaming hot concrete. Eventually we began to lose until mercifully, the match ended in a score of two to one.

I limped off the court, and someone drove me back to the host house. My colleagues had not yet returned from their tour, so I was alone in the kitchen with some maids who spoke little English. I asked for a cold drink. As I sculled my glass of orange juice I noticed that my hand was trembling. I then mimed for them to bring a bowl of water, and as my blistered bleeding feet dropped into the cool water a wave of weakness overwhelmed me. I dragged myself into the shower, and after dressing in a cotton shift, I flopped down on my bed. I stared at the ceiling and became aware that my breathing was irregular. Hearing the two girls returning to their bedroom next door, I tried to call out, but this room appeared to be soundproof. My heart began to jump out of rhythm and my fingers tingled. *Am I having a heart attack?* One of the girls put her head into the room. Seeing my distress she rushed to get help, and soon a doctor came and gave me some brandy. Within half an hour I was feeling better, suspecting my problems were a tangled mix of exhaustion, heatstroke, and dehydration.

By that evening I felt strong enough to go out with the girls to meet the Australian boys at a ten-pin bowling alley where we all ate rice cakes and laughed a lot. The Philippine bowling alleys weren't mechanised.

Instead, small Filipino boys scampered to send back the ball and set up the pins in the perfect triangle. They never stopped! I returned home at 10 P.M., ate some cheese and crackers, felt great, and got a reasonable night's sleep.

The sudden feeling of nausea woke me up. I got up and immediately fainted onto the floor. When I regained consciousness, severe pains racked my stomach, and for the entire day I felt too sick and weak to leave my bed. I lay there, and to keep my sanity I tried to imagine SJ entering the room, sitting down beside me, holding my hand and looking deeply into my eyes. For a while this game would help until my imagination wavered, and I'd feel worse because it wasn't real. When the time came for the ball, I didn't have the energy to drag myself up and put on the glamourous dress Mary had lent me. A miserable evening was spent in bed made worse by waves of agonizing homesickness.

The following morning, though weak, I felt in a fit enough condition to attend the city's grandest hotel where there were literally hundreds of Rotarians. The Rotary Exchange students were lined up along the stage, and each of us had to speak for five minutes. I was the very last to say my bit, and although I felt nervous and weak I surprised myself—not only did my speech go down exceptionally well, but when Charlie came to escort me off the stage, the crowd clapped and stomped their feet and cheered wildly. It seemed that I had scored the most popular Rotary president in the whole of the country. Even if only a small part of the cheering was for me, the accolade was uplifting—just what the doctor ordered. After a professional photography session we were set free to prepare ourselves for the Governor's Ball to be held that night, so after a siesta, I donned Mary's pretty, long dress, and we three girls were driven to the ball.

The venue was al fresco and magnificent. Thousands of glamorous guests stood around on vast lawns dotted with flares and flowers, and guitarists performed close to the many dance floors to ensure non-stop dancing to the irresistible Latino tunes and rhythms. When I was returned to the host house it was 3 A.M. which left two hours for sleeping. At 5.30 A.M. Charlie would pick me up and take me to the airport for a 6.30 A.M. flight back to Zambo. Or so I thought.

Charlie escorts me onstage at Cagyan de Oro.

Groaning with fatigue, I roused myself at the correct time and waited outside for Charlie. And waited. At 6 A.M. a servant came running out to say a Dr Marasigan was on the phone wondering where I was. My adrenalin had now reached dangerous heights, and I felt quite ill. "Can you please arrange to get me to the airport?" I asked, but the servants could not understand. In desperation, I pointed to the family jeep. "Please," I begged. "Quick!" It seemed like hours before a driver sauntered out of the house. I jumped into the jeep with my bag. But an excruciating ten minutes crawled by while the driver filled the vehicle with gasoline. It seemed like eons before we were heading (not fast enough for me) out of town to the airport.

Doc ushered me out onto the tarmac, explaining he had managed to delay the plane twenty minutes. I felt terrible, both emotionally and physically, hurrying down the aisle and slumping into my seat. "Where's Charlie?" I asked weakly. "I don't know," replied the Doc mildly, "but he is known for missing planes." From that moment I found it a great effort to speak, closing my eyes and trying to sit upright as I steeled myself against what became a rough journey. The turbulence threw us about, and while normally I have a cast-iron stomach for sea and air sickness, I was already so low that it took every ounce of willpower not to be sick. Quite frankly I couldn't have cared less if we'd crashed into a mountain.

When at last we landed in Zamboanga and the plane taxied to a stop, I tried in vain to get my body and brain to operate. Gently, Doc unbuckled my seat belt, helping me to my feet. He held me steady as we made our way out into the glaring sunshine. The Brent Hospital van was at the airport, presumably driven by Mary, and all I can remember is the van parking outside Brent Hospital and me being taken in a wheelchair up to the second floor. In a private room I was put on a drip, and that is where and how I lay for a total of two days and two nights. By the third day I began to eat heartily again, and felt much stronger, although even climbing the stairs to my room left me breathless, and I had lost a great deal of weight.

* * *

Immediately the rounds of invitations to all kinds of events resumed, and many of these could not be refused without giving offence. On Easter Thursday Jo-Jo once again took me to dinner at the Byot Hotel overlooking the sea, and apart from the boat people trying to sell us corals and shells, there was a freighter docked at the wharf, the *London Citizen*. Someone told us that the Chinese crew had mutinied against their British captain. The Western owners of such freighters tended to employ Indian and Chinese crewmen because they could pay them a pittance compared with European crews, so it was hardly surprising Asian crews mutinied every now and again.

While Jo-Jo and I were dining we were joined by Charlie and three of his friends—Will, a Canadian, Hank from the Netherlands, and his fiancé Chita. Someone got talking about Santa Cruz Island, and soon I was accepting the invitation by Hank, Chita and Will to accompany them to explore this low coral island.

I tried to get a few winks of sleep before dragging myself up at 7 A.M. on Good Friday. Someone drove us to the Byot Hotel, and from the decking we haggled with Muslim boatmen until we struck the bargain of sixty pesos for two vintas to take us to the island for the morning. With one boatman handling each vinta, and Hank and Chita in one boat and Will and me in the other, we sailed in glorious sunny weather for the island, beckoning to us with its low bright green shrubs and gleaming white coral sand. It looked much closer than four kilometres from the mainland.

My dad had always been a keen yachtie, so I had experienced many different types of sailing boats, large and small. But never had I seen anything as primitive as the vinta and the incredible skill required to sail it. In pairs we were crammed into each end of the narrow wooden hull while the sailors with tough dark feet danced along the rim of the canoe or the outriggers on either side, constantly handling ropes, the helmsman steering the tiller with his toes. Like an ancient scroll the square sail unfurled from its horizontal wooden beam, and as I examined the craft I noticed that every component was constructed of wood held together by cords or rope. As we approached the island the water became crystal clean and green, and below its surface bright corals of all shapes and sizes magically appeared.

For some reason we avoided the Greater Santa Cruz Island and "landed" on the lesser one, small and flat and completely constructed of white coral and shells. The glare from the sun's reflection on the white was fierce, and from that moment we all began to cook to a crisp. Will and Hank, who had goggles, floated over the beautiful vista below the sea while Chita and I began to collect coral and shells on the shore.

Every now and again one of the boatmen approached me with a tentative "Ma'am?" and would offer me a treasure he had just discovered. This was generous, because their income was meagre to say the least and they could have stashed their own finds to sell afterwards to rich Westerners like us.

Mischievously Hank told us about the Lapu Lapu, an infamous and gigantic grouper which tended to hang around this island and had been known to attack humans. So only when I was beyond boiling did I venture into the water, looking out for a large dark shadow which might be about to eat me. Port Lincoln had been dubbed the "Home of the Great White," and as a child I had walked out to the end of the town jetty to peer, mesmerised, at a shark strung up by his tail so that his nose touched the planks. As I stared into his open jaws, I was overcome by the sickening realization that this monster could have swallowed me like a small snack.

The sun shone glaringly hot on Santa Cruz. Every time I paused from my swimming and tried to stand up, the razor-sharp coral floor threatened to lacerate my feet, and those feet had recently suffered enough. No sooner had I emerged onto the gritty white sand than I became aware that Will and Hank had stopped snorkelling and they and the boatmen were squinting at a thick black cloud on the horizon. Suddenly all the males seemed very keen to head back to the mainland, and for good reason. The strait was known for its strong currents and its sudden storms.

Once again we took our places on those narrow canoes, but this was a different journey altogether, and even if we had thought of lifejackets, there weren't any. The storm hit within minutes of us leaving the island, and the other vinta was lost to view as a ferocious gust picked up the right outrigger, threatening to hurl the entire boat across the water in a giant cartwheel. One of our boatmen sprang to sit with his full weight on the outrigger. The waves piled higher and began to rush into the canoe and drench us repeatedly. Suddenly the rope securing a corner of the sail snapped. As the sail whipped and flapped dangerously one sailor began to bail furiously. The more water we shipped in, the lower the boat sank and the more waves we copped. But the second sailor was sidling nimbly along the upper side of the boat, reaching out for the flailing rope to rein it in. Sometimes we were slicing through the crests of the waves, but mostly we were plunging into the trenches with brutal force, leaving the boat floundering and helpless. And what did I write home? "Oh boy, was it terrific! I really expected us to capsize."

At last both small vintas limped into the shelter of the harbor, sailing past their larger brothers from which little brown and naked boys swam like torpedoes towards us and begged for coins. Those kids could have easily won gold at the Olympics.

* * *

On Good Friday afternoon friends and I gathered on the second floor of Laura's Bakeshop, a café-style bakery with a casual restaurant upstairs, to watch the Easter procession. Although this was due to file past at 5 P.M., and although people had already been lining the narrow streets for an hour before, no event in the Philippines ever started on time.

Not until 6 P.M. did all seven floats crawl into view on the street below us. They were simple carts, each carrying a brightly lit statue depicting the story of the Cross, carried high by men. In between the floats walked crowds of people, the women in black lace veils, all bearing candles or rosaries. But the impressive part of the whole show, which took more than an hour to pass, was that everyone was totally, utterly silent. As the sun was going down, that silence was powerful, until a disgusting incident in a side street marred the holy ceremony. An exhausted calesa pony collapsed in the shafts, the driver eventually hauling the little horse to its feet, re-harnessing him, and loading the cart with passengers once more.

On Monday morning someone mentioned an Easter egg hunt, and instantly I envisaged a choc-fest. But it soon became clear that chocolate doesn't do well in the tropics, and the Catholic custom of hollowing out hens eggs and painting them had been around for hundreds of years. The Filipino children seemed just as excited to receive their painted eggshells as we had been back in Oz to receive chocolate, and I secretly admired this custom for several reasons. Firstly, the kids had decorated the eggshells themselves, so there was no commercialism involved. Secondly the symbol of new life from a real egg seemed far more potent than the commercial equivalent. And thirdly, the "little devils" didn't end up smeared with chocolate from chin to hair.

That afternoon the whole family and I went for a stroll along the boulevard. It was a spontaneous decision, so Doc, Mary, the kids and I left for the walk without changing clothes. Doc was wearing the equivalent of a singlet on top, the most casual I had ever seen him, and as usual I was barefoot. We chatted as we walked, and in no time at all we were standing below a restaurant where the dining section was al fresco and overlooking the sea. "Shall we go up and have some barbeque?" said Mary. The kids piped up, eager to go upstairs, but Doc Marasigan reminded us quietly that I had no shoes and he had no proper shirt.

We were about to turn back when I said, "Who cares what people think?" The Marasigans stopped, staring at me. Then Mary smiled and nudged her husband. We crept upstairs like thieves, sat in the darkest corner, and ate roasted pork bits on a skewer. But Murphy's Law dictates we would be discovered, and within five minutes, six of Dr Marasigan's patients wandered in. I knew my bare feet would be undetected as long as I kept my legs under the table, but Doc squirmed, trying to conceal his torso behind his small son who was sitting on his knee. However, all too soon his patients approached us for a chat, the white singlet shining out like a beacon from the gloom. I got the giggles, and I think Mary did too, but poor shy Doc looked as if he had landed in Hell.

* * *

Back in the southern hemisphere a certain vibe told me that Mum and Dad were getting restless, my letters home describing idyllic days on beaches and spectacular nights at balls and nightclubs. "When will you actually start to study?" they asked in their letters. I struggled to explain that, apart from the typing school which I would soon be attending, the summer holidays for Filipino students covered those first two months of my stay in the Philippines.

There were numerous glorious swimming days, mostly in the green sea at Caragasan, and in the Pasonanca mountain pool where I practiced my diving. Afterwards my friends and I often walked up into the beautiful park to purchase fried bananas on sticks from ragamuffins. Because the stumpy bananas had been dipped in brown sugar then turned over a flame, they ended up thinly covered with toffee—delicioso!

**Five months before meeting President Ferdinand Marcos
Location: Reiths' second house, Madrid Street, Zamboanga**

It was time to leave the Marasigans and transfer to the Reiths' second house, inhabited by Hans, Rosie and Charlie, and infrequently by Mrs Reith and George visiting from Manila. After I had taken the Marasigan boys for a farewell walk along the beach in front of Brent Hospital, it was time for Charlie to pick me up and settle me into his spacious home. There were two maids and Sy the cook, the old chef who had been with the Reith family even in the pre-war days. And there was one other right-royal inhabitant—the aloof Siamese cat who looked upon humans as inferior beings. The rooms were light and gorgeously furnished—copper and dark wood gleaming, shell lampshades shining—and to my delight there was a piano. The back of the house led down to a sheltered rocky foreshore from where the Hotel Byot was visible, and further away across a grassy treed area stood those substantial ruins of the ancient Fort Pilar. Encroaching out into the sea from the fort was the high breakwater that hid from view the swampy Muslim village, except for the top of the mosque's dome.

The Reiths' maids and man servants always seemed happy, which gave me an even higher opinion of this big Austrian-Filipino family. Even the turkeys in an enclosed area at the back seemed content, gobbling away and blissfully unaware that they would be providing the family with meals from time to time.

My room was luxurious, featuring a double bed with embroidered sheets and pillowslips, and my own little spotless bathroom with—joy of joys, hot water every time I turned on the tap! And something else I prized . . . the sounds of silence, except occasionally happy laughter or singing from the servants. No children crying or shouting. There was yet another feeling less tangible, having something to do with freedom. The Marasigans had guarded me as closely as was possible without formally chaperoning me, bless their hearts. But here with Charlie and Hans and Rosie, I sensed with secretive joy that I would not need to account for my whereabouts every minute of the day, especially as so many of my new friends were offering to take me out swimming, or to parties and special events. On some occasions a special delicacy called "lechon" was offered, a whole pig roasted on a spit, the crackling reserved for the VIP guests. I adore crackling, and although I knew too much of it could swell me to the size of a nipa hut, to refuse this honour would have been offensive to the host. That was my excuse anyway.

* * *

Charlie was out somewhere as usual, and Hans and Rosie were busy elsewhere. Even the cat was invisible. Sensing that the Reiths trusted me, I decided to stroll into town alone. At one stage I became disorientated, and the smell in some of the dirty streets nearly knocked me over. I figured that was partly due to the dried fish hanging out the front of meagre wooden shops, and no doubt some uncontrolled sewage, the putrid mix hanging heavily in the air.

The male "wolves" stared and made comments in Chavacano or pigeon-English as I passed by. Sometimes they turned, faced a wall, and urinated. The Muslim men, who evidently were forbidden to swallow their saliva, did a lot of spitting. While I hoped they would never spit at me, it was disconcerting to have to dodge the globs on the pavement.

By now I had taught myself the cool, calm and collected look, and felt more able to withstand the odors, the urine, the spit, and the unwanted attention. I had also learned to ask for items in shops, and to make myself understood by calesa drivers. After I had caught a calesa back to the Reiths' and indulged in a siesta, Jo-Jo magically appeared. He taught me some Spanish, while Sy cooked us a meal fit for a king and queen, serving up a main course of sliced beef and vegetables and rice, with a choice of mango pie or creamed bananas for dessert. Because I adored both and couldn't resist, it seemed only right to have some of each.

* * *

I begged Charlie to let me go horse riding. He knew this was coming and grinned, a grin that told me I was in for a hard time. "Are you a good rider?" Charlie asked. I hesitated. When I was seven Mum was given a glorious Arab mare called Silver Dash, and from that time I had been taught to ride. Some of the most exciting days of my life were when the float was hitched up with Silver D safely aboard, and off we'd drive to one of the country shows. If my brother and I were lucky, one of the farmers would bring a spare horse for us. We'd hop on this untried brumby (Australian wild horse) to compete in "Best Boy" or "Best Girl" rider, but these animals came straight from the paddock where they had been grazing unchecked for months. Understandably annoyed to find themselves saddled and bridled and someone on their backs urging them to do what they didn't want to do, they always tested us out, so we had learned to stick like glue to a troublesome horse. Now at Patalon I'd be on full alert.

Charlie produced a bay gelding called Roger who had a glint in his eye that set off warning bells. An estate worker put on his bridle, trying to avoid being bitten at the same time, and then threw a cowboy saddle on his back, drew the girth super tight, and disappeared. Hans and Rosie, Judy and Charlie all stood at a distance and watched with glee as I held the long ropes that passed for reins. I tried to slip my hand under the girth and couldn't. I loosened it a notch before swinging into the massive cowboy saddle with its high pommel. Immediately Roger bucked. I was expecting that, but I hadn't realized the stirrups were dangling below my feet. I gripped with my knees for dear life as rascally Roger put me through the full test of kicking and bolting and trying to wipe me off on a rubber tree. Somewhere in the distance my audience was hooting with laughter, but it took all my concentration and a good five minutes before I brought Roger under control. I dismounted and was raising the stirrups as Charlie approached with some advice. "If you want him to go to the right, don't pull his mouth to the right, just lean to the right and let the left rope come up against his neck." From that moment I really enjoyed myself, riding with one hand only, the other on the high pummel as I lazily swung the free section of rope in my new cowgirl style.

I headed for the hills along soft dirt tracks pushing their way through the lush jungle. Then, turning back towards the sea, I took another route, my hair flying free during a fast gallop. On the beach we turned and cantered for miles along the shoreline, and I had a sneaking feeling that Roger was enjoying himself too.

In my beautiful bedroom that night, as my pen was describing details of the day to my family, the Siamese cat suddenly decided I was worthy of him. Plonking himself on my lap, he demanded I stop writing and caress him. At that moment the lights went out. Yet another blackout! The maid brought in candles so that I was able to finish off my letter with "Tons and tons of love, Estefania (as Hans calls me)."

* * *

I started to spend time with Rosie, who was famous throughout the country as a choreographer and teacher of ballet and Spanish dance. Since marrying Hans her teaching was confined to Zamboanga where she was widely respected. In fact, just being part of the Reith family seemed to earn immediate credits from the community. One night she was given two front seats for us both to witness the coronation of the "queen" of nursing school graduates. This event was presented as a performance where the winner of the crown played Queen Isabella of Spain. The stage was awash with spangles and speeches and loud blasts of the trumpet. It seemed that while most Filipinos became easily bored with subtlety, everyone onstage and off had a rollicking good time, which was all that mattered.

One day Rosie took me to meet a French Vietnamese woman called Nicko who was drop dead gorgeous both inside and out. I spent some time practicing my school-girl French with her, and it was a pleasant surprise to find that I could understand most of what she said. Nicko and I asked Rosie if we could be part of her slimnastic classes in her studio. We leapt, twirled and twisted to throbbing music—good infectious fun.

There was the Hula and Hawaiian dance, perilously close to belly dancing, where you must throw each hip forwards as you move. I had trouble from the start. While the other women seemed to have substantial hips to "throw" forwards, my hips were so slim they were almost non-existent and simply couldn't be thrown. At one stage I tried so hard I nearly threw my back out instead. One afternoon the three of us were in the change room when suddenly mischievous Rosie asked if we'd ever heard of "Princess Papooya." Before we could reply she was gliding forwards, her hips swinging as she sang "Princess Papooya," her hands insinuating the shape of a curvaceous female, "has plenty papaya," her hands outlining breasts, her arms opening outwards "she love to give them away!" Nicko and I stared, then exploded into paroxysms of laughter.

* * *

One of the hen turkeys in the Reiths' back garden suddenly produced very strange looking poults, and Rosie remembered that three months earlier a big white rooster had hopped over the fence and into the turkey enclosure. Two of the "turkeylets" had features suspiciously like a chicken. One was bright yellow! Turkeys were prized meat in the Philippines, but rookeys or turkhens were worthless. A furious Sy stomped about threatening to "put dat damn rooster in the pot."

George, who this time was visiting without his mother, was as eccentric as ever. As usual we got on famously, ribbing each other and sometimes having quite deep and meaningful discussions. One night as I was applying makeup, getting ready for a party, George appraised me. "You know Steffie, I hate to be so frank and blunt but I think you need a new face!" Another time, when I was describing my beloved SJ, he squirted me with water exclaiming, "You know you're a lovesick sentimental fool." When I enthusiastically agreed he sighed, saying "I give you my blessing my children."

* * *

After lunch one afternoon, the weather was sweltering. Hans felt unwell and he and Rosie disappeared to take a siesta. George too had hit the sack, and suddenly the house became unnaturally quiet. I set off alone after stuffing a few pesos into my handbag. This time, instead of heading towards the town square I turned right towards the great fort. I yearned to explore it, even though I knew the interior was only open to the public on special occasions, usually parties held by the town's elite.

On that scorching afternoon I walked over a lawn shaded by a few trees towards the massive wooden gates which were firmly closed. I skirted the wall that curved towards the breakwater stretching out into the sea, that breakwater I had seen from a distance sheltering the small Muslim village with its dominating domed mosque. The grass finished abruptly—now I was walking on a stony road which circled the fort. Unrelentingly the sun blazed down. Up high in the wall facing the sea I spotted an empty niche which I suspected once contained a bass relief of the Virgin Mary. Perhaps the carving had worn away over time.

Lined up at the entrance to the breakwater and parallel to the shore, directly in front of the Madonna niche, were three long trestle tables laden with red candles of different sizes. And behind the stalls stood female Muslim vendors, all highly excited to see me and chattering in their dialect, desperate to sell. It took me a few moments to appreciate the irony—the Muslims were selling candles to Christians who came to pray to the Virgin so that their sins might be forgiven while burning a redemptive candle.

I understood only two words the vendors were saying—"Cara Benita" (beautiful face), but one thing was certain—this Cara Benita was now perspiring profusely. I tried to make the vendors understand that I would like to purchase "le mas grande" candle—the biggest they had on offer. They clambered to find their largest specimen, and one old lady held up a candle that eclipsed all the others. The women exploded with mirth. It was clear I had committed such a massive sin that only a candle the size of a fire extinguisher would atone! I paid a whole peso for that huge red cylinder of wax, and then my eyes lifted to the silver dome beyond the old vendor. Clumsily I indicated to the old woman that I would come back for the candle after I had walked "out there," pointing to the village nestling against the eastern side of the breakwater. The laughter stopped. The women were suddenly uneasy. I hesitated, then decided that this might be my only chance to see for myself what the inside of a mosque looked like. Besides, I couldn't back off now—not in front of this audience who obviously inhabited the wooden huts around the mosque.

I must have been an odd sight, in cotton dress and sandals, clutching my handbag and heading out alone on that dusty track atop the ridge of rocks making up the breakwater. The walk seemed endless. When in line with the mosque I turned off down the bank and found a squelchy track through the raised wooden huts. Not one face did I see. Extremely eerie. Soon I arrived at the mosque's entrance, a small porch area where the faithful had left their shoes. That reminded me to slip my sandals off, and I stepped barefoot into the enormous circular area, the clean shiny floor stretching to the curved walls of the mosque. The sun's rays streamed through a gilded window high above indicating the direction of Mecca. Even though my belief in any God had waned, I felt overwhelmed by the glorious feeling of peace in that vast, cool space. Gazing up at the sunlit window, I gradually became aware of low mutterings breaking the silence, and before I could collect my wits I was surrounded by a crowd of men.

Jabbering at me in a dialect I could not understand, there was no mistaking their anger. I pointed to my bare feet. "Zapatos," I said, pointing towards the entrance. In other words, I had remembered to take off my shoes. They shook their heads, their voices rising to a dangerous level. And that's when I picked up a vital word—"mujer." Some were pointing their fingers at me, while others were pointing up to a mezzanine floor with a guard rail. And then it hit me. While remembering to take my shoes off, I had forgotten that I was a woman! Struggling to appear calm, I threw out a relieved and apologetic smile. "Aaah, si, perdon. Would you be kind enough to show me, por favor?" And I pointed upwards, at the women's gallery. The tension around me switched to confusion, a heated debate starting up until the collective mind reached consensus. Most disappeared, but a few stayed back to escort me to the gallery entrance which was outside the mosque proper. As we passed through the porch I pointed to my sandals and asked in English whether it was okay to put these on to go to the gallery. They understood, and nodded, before ushering me further around to some rickety wooden steps leading up to the mezzanine. Behind three men I climbed the stairs until I reached the area where thirty equally rickety wooden chairs stepped up in rows. With much nodding and many approving little ums and aahs, I then turned to my escorts. "Muchas gracias."

As we made our way back down the stairs I breathed easier, knowing that the inflammatory situation was defused, even though none of them looked happy as they guided me along a track leading out of the village. We were almost at the base of the breakwater when a hot and bothered Ali came hurrying towards me.

Ali was one of the few Muslims in the town of Zamboanga who had managed, because of his buoyant personality and intelligence, to secure himself a job as DJ at a radio station. About twenty years of age, Ali had a wonderful smile from ear to ear, but apart from that I knew little about him, and had never thought of asking where he lived. I could not fathom how Ali had been alerted that the "Australian girl" had appeared in his village. When he saw that I was all right, he asked me to backtrack with him a little way so that I could meet his mother. There, amongst a cluster of wooden huts, his mum sat sewing on a Singer treadle machine. She seemed delighted to meet me, and we had a stilted conversation as I admired some of her handiwork. Ali's face clearly showed he was proud of his mum, and of himself for earning the money to buy her that sewing machine.

A jeepney crammed with men was waiting on the ridge of the breakwater to ferry me back to town, but I didn't feel comfortable climbing into a confined space with a mob of males. Besides, I had promised the candle vendors that I would return for the "mas grande" candle. Waving Ali farewell in the jeepney, I returned along the breakwater. By midafternoon I arrived back at the Reith house, armed with my huge red cylinder. Instantly, eagle-eyed George spotted it and demanded to know where I'd got it. At the very moment I told him, using my acting skills to sound offhand, Hans and Rosie appeared. *Red alert*. Questions were fired until I was forced to admit I had ventured from the fort and had strolled over to the "swamp village" to visit the mosque.

Well! Hans nearly had a heart attack, Rosie gave me a lecture, and George said I could have been killed. He made me promise to never,

ever, go anywhere near a Muslim village again. When Hans had recovered, he told me about the Muslim concept of Jihad. It was the first time I had ever heard of the horrible belief that it was okay to kill all those who didn't believe in Allah. Hans became specific, explaining that every so often a Moro would appear in a bustling Christian market with a kris and do a whirling Dervish dance with the multi-curved scimitar, killing as many infidels as he could before he would inevitably be overpowered.

That day gave me food for thought. Although I would continue to take every individual as they came, some belief systems offended me. How dare men from any religion treat women as inferior people, in this case inferring that women would profane the mosque proper by entering that holy space. This was an offensive notion to a free-thinking girl who had never experienced anything other than equality. As for Jihad, which shows zero tolerance to any creed other than Islam, I could not understand why Muslims like Ali and his loving family didn't denounce it loudly and publicly. On the other hand, I realized it would take a brave individual to stand against the tide and risk being ostracized, or worse.

One day I broached the subject of birth control to Hans and Rosie, who I knew were Catholic but always seemed so liberal minded. I asked them why, when I had seen children living in such poverty and beggars starving in the streets, did the pope not promote birth control so that the population of the Philippines could be reduced along with much suffering. Rosie was shocked, with me equally shocked at her reaction. She told me that the Holy Father spoke on behalf of God himself, and because God was against birth control, then that was the last word on the matter—the Word of God.

The population of the Philippines in 1968 was around 33 million, in 1977 55 million, and in 2020 more than 109 million!

* * *

At the Reith house the situation was constantly changing. George left for Manila one night to resume his studies, and Charlie vanished the following morning for his overseas trip which would include Sydney.

Naturally I loaded him up with gifts for my loved ones and assured him that if he could just "pop" down to Adelaide, Mum and Dad were under strict orders to spoil him rotten.

My family never got to meet Charlie, but faithfully he posted the gifts which arrived safely.

At this time I began my typing lessons at Southern City Colleges, a short walk away from the Reith household. The few classrooms were basic with wooden chairs and desks. Because I had already used a typewriter with the wrong fingering and needed to sight the keyboard, I sensed my secretarial career wouldn't get far. The typewriters were antiquated. Each key needed a lot of persuasion to depress, and of course the ribbon was always running out or getting twisted. During the first lesson I spent two frustrating hours wrestling with those infernal machines before trudging home and indulging in a siesta for the entire afternoon.

That night, as I was scribbling a letter to Australia, once again Zamboanga was plunged into blackout. The maid brought me a candle, but after I had written a few more words I became aware the curtain was alight. Panicked, I stifled the flames with a piece of tablecloth. This worked, but I needed to confess to Rosie and Hans that some of their furnishings were singed. They were very gracious about it, but for several days my imagination ran riot and I felt a little sick. If I hadn't quickly snuffed out those flames, I would have become infamous as the Aussie who burnt down her hosts' home!

It was during my typing lessons that I met Bing, a Filipina from the poorer end of town. Discovering that she collected stamps from around the world, I invited her back to my "home" to give her some Australian stamps. Bing looked a little embarrassed, so I asked if she had any Filipino stamps and would she like to swap. Her face lit up. I held a tin of Aussie stamps as Bing and I sauntered not far away to where she boarded at her Auntie's (Mrs Bader's) home. It was a humble abode compared with the Reiths' residence. The backyard was small and the furnishings sparse. Bing's parents lived on a modest coconut plantation on Basilan Island, two hours ferry ride away to the south. Every workday morning, I met up with Bing and walked to Southern City Colleges where we sat side by side and dutifully typed, sometimes with a cover over the keyboard so we couldn't cheat.

* * *

Towards the end of my stay with the Reiths a mestizo called Artu Lopez began to feature in my life. His family, one of the wealthiest in Zamboanga, owned Laura's Bakeshop, the two-level bakery selling homemade ice-cream and all kinds of pies, including banana and coconut. It was this shop from which I had viewed the Easter procession. His mother I only met once, in her big kitchen at home from where she baked all those delicious pies, so I presume her name was Laura. Artu's dad owned a radio station called DXLL, and it was this station that employed Ali, the delightful Muslim boy with the big grin from the "swamp village," officially called Rio Hondo.

Like Jo-Jo, Artu was part Spanish and part Filipino, stocky, well-built, and hair black as coal while his skin was as fair as any Anglo. He drove a Toyota two-seater bright red sports car and was a star student in commerce at the University of Santo Tomas in Manila, an institution founded in 1611. Within days of our first meeting Artu fell madly in love, insisting he could not sleep for thinking about me, often luring me to the bakeshop for ice cream or a slice of his mother's famous coconut cream pie. I admitted all this to my SJ, assuring him that while I was shamelessly addicted to coconut cream pies, I had not lost one second of sleep pining for Artu.

I must stress that (so far) none of the Filipinos who had taken me out and lavished me with gifts and proclaimed their undying love, ever took advantage of me in any way. I always made it plain from the start that I was in love with SJ who was waiting for me back home. The worst I had suffered by the end of May were some pangs of embarrassment when suitors like Artu brought me treats, and all I could offer them in return was my friendship. One Friday morning Artu called by in his red machine, and although the rain hammered down we roared out to Caragasan Beach and had a swim where for once the water was cool. After our swim we continued to be drenched as we sat on the beach and ate lobster salad sandwiches, probably made by his mum. During the afternoon Artu took me to radio station DXLL where Ali interviewed me, Artu hovering outside the glass of the soundproof studio while Ali asked intelligent questions on far-ranging topics.

That evening I was subjected to another completely different experience as I accompanied Artu to the last prayers for Mr Wee Sit, a prominent Chinese man of the town who had died nine days before. Every evening of the nine days friends had gathered at his home to pray for his soul, afterwards sitting around gambling. This rather shocked me until Artu explained that the gamblers were expected to donate all winnings to the family to help pay for the deceased's funeral—a win-win activity! Anyway, because this was the ninth and last day, the family hosted a full-on celebration with an excess of food including the very fatty and fattening "lechon" (pig on a spit).

* * *

I prepared to move again. Although my new parents looked mostly Chinese, their name was Alvarez—he was a doctor and she the principal of the Chinese school. It had been common practice for Filipinos over the centuries to give themselves Spanish surnames, a sensible move given that their colonial conquerors were the elite wealthy. The more the Filipinos emulated them, the greater their chance of advancing themselves. Dr and Mrs Alvarez lived in the barrio of Santa Maria, and while this was much further away from the typing school than the Reiths', it was also closer to the mountain pool of Pasonanca.

I had mixed feelings about the move. Hans and Rosie had been like older siblings to me, granting me lots of freedom and treating me as an adult. But at the Alvarez home my female companion would be their daughter Diana who, like Linda Gonda, was studying to become a nurse, and had returned home for a few weeks' vacation. She was also very reserved, which for me conjured up scary visions of days inside reading and cooking.

My last day at the Reith house proved significant on many levels. First thing in the morning Artu appeared at the front door with a box of chocolates, wistfully explaining he had to fly to Manila that afternoon for a very important meeting. After dropping me off for my typing lesson and with a last longing glance, he roared off in his red car.

Bing once again invited me to her Auntie's house, telling me her cousin and some of his friends, who studied in Manila and were home on holidays, would be there. We walked straight from typing to her Aunt's modest home where a group of boys milled around the tiny backyard, some seated on benches and playing guitars. Two of these were her cousins Teddy and Raymond, taller than most Filipinos and slender with shy smiles. Bing took me amongst the group, introducing me to each one, and it was during this process that a boy who was softly strumming his guitar looked up at me. Bing introduced him as Chito.

I never recorded this unique moment in a letter home. How could I explain to my family and especially to SJ that one look at a young man had knocked my world sideways, not because I desired to jump into bed with him, but because I felt sublimely happy in his company?

His mum and dad were both dentists, so like the Marasigans his family existed comfortably but not lavishly. Their one car was a jeep, and they employed a girl to help with cleaning and the children. Chito was strongly built and a good swimmer, but it was as a guitarist with The Serenaders that he came to spend most of his time with me. Not only could he play the guitar expertly but, like me, he preferred the folk songs of Bob Dylan, the Seekers, Peter Paul and Mary along with the more tuneful songs of the Beatles such as "Hey Jude" which had only just been released. From that first meeting with The Serenaders, I couldn't help but sing along with them, and soon the boys were harmonising with me so that each tune became not only more complex but charged with passion and excitement.

Reluctantly I left Mrs Bader's house to pack up for my move to the Alvarezes. No less than nine Serenaders escorted me back to the Reith residence, assuring me that one night soon they would visit me at the Alvarez home. I took my leave of them, floating happily into the Reith house with folksongs still ringing in my ears. Sy hovered, asking if there was anything at all he could do for me. I would miss this dear old man,

Chito on guitar.

but of course I intended to visit from time to time. The only Aussie souvenir remaining with me was an Australian tea-towel, so I gave it to him. He was as overcome with gratitude as if I had presented him with a bag of gold, thanking me over and over. When I escaped to my room to begin extracting my clothes from the wardrobe, there was a tap on the door. Head maid Marcy entered, shyly handing me a neat parcel. It was a beautiful five-year diary. I was touched but also embarrassed. As a wealthy Westerner it should have been me giving her a farewell present. My eyes flew desperately around the room, zooming in on Artu's chocolates. Scooping up the box I handed it over. Judging from her wide smile this gift was as successful as the tea-towel had been for Sy, so once again the balance of favours was restored by the time I left the house to be driven to my next place of residence.

Four and a half months before meeting President Ferdinand Marcos
Location: Santa Maria, Zamboanga
Host family — Alvarez

I moved in with the Alvarez family one afternoon in late May, that fortuitous day when I met Chito and The Serenaders. I barely had time to drag my bathers from my case before Diana and her nine-year-old brother Espy led me through their back gate into the lovely garden of their Uncle and Aunty Climaco. To my delight, there before me stretched a decent-sized pool. Espy jumped in with a monstrous splash at the deep end while Diana timidly slid into the shallow end. She could barely stay afloat, although she was keen to learn. Espy, on the other hand and to my relief, was a natural fish, and fearless. All I needed to do was to demonstrate the crawl, sidestroke, and backstroke, and he was off! We had just decided we were waterlogged enough to exit the pool when a sheepish-looking Artu, clutching a huge bouquet of roses, appeared at the gate. I stared at him. "Shouldn't you be in Manila at a very important meeting?"

"Yes," he said, staring down at his shiny shoes.

"Plane delay?" I guessed. Artu shook his head. "No. I took so long selecting your roses I missed the plane."

I couldn't help it. I began to laugh, especially when he threw me a sheepish grin, adding that all his luggage, mostly clothes, would now be in Manila without him being there to wear them!

* * *

In early June I wrote to SJ with good news and bad news. The bad news—no letters had arrived from Australia for over a month, and to make things worse, as if on a whim Zamboanga's airport had temporarily closed to all but light aircraft until September. This meant no newspapers from outside the city itself, and worse, a fearful uncertainty about whether my letters would ever reach Australia. From Zamboanga they would need to be carried by boat—a very uncertain and laborious transport. Every word I wrote to SJ or family might be a complete waste of time from now on. Against all rationale, I felt I'd been abandoned on a desert island.

However, the good news was that from the moment I entered the aura of the Alvarez home, I felt happy. Motherly and super kind, Ma Alvarez had a warmth and consideration that made her quite wonderful in my eyes. Her long black hair, lightly interspersed with grey, was pulled back into a tight bun. She maintained that she never felt quite at home speaking English, and like most people in Zamboanga she preferred the local Chavacano.

Diana, kind and gentle like her parents, was an easy and relaxing companion. Her father, Dr Espiridion Alvarez, slim and with glasses, was equally reserved and thoughtful. Only four years earlier he had instigated the building of a new hospital.

The whole family had no qualms about me going out from time to time. We two girls slept upstairs in an enclosed verandah, and although the house was not nearly as luxurious as the Reiths' residences, it felt like home. Downstairs in a big room which included pool and table tennis tables, slept Diana's four brothers, Gai, Butch, and Litong, who were nearer to my age, while Espy the fish was only nine. Litong was slightly mentally disabled. Two maids toiled in the kitchen, but very often Ma and Diana would work alongside them, helping to prepare food much more basic than the fancy delicacies old Sy had lovingly created for me. I was back to Marasigan-type meals—spiced pork, boiled rice, fried fish, and slivers of green beans.

Mind you, Ma Alvarez didn't just stick to the traditional basics when it came to food. During one lunch squid was served. I stared at it. *Eating squid!* My mind pictured those weekends my brother and I were allowed to go night-fishing on the Port Lincoln jetty, throwing out the potato lures for the squid attracted to the jetty lights. If we managed to hook one, the game was to haul it up onto the jetty in a way that directed the spurt of ink onto another kid. Always we would sell our catch to the fish-factory, thinking how weird it was that "New Australians" bought our slippery octopods for a handsome price, then actually ate them!

* * *

Jo-Jo arrived back on the same plane which Artu then boarded for the flight to Manila, the last passenger aircraft to leave the Zambo airport before it closed. Jo-Jo's feet had barely touched terra firma before he scooped me up to see the latest comedy *Who's Minding the Mint?* It provided a welcome and joyous distraction given my feelings of isolation from my family as well as adjusting to yet another home.

On my first Sunday at the Alvarez residence their extended family piled into jeeps and trailers and clattered off along the coast towards lovely Caragasan. But unexpectedly the convoy turned inland until we came to a grassy area in the jungle. Out of his jeep with the agility of a teenager hopped Ma Alvarez's brother, Cesar Climaco, with long hair streaking across wonderfully wicked eyes. He had a brief conversation with me, but it's the man I will always remember rather than the conversation.

Diana told me that her Uncle Cesar was quite famous. A real character, he had been the first elected mayor of his city from 1956 until 1961 and was known for saying and doing surprising things, including refusing to cut his hair for no apparent reason. Another car pulled up and an insanely tall Anglo man uncoiled his legs, clambered awkwardly out of his seat and strode over to me. Peering at me through thick lenses, he grinned widely and held out his hand, introducing himself as Rob Parke, a Peace Corps man who had recently arrived in Zamboanga to board with one of the Alvarez cousins. Outrageously intelligent and broadly educated (science in particular), he possessed a crazy sense of humour.

I asked Rob whether he had visited Pasonanca Pool in the mountain park, and when he shook his head my foster brother Gai immediately offered to drive us there. I felt like a proud local as I showed Rob the diving board, followed by an equally proud demonstration of my handstand dive. When Rob walked the plank, some sixth sense told me that a funny display was about to happen. Using his ridiculously long legs and arms

At Pasonanca Pool – my handstand dive while friends watch on.

to maximum effect, he purposely performed the untidiest dive the world has ever seen, creating a tsunami before eventually surfacing and blinking like a stunned owl. Diana and Gai, who had remained firmly on dry land, broke out into big smiles while I bent double laughing. With this American living so close to my present residence, life couldn't help but be interesting from now on.

It was less fun the following morning when I had to rise bright and early to catch a jeepney then a calesa out to Southern City Colleges. There I was confronted with the touch-typing test containing all the letters of the alphabet—*The quick brown fox jumps over the lazy dog*—while the keyboard was masked and the clock was on. After completing the test I was allowed to leave early, so I headed to the main street to catch a jeepney. None came, and I was getting mightily frustrated when a friend of Artu's, corpulent Manny Yu, drove up in his glamourous car and offered me a lift back to the Alvarezes. Inside the car was a huge bunch of roses which Artu had instructed him to give to me. Since Artu had been confined to Manila he had sent a total of three bouquets of roses and the same number of passionate telegrams. This was getting embarrassing, but I refused to feel guilty. Repeatedly I had stressed to Artu that I was in love with SJ back home, and I can only assume that he decided to woo me so lavishly I would eventually succumb, marry him, and live happily ever after.

Talking of weddings, Diana and I sat together in a huge Catholic Church for the marriage of one of her cousins. Having been brought up a Protestant, the theatricality of the Mass always intrigued me—the statues and carvings, incense-swinging, and bell ringing. A small pageboy appeared bearing a satin cushion on which balanced two wedding rings. I felt nervous for the child as he proceeded slowly down the aisle with his precious cargo, trying not to wobble.

The reception afterwards was typical Zambo style, held under the stars on a massive area of lawn, with fairy lights entwined all through the palms and ferns, with at least 200 guests to enjoy it all. Diana and I needed to take our leave at 7.30 P.M. because I had promised my typing friend Bing that we would attend her Auntie's place for a jam session. Secretly I was yearning to join The Serenaders again.

The Bader house was worlds away from the magnificent venue from which we had just come. Young people were seated on benches along the back wall and The Serenaders, including Chito, were clustered at the edge of the tiny lawn area lit by a few paper lanterns. My heart leapt as the guitars began to strum, and soon we were all singing and dancing, and for the second time in a few days I was sublimely happy. When I wrote to my SJ about that night at the Baders', I simply mentioned that the ambience was more relaxed than at the previous party, and how I danced barefoot under the stars until 1.30 A.M. From that first look into each other's souls, Chito felt the same joy that I did.

* * *

Soon after I met Chito I began to teach children to swim at Pasonanca mountain pool, a task set for me by Dr Marasigan. Apart from the very poor Muslim children who lived on or by the sea, and the extremely affluent families with swimming pools, very few Filipino kids could swim. At first I had ten pupils, ranging in age from six to thirteen, mostly the sons and daughters of various local Rotarians. I was fearful. How would I keep such a great number safe and interested? Never having had a younger sibling, any child under ten scared the life out of me!

In the sixties and seventies, Australia did not insist on regulations in the teaching of children to swim, and the Philippines was even more casual with an attitude of "anything goes." There was simply the expectation that the person with more experience would somehow pass the knowledge on.

And so there I was—a seventeen-year-old alone with ten kids ranging from six to twelve years of age in a large mountain pool where the diving board end was extremely deep, and the colour of the water was blurry brown.

One afternoon in early June was D-Day (Drowning Day?)—my first attempt to teach swimming. That morning Diana and her brothers had taken me to Caragasan in their jeep, and off we set in torrential rain! On the beach we simply mucked around and ate noodles, bananas, and a type of brown coconut candy sold to us by a ragged boy. We cut it a bit fine to get back to the Alvarez residence, so I hastily changed into shorts and went out onto the road leading up to Pasonanca. Eventually I caught a jeepney, but it stopped way short of the park. I hovered on the verge, sweating and fretting. The Australian swim teacher was already fifteen minutes late for her first lesson, with no jeepney in sight. However, miracles do happen. My rescuer Artu roared up in his red sports car and raced me up to the pool. Recently returned from Manila, he had even thought to bring me sandwiches to eat after the lessons.

Eight kids were patiently waiting. And oh joy, The Serenaders were there too, on the side of the pool playing guitars and singing. Sometimes Chito put down his guitar and waded in beside me to help with the young ones. I tried to teach the obvious at first—the dog paddle, but quickly realized that the learners, struggling to keep their faces out of the water, hated every moment.

The following year, when I taught children to swim in the Australian Learn to Swim campaign in a seaside town, I put out the command for all students to bring a swim mask. I collected various curiosities such as corals and coins which I spread out on the white sand just beyond their reach, attractive "bait" to spark the kids' curiosity and overcome their fear.

But there was no pale sand at the bottom of Pasonanca Pool, and diving masks or goggles were scarce. So I struggled on, encouraging the kids to duck their heads below the surface to see what sort of shape I was making with my fingers, or what I might be holding in my hand—a centavo piece perhaps? Gradually I earned their trust, and with Chito's help a few began making good progress. I insisted upon everyone learning sidestroke, explaining this may save their lives one day.

That night Artu and I had a scrumptious meal at Hotel Byot while gazing out at the lamp-lit vintas in the bay and two ships illuminated by the fairy lights tied up at the wharf. After dinner we visited the night market at the docks. Hundreds of tiny tables lined the waterfront, each lit by two candles and piled high with cigarettes, bolts of cloth, jars of biscuits and other rather dubious items, probably smuggled from Borneo. Most tables were manned by Muslim women in head shawls and tattered robes. Sometimes a child lay asleep on a small bench behind her. I stood there, hating being badgered and targeted by so many vendors, yet fascinated by the whole scene. Artu indicated we should move on to our next venue—the Lucky 7 Nightclub. It was dark and dingy, but the band played non-stop and was excellent, not too loud and with good singers. Quite soon the strenuous activities of the day took their toll and by 10.30 P.M., I was ready to go home.

For a whole nine hours that night, unsurprisingly, I dreamt that I was swimming. Sunday, though less strenuous, was certainly busy. After breakfast The Serenaders called by to take me up to Pasonanca Park and there, on the summit, we sat on boulders and gazed out across the jungle-clad valleys to the Isle of Rock. The boys strummed and I let my voice soar to the heavens as we harmonized to Peter Paul and Mary's latest song, called "For Baby," created to celebrate the birth of Mary's baby daughter. Just when I thought it was impossible to feel any happier, the lanky Rob appeared out of nowhere. We all changed into bathers and frolicked in the pool—such fun, just clowning around with my new friends.

Although I was lukewarm about going to church, later in the day I agreed to accompany Rob to an Anglican service. Rob took his religion very seriously, but while I believed in trying to follow Christ's example, I also believed that people have a natural tendency to do good without having to go to church to be reminded. Tessie Climaco, Diana's sweet-natured cousin, was happy to debate various points about Catholicism versus Anglicanism, including the confessional which I had always believed was an easy cop-out for wrong doers. Perhaps Tessie's open-mindedness was not surprising given her father Cesar was the radical individual with the long hair who delighted in challenging the norm, but it also had something to do with her being a decade younger than Rosie Reith, who had proved to be immutable in her Catholic beliefs. I suspected that the next generation Filipinos were beginning to question doctrine that for hundreds of years had been set in stone.

That evening, I was about to change into pjs and get an early night when the sweet sounds of guitars floated up to me. I opened the French doors onto the little balcony, and there they were—twelve Serenaders under the palms below, directing their voices upwards, the very first time I had ever been serenaded. I found myself incredibly moved as I stood there under the moon, feeling over the moon.

Four months before meeting President Ferdinand Marcos

It was 12 June, Philippines Independence Day. I rose early and took a jeepney into town to watch the celebrations. The event was fiercely patriotic, with much flag waving and singing the national anthem. The rousing tune and words really meant something to the majority of Filipinos, whose army—not so many years before—had joined the Allied forces. Together they had eventually ousted the occupying Japanese army.

Mostly, Filipinos sang their special song in their native language of Tagalog, but the English version of the second verse—"Land dear and holy, Cradle of noble heroes, Ne'er shall invaders, Trample our sacred shores"—served to remind me that while the Japanese had got horribly close to invading Australia, events like the bombing of Darwin and the one-man submarines entering Sydney Harbor had been downplayed, perhaps to avoid mass panic. As a child of the 50s, I had always been confident that wars and invasions happened many miles away, overseas and therefore never a direct threat to our free and happy island continent. So, after witnessing such a fervent demonstration of patriotism as the one I experienced in the Philippines, I resolved never again to take peace for granted.

On that National Day I spent some time with Rob at Caragasan. He would soon become my Scrabble rival, and over the months I would learn much about him. He had studied various languages for two years before coming to the Philippines where he lived for ten weeks in the dreadful slums of Manila, at the same time learning all he could about malaria. During the first few weeks of arriving in Zambo, without proper food or a place to sleep, he would trudge for miles through mountains thick with jungle to reach remote communities where he would assess the level of malaria outbreaks. It is no wonder that I rarely won a game of Scrabble with this exceptional man. Graduating from Harvard with eight consecutive years of straight *A*s, Rob was the first of that college's pupils ever to do so.

* * *

A dozen Serenaders swarmed into and all over a jeep, and this time the agenda was not to sing, but to hike from Pasonanca Park up to the great Island of Rock. I think the boys had decided that if a visitor to their country had conquered Pulong Bato, then they must too. Diana and I maneuvered ourselves into the vehicle which was no longer recognizable. Somehow our water bottles, rucksacks, and medical supplies squeezed in with us.

After tumbling out of the jeep at the top of the park we kitted up and began to hike, always heading towards that massive dome clad in jungle greens. Since my first expedition the big rains had come. The jungle was even denser than before, and the ground underfoot was mushy. We got lost several times but eventually found the track leading to the base of the mountain. That trail then petered out, and the climb quite suddenly steepened as Raymond in the lead swung his bolo (a curved machete) to hack out an opening through the infuriatingly thick foliage, including that same sharp grass I remembered from the first experience. We clutched and dragged ourselves upwards, and as blood began to stream down my arms I wondered why I hadn't had the foresight to wear long sleeves.

At one stage the group became separated, and although a boy called Bong, Raymond, Chito and I were up ahead and higher than the others, we simply could not spot them through the thick jungle. We plonked ourselves down, and I felt quite the Florence Nightingale as I fixed up a gash on Bong's arm with a bandage. We drank a little of our water, but the others had the bulk of the water and all the food. For ages we waited, and shouted every few minutes, but no one came. Then one boy struggled through to us with the news that a Serenader had fainted, and that the rest of the group, including Diana, had decided to stay with him while we four climbed the mountain. The messenger disappeared into the undergrowth, and wearily we got to our feet.

Soon after resuming our climb, I tripped and began to roll steeply. Bong grabbed my leg as I tumbled past him, and he very nearly fell too. Then it was time to tackle the sheer cliff of the mountain. Clutching for rootholds or each other's hands, desperately seeking crevices in the rock for our toes, we made it as far as a narrow ledge on which we inched along. Raymond was ahead of me, and as he came to a gap of about three feet he steadied himself, eyed off a tree root to grab, and jumped. I was next in line, but I stopped. Heights have never bothered me much, but my nerve failed here. I looked down. If I misjudged my leap, then unless I developed wings I would definitely die. Chito maneuvered himself around me, using one arm as a psychological barrier to stop me from falling outwards while Raymond reached out to pull me across. Still I hesitated, more frozen by the second, becoming literally paralyzed.

Suddenly it hit me. If I failed to get across, the other three would refuse to go ahead and I would be the cause of their failure to summit. That thought outweighed the fear of death. Forcing my knees to relax slightly, and putting my trust in Chito's arm and Raymond's outstretched hand, I jumped the gap, hoping in that split second I wouldn't topple Raymond from his precarious perch as I landed, almost on top of him.

We made it up to what was an impenetrable jungle layer and once more Raymond used his bolo to hack an opening. My legs were aching badly, and I assumed the other three were suffering too. All of us were perspiring profusely. At one stage Raymond stopped, took off the towel around his neck, and wrung out at least a cup of sweat. I thought back to my original climb with Sierno, Linda, and Eddie, when we had set off with nothing but a bottle of sugar-laden Coke and a small tin of tomato juice. Even so, right now we had finished what little water we had packed, and it took all my mental strength to ignore my thirst.

At last we reached the topmost point, and without congratulating ourselves we immediately turned to descend, this time seeking another way down to avoid the gap where I had frozen. Our feet slid on the rotted leaves and our fingers grabbed vines and matted foliage as we stumbled and slipped down through valleys and up again. In some places little sunlight penetrated the canopy above, and so it took a leap of faith to place our feet on what we imagined to be solid ground.

When we made it back to the others we bombarded them with insults. "Traitors!" "Food-thieves!" But even though they forked out some baked beans, all I wanted was to drink a river dry. Further down the track we reached that same magic stream which had saved me before. It was too tempting. Fully clothed, Chito and I jumped into water that was cold and so clear we could see every stone as if we were looking through glass.

Although every muscle in my legs was screaming, I dressed up and dutifully accompanied Artu to a beauty contest where his beautiful sister was competing in the finals. There was a massive crowd, and the night was interminable. The final voting didn't happen until 1 A.M., but to our delight Tessie won, which meant lots of prizes including a fortnight for two in Hong Kong. The whole show didn't wind up until 2 A.M., so I fell into bed sometime in the wee hours.

* * *

Early one morning, Jo-Jo drove me to the home of Tony and Nina Veloso. Rotarian Tony was handsome and had married Nina when she was only seventeen years old. Quite quickly they had produced four children, yet Nina still only looked twenty and was strikingly beautiful.

We had been invited by the Veloso family for a picnic at Santa Cruz, the dazzling white coral island which I had visited with Hank, Will and Claro some months before—the visit that had ended with our two vintas making a race for the mainland in a dangerous storm. However, this time our mode of transport was Tony's speedboat with its cargo of two crates of beer and lemonade. In a quick fifteen minutes, the hull flying from wave to wave, we arrived at the white coral beach of Santa Cruz. Nina and I had goggles, and as we floated over a fairyland in water clear and green, I realized that yet again I was burning to a crisp from the glare of sun reflected from white coral.

We heard a yell. Tony and Jo-Jo were beckoning frantically from the shore. Something about their body language was telling me this was serious. I looked up at the sky, expecting to see an approaching storm, but all was clear. Tony was running to his boat that was beached nearby, then emerged with a revolver. Shepherding Nina and me up to some bushes, he ordered us to stay down and keep still and quiet. The foliage was so meagre Nina and I needed to lie flat on our stomachs to stay hidden. My heart thumped against the sand. We peered through leaves. Tony and Jo-Jo were leaning against the hull of the boat, brandishing their guns deliberately in full sight. We became aware of a faint putter-putter as a longboat came into view, crammed with men bearing carbines. I was thinking, *if they decide to attack us, they can, easily*. The consequences didn't bear thinking about, but the image of Werner's beautiful cousin, raped, blinded and lying in the Manila hospital, returned to haunt me.

It seemed an eternity before the longboat passed. Only when we could neither hear nor see the boat did Tony give us the all-clear. He explained that very recently pirates had raided Basilan Island further south, and only a week ago a lumber vessel had been attacked along the east coast. Without another word we hurried to the speedboat and Jo-Jo drove it at full throttle across the strait. We dropped Nina off at the docks, and I assumed this was because she had been rattled by the experience and wanted to go home. Jo-Jo, Tony and I continued along the coastline westwards, more slowly this time as Tony kindly let me take the wheel. We passed beautiful Caragasan Beach which was deserted. Eventually we tied up at a local shipyard, Tony collected some boat parts, and we headed back to Caragasan where—I couldn't believe my eyes! Chito and at least sixteen Serenaders had set themselves up at the base of the coconut palms, some with guitars and all singing at full voice. After securing the boat in the shallows we hopped off and waded ashore, and not long afterwards it became clear why Nina had been dropped off at the docks. She appeared in her car complete with children and a crate of food before setting up a picnic lunch in the shade, not far from the group of singers.

The day had been interesting, and now it was turning into a little slice of heaven. I wandered back and forth between the Veloso camp and The Serenaders. There were marked differences in the two picnics—the wealthy lot were gobbling lobster and other such delicacies, while the boy singers enjoyed cheaper fare like noodles. But what mattered to me was that we swam, we talked, we sang—pure happiness. At first with The Serenaders my voice had been embarrassingly thin, due to that Aussie self-consciousness. Yet as I evolved into their honorary female singer, my voice found greater strength. Every boy in the band had a good singing voice and their ability to spontaneously harmonize was uncanny and thrilling.

During the afternoon a bulky vinta sailed laboriously along the coastline from the east. Its sails half-filled and drooping, the hull low in the water, it was an unusual sight in this part of the world which boasted expert Moro sailors. When the vinta levelled with Caragasan, two young Western men stood up, wobbling as they tried to roll the sail down, and at the same time I glimpsed a floppy orange mushroom peeping over the side. Soon all was revealed when the motley crew tumbled out from the ancient boat which the Peace Corps had obviously bought for a song and kept at HQ for their own use. The hapless mariners were six PC men, their noses smeared with white sunburn cream, and the mushroom turned out to be a floppy hat atop the one female, a PC with a flamboyant personality whom I would come to know as Nancy.

The afternoon sparkled happily on, the three groups intermingling with each other either in the sea or on the sand. Nina Veloso tended to sit under the palms to protect her flawless skin, and at one stage she gently advised me that I should do the same unless I wanted to turn my skin brown. "Oh, but I do!" I told her. "In Australia we always try to get a tan!"

Many years later I didn't feel nearly as smug when my first melanoma was removed!

At about 4 P.M. a stiff breeze blew up from the east, and Tony asked one of the PCs how he thought they could sail back against the wind. With a wide grin the American retorted "Well gee, with a fair amount of difficulty I guess." With that Tony offered to give them a tow back to base. They eagerly accepted, tumbling into the dilapidated craft and sitting one behind the other, the orange mushroom somewhere in the middle. After securing the towrope Jo-Jo, Tony and I boarded the speedboat, up-anchored and with Tony at the helm we set off at a cautious speed. I was at the stern, waving to my new friends, and as the cruiser slowly picked up the pace the PC contingent smiled, feeling the unfamiliar sensation of speed in the vinta. I turned my head towards the bow, the wind in my face and hair as Tony pushed the throttle forwards—full speed ahead!

I glanced behind. The PCs were making frantic signals. Water was pouring in over their gunnels. I yelled at Tony to stop, and with one look astern he did exactly that. The boat propped as if it had hit a wall, the wake surging up like a small tsunami, washing over the craft until it disappeared entirely. All we could see was a flurry of floating sandwiches, an orange hat, flip-flops, arms and legs, paddles and bubbles. I doubled over with laughter. The Americans were drenched and bewildered. But soon, bless them, they were laughing so hard it was a miracle none of them drowned. We hauled each one up and over into the speed boat. Tony started up the motor and circled his boat slowly, allowing us to salvage any flotsam still on the surface. That done, he turned back to the wheel and headed east. However, not seeming to understand that a vinta full of water would be a formidably heavy object, he hit full throttle. The rope snapped, jerking the speedboat and leaving the vinta floundering in our wake. Again we hooked up the rope, and this time Tony maintained such a slow speed that it took over an hour to deliver the vinta and its sailors back to base.

The rest of the afternoon was spent lazing away the day at Caragasan, singing, eating, swimming, and laughing. I helped Nina pack up and at sunset she headed home with the children in the car. As Tony and Jo-Jo drove the speedboat back to the docks I stood like a figurehead in the bow, enjoying the coolness of the breeze in my face and a strange sensation of power. The water was like glass and the sunset was a mass of oranges, pinks, and streaks of purple, all reflected in that glassy sea. I recall, vividly, that feeling of unutterable joy.

The next morning as I gingerly climbed out of bed, all joy had vanished. My skin was so sore and tight it felt as though I had been poured into a mold several sizes too small. When I dared to glance in the mirror I saw a monster resembling a cooked crayfish.

* * *

Sitting at a table with sheets of skin peeling off, I wrote a very impassioned letter to SJ. It was about different types of love, describing those who were physically attractive to you but for whom you had no deep love to "last through sickness, old age, changes of mood, etc." Then there were all those people for whom you could hold a great love, but whom you were not sexually attracted to in the slightest. Thirdly, as I explained in my newfound wisdom, there were a few people with whom chemistry was right and whom you liked, but you were still not "in love" with them. That "in-love" feeling was something indefinable, like magic. I think I was trying to analyse for myself the differences in my loves for Chito, Jo-Jo, Artu, Rob, and of course, SJ himself. I reached the conclusion that although I had relationships in the Philippines that fitted with all three descriptions, SJ was the only person with whom I was "actually *in love.*"

However, I felt real confusion about my powerful feelings for Chito, this twenty-year-old Serenader with the warm brown eyes. Two days earlier he had announced he was packing his bags to return to study in Manila, and in a kind of shock we had sat together in his parents' jeep while the tropical rain trickled like tears down the windscreen. Occasionally he played a song, but our voices faltered. We just didn't have the heart to sing. He promised to send me all the lyrics from our favourites, and one of these would be Simon and Garfunkel's "Sounds of Silence" which seemed appropriate given that we sat in the jeep, mostly silent. I do remember Chito saying, "I will miss you badly Stephie." My reply sounded lame. "I will miss you too." Although true, I knew I must curb any show of emotion for both our sakes. Chito later confessed that "I love you" was on the tip of his tongue that night. It was just as well he didn't, because I couldn't have coped with his pain or with mine.

Several of my other friends were also leaving to resume studies in Manila. Most were forced to travel north by boat, because Zambo airport was still effectively closed to all but very small aircraft. Big changes were happening. In a few days Chito would depart, I would sit my typing exam at Southern City Colleges, and on 8 July my own studies at Ateneo were set to begin.

* * *

Monday 24 June was horribly humid and scorching hot. It was also a special day to mark St John the Baptist. Cesar Climaco, that larger than life character living beside the Alvarez house, scooped me up in a jeep with the aim of giving me the experience of a Filipino St John's Day. The entire route from our suburb in Santa Maria to downtown Zambo was lined with adults and kids armed with buckets and bowls, bombarding us with water. Drenched to the skin, we enjoyed ourselves immensely. It was a given that St John's Day was never going to happen in South Australia—the driest state in the driest continent on earth!

Cesar Climaco dropped a sodden me at typing class, after which Artu picked me up and took me to his family's radio station DXLL to rehearse two songs I had chosen to sing at a special Rotary induction ceremony the following Friday evening. The guitarist Zingy was perched on a stool, tuning up in the glass soundproofed room surrounded by mics and huge tape recorders, and although I was now drenched with perspiration rather than fresh water, I sang strongly and well.

After the rehearsal I joined the entire Climaco clan plus Rob at the private pool for a refreshing dip. With characters like Cesar and Rob present it was great fun, but eventually I wandered out through the gate and back to my room at the Alvarezes to take a siesta. A feeling of sickness roused me.

All evening and night I tossed and turned with a fever, trying to suppress waves of nausea. Next morning I was too ill to attend typing class, and poor Ma Alvarez was fussing around and quite worried, especially when I refused food. By evening I relented, accepting a bowl of soup, and just as I finished the last spoonful Rob wandered over the road from where he boarded and sat by my bedside. Talking about all and sundry, Rob's droll humour kept me wonderfully distracted. After a better night, but still feeling average, I dragged myself off to typing school in tropical heat which seemed more oppressive than usual. The final exam was on Friday, and I needed all the practice I could get. Once again Artu picked me up, but this time it was to take me to swimming classes. To my relief, because it had been raining so heavily in the mountains, the pool was too muddy for safe swimming.

I still felt below par when Artu drove me to DXLL for another rehearsal. This time my voice was truly terrible, a scary situation given that I would need to perform at the special Rotary induction in two days' time. After rehearsal Artu, because my every wish was his command, drove me straight to Laura's Bakeshop where I consumed a big bowl of tomato soup and magically felt a whole lot better.

The next day, still weak, I forced myself to go to my typing lesson, afterwards visiting the Philippine National Bank to collect my allowance. The manager was not in, and so I was forced to leave with the few remaining pesos and centavos in my purse. At the old Spanish colonial post office, the stamps for three letters swallowed a precious two pesos in total, then I used up another to take a taxi to Ateneo where I tried to enroll. Confusion reigned throughout the building, and I was told to come back later. *Why is everything so difficult today?*

I had an hour's reprieve at Angie's House of Charm over the road, getting a free manicure and hair set in readiness for the big event the following night. Mrs Ebby had struck a deal with me whereby in exchange for teaching her three small daughters and son how to swim, all services would be "on the house." In my present financial straits, it took me a split second to accept her proposal.

After my beautification I wandered half a mile away to a tiny wooden hut where a seamstress did the final fitting of my new fuchsia pink gown. The lace fabric from the waterside market had been a welcome gift from Ma Alvarez, but the dress needed to be ready the next day, so I was cutting things fine. Outside the heat was unbearably oppressive. I thought I had acclimatized to the pungent smells in the smog of downtown Zambo, but this morning all odors assaulted me. I wilted on the pavement, waiting for a jeepney to return me to Ateneo.

An American Peace Corps boy (one of the cheerful but inept sailors of the doomed vinta) appeared out of the blue and asked me around the back of a nearby shop to join his friends for some Coke and cookies. Seated around a rustic table were several PCs, including Nancy minus her orange hat. I can't remember her face exactly—I think her looks were overwhelmed by her personality!

After funny conversations and welcome refreshment, I hailed a jeepney and sorted out the enrolment at Ateneo. I was hugely surprised, almost embarrassed, at the few hours per week I would be spending at lectures—one hour for Spanish, one for English, and one for Philippine History. I justified this to myself and my family by asserting that my Spanish teacher Mrs Araneta, soon to be my host mother, could give me private Spanish lessons. The enrolment completed, I stood outside waiting for a jeepney pointing towards Santa Maria. But after a quarter of an hour in that baking sun, as had happened so many times before, Artu appeared in his red sports car and rescued me. It was uncanny how many times he found me and scooped me up from the dirty verges of this ancient city.

We drove to the main roundabout where we came to a halt in an untidy traffic jam at a four-way crossing. Suddenly I saw the cause. Yet again an emaciated calesa pony had collapsed in the shafts, but this time the owner was whipping it, lashing that bony body all over. "Stop!" I yelled. My hand was already trying to open the door when Artu warned me that it was dangerous to interfere and he would physically prevent me if he had to. My heart was pounding with horror as I was forced to watch the brutal beating for what seemed like an eternity. And then (I could scarcely believe it) the little horse struggled to its feet and staggered on.

I felt sicker than ever, and we drove on up to Santa Maria in silence. There and then I decided to write a scathing article about the calesa in the Ateneo newspaper, the *Beacon*. Next day I would be advised by concerned colleagues to keep it anonymous, because it was obviously written by a foreign visitor, and I was becoming a familiar sight in the city. I restrained myself from arguing for the abolition of the calesa, because I knew how much that would cost the city in terms of compensation and loss of public transport in a district with few taxicabs. Instead, I promoted the idea of a regulatory body which would include a vet and which would impose fines for mistreating the horses in all ways. Such an authority would also enforce the bag-under-the-tail idea to catch the manure. As things stood, Zamboanga was a dirty town, not helped by the steaming piles of manure crested with flies all over the roads. Mind you, a tail bag could not stop the urine. And not even a regulatory body could prevent the Zambo's male humans turning towards any building and urinating against its wall.

Today these cruel horse-drawn vehicles are a thing of the past, and I can only hope my public condemnation hastened their extinction.

With kindness as their trademark, all the Alvarez family treated their guard dogs and their white cat (with one blue eye and one green eye) as treasured pets. Every day the dogs and the cat gathered around for a pat from me, but because each was furiously jealous of the other, caressing these animals became an enjoyable love-in circus.

But that frustrating Thursday afternoon, still feeling unwell, I conducted my swimming lessons from the side of the pool. Afterwards my chauffeur Artu once again took me to DXLL for a rehearsal, and although my voice had improved slightly since last time, it was still too thin and scratchy to give me confidence, especially for "Hurry Sundown" which needs to be belted out to do it justice. All I could do was to convince myself it would be "all right on the night."

The following morning was the final typing exam. Adrenalin must have kicked in because on that day I came top of the class. After the exam I drank grape juice with Bing who was despondent knowing that she would see less of me from now on, but I reminded her that in a few weeks I would accompany her to Basilan, that large island which had beckoned to me from across the water ever since my first day in Zamboanga.

* * *

Charlie Reith was still overseas so Tony Mas, who was about to be inducted as the new president of the Zamboanga Rotary Club, was expected to shoulder extra responsibilities. One of these included welcoming guest speaker Senator (Jovito) Salonga to Zamboanga for the grand Rotary event that night. Tony called by to pick me up in his limousine, probably the only "limo" in town at that time. We headed to the airport which, although still under construction, could now accommodate passenger planes the size of DC3s. Doc Marasigan puttered up in his Brent Hospital Kombi van, and when the plane appeared in the sky we lined up on the tarmac. As soon as the senator had set foot on land I placed a sampaguita lei around his neck, introducing myself and uttering pleasantries. Salonga then turned to greet the Doc and Tony, and as he did so, someone touched my arm. It was Chito's mother, Mrs Limcango, who had also been on the plane from Manila. She handed me a recently released Peter Paul and Mary LP from Chito. I had never actually met his mother before, but instantly I recognized the same kind brown eyes and heart-shaped face she had given to her son. Dr Limcango stood nearby, but there was barely time to greet either of them before I was bustled into the back of the limousine alongside Senator Salonga, while Dr Marasigan sat next to driver Tony Mas in the front.

Well, there I was, making polite conversation with this special guest, having no idea of exactly why Jovito Salonga was so special. All I had heard about the senator was the general gossip that "everyone thinks he will be president next after Marcos."

The sad truth was that I was seventeen, and I simply saw Salonga as an elderly politician who was not relevant to any part of my life at that time. I had no idea that he was born in humble circumstances with no advantages except superior intelligence. Without wealth, intelligence alone is usually not enough in a country such as the Philippines to become a successful politician. But Salonga possessed three other characteristics which impressed all decent people—courage, humility and cast-iron integrity. In 1965, despite limited financial resources, Salonga had been elected senator by a huge majority. From that moment he became a persistent thorn in Marcos's side, as early as 1965 writing several exposés laying bare Ferdinand and Imelda's "secret" Swiss bank accounts. It seems certain that the "old man" who sat next to me in the limousine in late June of 1968 must have been acutely aware that for as long as Marcos struggled to hold on to power, he would be a marked man.

Our limo arrived at the Zamboanga Hotel. Amongst the flowers on the rooftop the four of us sat at a table enjoying afternoon tea (merienda). At last the senator took his leave for a well-earned siesta in one of the hotel rooms, while Tony Mas returned me to the Alavezes.

After a short rest I dressed in my new bright pink gown, adorning myself with simple earrings and a bracelet made from pearl shell—a gift from the Marasigans. I knew that every wife from the Inner Wheel of Rotary would be festooned with diamonds, gemstones and gold for this occasion, but shells felt right for me.

It was a lovely cool night when Rob, Dr and Ma Alvarez and I set off in the big Chevrolet for the night of nights. The rooftop had been transformed into an even more magical space, glittering lights and flowers under a black velvet sky. Much to my surprise I was ushered to the official table, and the night began with an hour or more of flowery speeches, including "the most painful speech I had ever heard" from one particular Inner Wheel lady. I made the big mistake of peeking across to the Alvarez table where Rob threw me a wicked smirk, and from that moment on I studiously kept my eyes on the floor.

Last of all the extremely eloquent senator came to the podium, but I paid little attention to what he said. This was partly due to frayed nerves—any moment now I'd be called to the microphone to perform. When that time came all went without a hitch, my voice reasonably strong and steady. Sitting down amidst a flurry of applause and congratulations, I was still shaking when Rob approached and asked for a dance. As soon as this "show dance" finished I was led from table to table, having to linger diplomatically at each, engaging in small talk. Then full-on revelry seemed to be the order of the evening, and who better to revel than Nancy. I marveled as she flung off her shoes and leapt and gyrated around the dance floor without caring what anyone thought. It was hard not to smile, and I remembered her recent kindness when she had trudged round Manila to find me a pair of bras capacious enough to accommodate me. These had cost a small fortune—"twenty pesos, but worth it," I wrote in a letter home.

Two mornings after the induction, Artu drove me to DXLL to thank Jingi, the guitarist who had accompanied me so skillfully. After we enjoyed a debriefing of the evening Artu led me further into the building where the printing presses of *Zamboanga Times* were noisily clattering away. He had failed to tell me that his family owned not just the radio station, but the town's major newspaper! I glanced at one page coming hot off the press, and my eyes went straight to a section nauseatingly titled "Society Whirlpool." It seemed that I had dived successfully into this whirlpool, for in print were the words, "the lovely Australian Rotary scholar who sang two very haunting folk songs . . ."

By this time all thoughts of Senator Salonga had vanished.

* * *

When I read the letter which had accompanied Chito's gift, I was deeply disturbed. A few days after he left Zambo he had sent me a telegram with three simple words "I love you." Warning bells rang loud. I had a problem.

The letter dated 26 June contained a declaration of love so genuine, so forceful, that any answer I could give would be bound to hurt him. Part of Chito's letter declared, "That day when we first met I said to myself that it was just an infatuation. But as the summer days grew shorter and shorter, each day I found out that it wasn't just infatuation, but love. I began to see your face, your smiling face and even hear your voice when I played my guitar and in my dreams at night. I don't know what this means to you. But for me it means everything Stephie, everything. I love you Stephie, for in you I saw everything that a lady should have. I hope you won't change now that you know my true feelings for you. I hope that the flame which burns our friendship will continue to burn for a long time."

I re-read the full letter many times, and the tears ran because I couldn't fathom a way to reply without the risk of killing him emotionally. With great difficulty, because no words could be the "right" words, I wrote back as gently as possible, but in the end the brutal truth needed to be stated. Yes, while I loved him dearly, and was incredibly happy in his company, the person I was *in love* with was SJ, the boy whom I had mentioned frequently in case there was any misunderstanding.

Promptly afterwards, in a letter to my family, I admitted that I was out of my depth with this problem. I wrote, "With Artu and Jo-Jo it's mainly infatuation. It's not the same with Chito because there's real liking and friendship between us. This makes the whole thing much harder."

* * *

The morning had not started well. While racing down to the Alvarez kitchen I tumbled down the stairs. Nothing was broken, but I felt as if I'd been run over by a small truck. I couldn't hang around groaning because many children were waiting for their swim lessons up at the pool. These lessons had become so popular and were now incorporating such a vast range of ages that I was forced to expand into two classes. Sometimes the parents gave me gifts as a token of their appreciation, but my greatest reward was in repaying the kindness of my Rotarian hosts. It gave me a real buzz to see how quickly my pupils progressed, and in the process of teaching, I was learning too. Artu picked me up as usual, and I taught two consecutive classes, the first involving the smaller kids, and the second the bigger ones. We finished up, but Artu had not yet arrived to drive me home. The more competent of my students were mucking around at the deep end of the pool while I practiced a couple of dives before resting, leaning on the edge of the dive steps, gazing dreamily at the water. A few boys were jumping off the diving board with the aim of creating the biggest "bomb," and through the splashes I made out two of my female pupils, ten-year-olds who seemed to be playing together. With a start I realized that only an hour earlier I had been teaching one of them how to dogpaddle in the shallow part of the pool. The other girl, who could barely swim, was desperately trying to hold up her friend, but they kept sinking and swallowing water.

Diving in, I surfaced nearby and managed to grab them both. They latched onto me, pushing me down so that they could stay up. After copping a few mouthfuls of water, I used every last ounce of strength to deliver them safely to the side of the pool. I was exhausted. It had been a close shave.

Shortly after returning to the Alvarez household my right ear went deaf and was sore to touch. Ma drove me to a doctor on the other side of town, leaving me there while she went off to the Chinese Temple for a teachers' meeting. The doctor diagnosed a swollen eardrum and advised me not to swim for a week in case it ruptured. Popping a thermometer under my tongue he promptly proceeded to jab a whopping injection into my arm, telling me he would need to do that for the next two days.

There were no phone boxes in Zambo, so I came out from the doctor's surgery into the heat and humidity of the outskirts of the city with Ma nowhere in sight. I had no option but to try to make it back to Santa Maria, walking under the blazing sun until I got near enough to the heart of the city to be able to hail a jeepney going in the right direction. When I finally arrived home there was not a soul to be seen except a maid who couldn't speak English, so I dragged my weary body upstairs (careful not to fall down this time) and wrote a letter to my SJ. "I feel bruised, I'm hot, my ear is sore, I can't swim and I think Artu is leaving next week which will mean yet another friend gone to Manila."

When the time came, of course, I would miss being spoilt by Artu—being taken to the movies, given banana caramel pies, offered anything I desired at Laura's Bakeshop, and driven to swimming lessons. However, some significant other appeared in my life at the beginning of July. "Jun" (nickname for Junior) came to board in the Alvarez house. Apart from his job as a carer for the mentally disabled Litong, he created scripts for radio station DXJW, writing most nights and somehow managing to study something (I can't remember exactly what) during the day. He needed a foreigner to play a major part in one of his series, so of course I offered to fill the gap.

Jun was tenacious, wiry, and fiercely loyal to those he loved. He came from the poorer side of the tracks, and I don't know how he managed to exist on such little sleep in his quest to gain education and provide the necessities of life.

What I didn't fully understand until almost two years after I returned to Australia was that Jun was also a fierce patriot, prizing his country's democracy, and he was determined to defend it when freedom was threatened. Needless to say this would prove a dangerous attribute when President Marcos began his brutal war against democratic freedoms for his own evil ends.

It was during July that I became more popular than ham and eggs for breakfast. It grew to be a joke in the Alvarez family that the phone was going constantly. "Can I speak to Mees Weeks please?" and this would nearly always be an invitation for a beach picnic, a party, or a movie.

On the surface, at least, life was busy but always entertaining with new experiences that were usually fun, sometimes challenging, and occasionally downright scary.

Three months before meeting President Ferdinand Marcos

At long last I would step upon Basilan Island, although for just a short trip. With my typing friend Bing and her aunt Mrs Bader, I boarded the ferry for the two-hour journey across the very unpredictable strait. When we arrived on the Island we transferred to an old jeep, and although Mrs Bader took the wheel, after a while it was plain she was struggling to drive over the rutted dirt roads of the island. With great confidence I offered to take over, and she was only too keen to let me. We arrived (alive!) at her family's modest coconut plantation, and after wandering amongst the trees Bing and I enjoyed a drink of coconut water inside the small wooden house.

By some strange twist of fate Nancy and some of her PC colleagues were visiting Basilan Island at the same time, inexplicably to attend some sort of Chinese "coronation." Hearing this, Mrs Bader encouraged me to stay on for another night with my friends, saying it was diplomatic for me to experience this debutante ball. It may have been diplomatic for we foreigners to attend, but that's where diplomacy ended. After the event, at about 11 P.M. on a quiet Sunday night in the middle of the main town of Lamitan, an incident occurred where I suffered huge embarrassment from being in a group of culturally insensitive Westerners. And the chief instigator of this bad behaviour? Nancy of course!

The Beatles had just released "Hey Jude," and Nancy was teaching it to us as we strolled back to our digs through the backstreets of Lamitan. She sang full throat, and some of us began to sing too, not quite as loudly but noisy enough. As we passed yet another modest house with its curtains drawn, I became aware of how we must have sounded to the town's occupants, and I urged Nancy to tone it down. "They'll think we're a mob of Anglo drunkards!" I whispered, but Nancy thought that was hilarious and upped her volume loud enough to wake the dead. I faltered, then abruptly stopped singing. Some of her colleagues were equally aware and stopped too, but as far as I was concerned the damage had been done.

That Sunday night we all slept in a massive monolith of a house, three floors high, open to the weather and constructed of very unlovely concrete blocks. It belonged to an extended Chinese family, each son living in one big room with his wife, and the kitchen a huge space teeming with women who adhered to a strict hierarchy based on seniority. I felt sorry for the younger ones, who seemed to be virtual slaves. The bathroom was a vast area of smooth concrete, with a giant tap protruding from one wall, and a toilet consisting of a hole near a bucket of water. No toilet paper, no porcelain bowl on which to sit. I decided to stay sweaty rather than shower, knowing also that I would need an iron-clad bladder.

Nancy and the others disappeared off to various rooms, while I was shown to a pokey bedroom with one single bed and four females wishing to sleep. Luckily for me, as a guest, I was offered the bed—it was just a hard mattress, but it was better than a mat on that unforgiving wood floor.

In the tropical heat of the night outside, all kinds of creatures flapped and scuttled. It must have been three in the morning when my tired eyes began to close . . . shadows swarmed around me and something fiendish squealed overhead. I sat bolt upright, staring, and those animals I had never learnt to love flew out. Bats! I looked down at the three sleeping figures on the floor. Not one had stirred. Once again, I was forced to admit how I had taken for granted the comfortable living in affluent Australia.

On Monday morning we Westerners straggled back to the mainland via ferry and made our way to our various "homes." I enjoyed a decent but short shower at the Alvarez house, then headed for Ateneo College where I had a preliminary meeting with Father McNally, the dean, a big, broad-shouldered, six-foot American Jesuit priest who impressed me on many levels. Part of the conversation was his reassurance that all my expenses would be covered, and it was only at that point I began to truly understand the extent of the organization undertaken by Zamboanga's local Rotarians to accommodate me as a student and their guest.

My very first lesson that day was Advanced Spanish, taught by my teacher and future foster mother Señora Araneta. She was a natural teacher, and I was surprised to find myself able to understand parts of her perfect classic Spanish. Mind you, all hubris died when at the end of the lesson "Mum" quietly suggested I attend the more basic Spanish class from now on. After that experience I found my way to the Philippines History class where I sadly discovered my teacher had zero personality and taught by the book. It became clear that Philippine history would never be brought alive for me at Ateneo. All I would have to do for good marks was to memorize the facts and figures in *Political and Cultural History of the Philippines Volume 1: Since time began to British Occupation*—if I didn't die from boredom in the meantime.

That night I was sitting playing a hilarious game of Scrabble with Jun when Nancy and a boy called Tonyito burst into the room to kidnap me for a party with her PC colleagues. Bursting into rooms came naturally to Nancy. I agreed to be kidnapped, hoping my new friend Jun wouldn't be too disappointed, reassuring myself that he probably needed to beaver away all night creating episodes for his radio serial.

We ended up in a small house with Artu, Nancy, her much-quieter colleague Lenelle, and boys. Darts was the game of choice, and it was a miracle Nancy didn't fatally wound one of us with her wild throws. At 11 P.M. one of the boys, Tonyito, drove Nancy into the city to try to find some food. When midnight came and they still had not appeared, the rest of us ate cold baked beans from cans and I can remember laughing a lot. Half an hour later we were packing up to go home when Nancy came staggering into the house, behaving in an uncharacteristically subdued manner, telling us that Tonyito was at the police station reporting the accident they had just experienced between their Volkswagen and a motorcycle with a pillion passenger. Nancy's head had hit the windshield, cracking the glass. Promptly vomiting, she then found she had blurred vision. Tonyito was unhurt, but the motorbike passenger was suffering a broken thigh and cuts.

Lenelle insisted on taking Nancy to the General Hospital, so we all squashed into vehicles and delivered the patient. As we trundled along the passage I glanced through the theatre window to see the surgeon operating on the motorbike passenger's thigh, a grisly sight. The doctor on duty refused to x-ray Nancy, so we decided to transfer her to the more friendly Brent Hospital where thankfully she was admitted and assigned a bed. Eventually Artu drove me home while Lenelle presumably spent the rest of the night sitting with her colleague.

Early the following morning Jun and I caught a jeepney to radio station DXJW for the recording of his series *La Cadena de Amor* (*The Chain of Love*). The building contained several rooms, some stacked with hundreds of different sized records, and others that were soundproofed with glass windows through which I spied announcers speaking into microphones or lounging back while they played various music records for the unseen listeners. Jun led me to a generous space with a low stage up at one end and five seats each facing three microphones. He introduced me to the four Filipino actors, then perched nearby on a stool to direct us. Through the soundproofed glass partition we could clearly see the manager in charge of the recording, and he would indicate when we should speak, and when we were "on" or "off" air.

In the series I played a foreigner called Stefani, although how the listener was to be made aware of the new more exotic spelling of my name was a mystery. Jun allowed me to alter my own speeches at random, so I could utter phrases and words which rolled more naturally off the tongue. I began to enjoy myself immensely—I was born to do this. Most of the nine episodes used Zambo's lingo Chavacano, but Jun had written what became a hilarious sequence, the "father" of the hero trying to talk to me in tangled English. I admired a female in the cast who was required to cry convincingly an exhausting number of times with each "take." The creation of the sound effects intrigued me, and even though I was bathed in sweat I was on a high, especially as the Filipino cast was also pumped up and repeatedly complimented me.

As a way of thanking me for starring in his radio series, Jun took me into town and bought me an ice cream from Laura's Bakeshop. This he adopted as a weekly ritual, never allowing me to pay but never buying one for himself, most likely because he could not afford it.

At noon I was interviewed by Vic Solis, editor of Ateneo's *Beacon*. Keen to start as one of its journalists, I was directed to a wood-paneled room separate from the main two-floor lecture building. Standing on the edge of the grassed area which served to create an impressive frontage to the university college, it had a surprisingly professional look about it, boasting four typewriters, filing cabinets, a record player, one desk for the editor (Vic), and others for the feature writers, of which I would be one. After a short interview my "professional" photo was taken before I wandered across to my more basic Spanish class. All the local students knew the hybrid Spanish (Chavacano), so I had to concentrate doubly hard to get a handle on what was being said or written.

Following that was my first English Drama lesson, which disappointingly for me consisted of studying Shakespeare's comedies. After cursory readings of works such as *Much Ado about Nothing* I had decided that most of his comedies were exactly that, much ado about nothing, and I preferred his dramas. However, a year earlier I had played the lead part of Kate in *The Taming of the Shrew* at Woodlands school, and while I always enjoyed the challenge of putting myself into a character's shoes, this play, including its title, offended me. The idea that a feisty girl needed to be "tamed" by her father so that she would fall into line and marry the man *he* wanted her to marry, was repugnant to me. I couldn't understand why it wasn't abhorrent to an all-girls school which purported to be progressive. While I understood that the concept of women being chattels was the norm during Shakespeare's times, it didn't mean I had to like it.

The English class included Vic Solis from the *Beacon* and the few boys from The Serenaders who had not disappeared to Manila. Instantly I knew this was going to be an unruly class, especially as the male teacher was far too good-natured to discipline the boys who kept asking mad questions like "Where was Australia in Shakespeare's time sir?" Poor Sir struggled helplessly to control them. In the boys' defence, Shakespearean language for them might just as well have had its origins in Outer Mongolia.

When lessons were over Artu scooped me up and took me to Laura's. Already seated playing a game of dice were several of his male friends, so I sat nearby and tried to concentrate on my Spanish assignment while I drank coffee and ate a purple yam (ube) ice-cream. The boys began to play for stakes such as "an ube for Stephie!" and so my efforts at learning Spanish became ruined with helpless laughter.

Artu described an event earlier that week when he had been gambling and started with five pesos, his luck so great he went on to win 400 pesos. My jaw dropped! This was a fortune too great to imagine for a girl who had to survive on two pesos a day. Then with a careless laugh he admitted that he had proceeded to lose until not one peso remained. Horrified, I scolded him. "Any good gambler knows that when you start to lose is the time to stop."

"Prove it," said Artu, and ushered me to a seat at the gambling table. I put up two days' allowance against the dice. At first I lost a few centavos, and won a few, and the die were rolled and juggled until I couldn't quite keep up with what was happening. I suspect the boys were cheating in my favour because in some mysterious way I ended up winning five pesos and sixty centavos. Righteously I stood up and declared I would withdraw from the game whilst I was ahead. Mightily amused, Artu declared that he had learnt a lot from me that night (sure, right!). At that moment the shop phone rang. It was uncanny. As if she had guessed we were at Laura's, Nancy was ringing from Brent Hospital to say she was bored and demanded we visit and bring flowers. Artu and I jumped to comply. Nancy had to be obeyed.

Because we couldn't find flowers that late in the evening, we took an obscenely large tub of ube to Nancy's room instead. Whether or not Nancy swallowed a spoonful of this delicious purple medicine I have no idea, but we did. Artu and I sat round the room with several PCs, gobbling ice-cream and making a dreadful racket. It seemed that wherever Nancy was, unholy noise was made in the most inappropriate situations, not that Nancy alone should have shouldered the blame. Not this time anyway.

* * *

Artu once again took me to the movies, and afterwards to Laura's for dinner. We climbed the narrow wooden stairs to the cocktail lounge to avoid the raucous gamblers on ground level. The lounge was long and narrow, and we had it all to ourselves. At the window end there was a nice arrangement of a fake Japanese willow overlooking a small fake lake, and I stood there examining it while Artu excused himself and disappeared down the stairs. Suddenly, unexpectedly, I was swept up in a terrible longing to be home in Australia with my family and friends. I hadn't been outwardly homesick since I had left the Reiths', and there was no apparent reason for homesickness to strike now, but it did, with a vengeance. I felt physically sick because of the fierce need which I knew could not be met, even to a minor degree such as connecting with a phone call.

Poor Artu arrived upstairs with a tray of food to find me barely able to speak, and certainly unable to eat. He was concerned for me, but I assured him there was nothing he could do except to have a go at consuming all the food, and to leave me by myself over by the window. He did this, then drove me home. Thanking him profusely, I apologized for my annoying behaviour, trudged upstairs, and only when I was safely tucked up in bed did I permit the tears to flow, until merciful sleep overwhelmed me.

With the sunlight I woke feeling slightly more cheerful, putting a concerted effort into studying some Spanish. Then the call came through from Rotarian Mr Bernado, telling me that his daughter had just arrived from Manila and his family was ready to have me stay with them. Instantly I felt miserable again. The idea of having to leave the Alvarez family as well as Rob and Jun, left me bereft. Also, on the few times I had met the sturdy Mr Bernado, he had seemed grim and without a sense of humour, a very different character from Charlie Reith who was quick to laugh, or Doc Marasigan with his ever-present shy smile, or Ma and Pa Alvarez who were so warm and caring. There was one other reason too, adding to my dread. The word around the traps was that the Bernados' daughter Maria was the holy type who didn't like to go out—except to church. At this point I wondered how I would survive.

I confided my fears to Ma, and the darling woman suggested I postpone the move for as long as possible. My heart leapt at this plan, but my brain told me that Mr Bernado would disapprove strongly of such tomfoolery. Already I had overstayed my month at the Alvarez home. That night the first episode of *La Cadena d'Amor* came to air, and all the family including boarders and maids huddled around the radio. I was mildly bemused at their wonder and praise, because it hadn't seemed like skill or work for me. It was just fun.

Once again Jun accompanied me to DXJW to rehearse and record the last two episodes. My part was bigger this time, and my spirits soared as the manager of the radio station said he had received numerous phone calls asking for the identity of the new talent. Jun just stood there, smiling with his buck-toothed smile, as if he were a fan just pleased to be in my presence. (Later I wrote to my mother, who had starred so many times in the Port Lincoln Players, crowing, "Aren't you jealous Mama?") Just like the recording session the week before, it was almost unbearably hot within the glass walls of the performance space, but my enjoyment far outweighed the discomfort.

The next day Mr Bernado rang again, this time demanding I move in straight away. I told him that I could not easily arrive sooner than the next Sunday afternoon, but as I hung up I felt something akin to panic. Immediately I contacted Rob and arranged to go to early church with him. It was more a ruse to be with Rob for a little longer, rather than a sudden desire to commune with the Almighty.

Late on Sunday morning I hurriedly packed, before asking all the younger residents of the Alvarez household to accompany me to Pasonanca Pool. I got more company than I bargained for. Jun and all three Alvarez brothers wanted to go, and so after the eldest brother managed to commandeer the family jeep, we climbed in and headed up to the lovely hilltop where I always felt so happy. Pasonanca Park was as uplifting as ever, but when we got to the pool we found it was impossibly dirty. It had been raining cats and dogs upstream, so rather than go home I suggested we keep driving up and over the crest of the park and into the valley below. We went along the small dirt track as far as we could towards Pulong Bato where the big river ran, that same river that Chito and I had plunged into after our sweaty ordeal in climbing the mountain.

The jungle track became narrower and narrower, until we could go no further. The others had never been here before, and so in a sudden burst of leadership I offered to guide them all to the river. Choosing the track which seemed to head straight for the Island of Rock, I threw out a childish and hypocritical prayer. *Dear God, please reward me for going to church this morning by leading me in the right direction.*

After a half hour we came to the first of the six streams we needed to cross before reaching the main river. *Thank you, God!* However, each of these streams took us fifteen minutes to safely cross as we toiled against the currents up to our thighs, holding hands so that no one slipped. All of us were fully clothed and were sodden by the time we reached the big river. We stopped and stared. It was rushing deep and furious, unrecognizable from the clear calm water which had refreshed Chito and me a month previously. As all of us assessed the situation, we began to realize the degree of danger in that swirling water, especially for the two brothers who were not strong swimmers. Espy was a little fish, but not a strong fish, and Litong had never shown the remotest interest in water sports.

I looked at the cliffs on the far side and spied a ledge from which, if I could somehow climb to it, I could dive into the river below. Then common sense kicked in. For a start, just swimming across to the other side would have been suicidal, far less climbing to a ledge and diving into a raging torrent. Without mentioning it to the others, I bore it in mind for another safer time.

Jun, Butch Alvarez and I decided to risk at least braving the water after rationalizing there was safety in numbers. Espy was mortified he couldn't join us, but Litong was relieved to sit on the bank and have the sole job of restraining his young brother. We stronger swimmers hung our shorts and shirts on branches, then turned to reassess the river.

Gingerly we tested the waters, venturing further and further, feeling the force of the flood. We cooked up a game where each of us would take turns at walking upstream before plunging in and allowing the current to hurl us down into the waiting arms of the "catcher" whose role was to save us from being swirled off to goodness knows where.

The fun had to cease, and quickly too. It was time to head back home. Maria would be arriving in a taxi at exactly 5 P.M. to collect me, and I sensed Mr B was a stickler for punctuality. My heart was heavy. Life at the Bernado household was about to begin, literally in earnest.

Three months before meeting President Ferdinand Marcos
Location: Madrid Street, Zamboanga
Host family — Bernado

The house was one of the few Spanish-style buildings which had survived the war. It was large and spacious, and made of whitewashed wood. Not far from the Reiths', its second floor balconies overlooked grand Madrid Street. Most furniture and inner walls were of wood, but unlike the Reiths', the Spanish-style structure was completely open. This meant that every bed needed to have mosquito netting, which I thought looked romantic. I had a separate room with a four-poster double bed carved intricately from polished wood. Five maids did everything from making the beds to setting up the table, serving and clearing away afterwards.

Within a short while I discovered that Mr Bernado, while he never exactly let his hair down, did have a wry sense of humour. His wife on the other hand had little warmth or personality, tending to giggle over nothing much. Her daughter, my companion Maria, was a practicing nurse who had just graduated and worked in Manila. She rarely went out except to Mass—every morning with no exceptions. It was also true that like most Filipinas she had never been given opportunities to enjoy good healthy fun. I thought of my first Filipina companion Linda Gonda, who had been introduced the hard way to our hiking adventure to Pulong Bato when we suffered with thirst, then shredded our feet in the long walk home. That experience probably influenced her ideas forever, about what girls should be encouraged to try.

My first breakfast was wonderful—fried egg with bacon, a bottle of fresh milk from the Bernado's small hobby farm, toast and honey, and papaya. On the second morning after an equally wonderful breakfast and feeling like I had nothing to lose, I asked Maria whether she'd like to come swimming with me up at Pasonanca. Shell-shocked, nevertheless she agreed. Surprisingly she owned bathers, so armed with swim bags we caught two jeepneys to reach our destination. For once the pool was completely devoid of people. Sensing that Maria was nervous, I entered at the shallow end, just floating around for a while to encourage her. At last, with great trepidation, she crossed herself and entered the water. When her feet left the ground she began to swim, awkwardly. She seemed keen to learn which warmed me to her. After I had demonstrated a few basics and was confident she wasn't going to drown under my watch, I began to practice my diving, uninhibited because I didn't have my usual band of onlookers.

All went well until I tried a somersault, and landed flat on my back, a real "ouch" moment. I swam to the ledge and laughed a fake laugh, but Maria seemed genuinely concerned, asking if I would like to go home. Secretly I was pleased that I now had an excuse not to revisit the diving board, and with my back smarting I showed Maria how to buy toffee bananas on sticks from the urchins in the park before we caught jeepneys home to Madrid Street. That night we had wild duck for dinner, an exotic food which I had never tasted. Another luxury available to me was a first-class typewriter, so during my stay at the Bernados' my letters home were typed, the bonus being that, with typeface, so much more fits onto each page.

But all the luxury in the world could not make up for the Alvarez homeliness, and as I lay in my four-poster with the romantic white netting draped over me like a wedding tent, I suffered that terrible longing to see my loved ones. Out of the corner of my eye I spotted movement above, and there was the cutest gecko, only two inches long, with splayed toes and bulging eyes, intently stalking a mosquito across the net. It seemed that she could only see straight ahead, so when a mozzie landed behind her I would whisper "Hey, Lizzie!" and she would whirl around and leap after her prey. It was a great distraction, better than watching a movie. This little sweetheart put on her best performance for me every night, helping to ward off the dreaded homesickness.

During the first week I refused all invitations for a night out. I had discovered two of the Bernado brothers and Maria were Scrabble-players. Freddy was quite hard to beat, but Toti could only come up with four-letter words. As we "Scrabbled," my liking for Maria grew. Like her dad, she actually had a sense of humour and was kind. However, after only eight days she had to board a boat for Manila, leaving me with two young teenage boys and their parents. It seemed that the Zambo airport was presenting another construction problem, so yet again I suffered that dread that the postal service would be compromised.

One Saturday late in July, I visited Angie's. I needed a simpler style of cut, one that didn't need curling or tending after I swam, which was almost every day. Afterwards I walked across to Ateneo for my first lesson, English Drama, discussing *Much Ado about Nothing*. Vic Solis and the other boys managed to be thoroughly entertaining. By the end of the lesson night had fallen, and I headed off along the corridor to the mind-numbing History of the Philippines. There we had a test laid out for us, so we put our heads down to work and were halfway through when a blackout hit. To my astonishment all students made a run for it in a deliberate effort to be gone by the time the lights came back on!

On Sunday morning, still groggy from partying with Jo-Jo and a group of friends at Lucky 7, I woke early and ran into town, hoping to catch some sort of transport to the Anglican service where Rob my Peace Corp friend would be. The humble church was on Cawa Cawa Boulevard, ironically bordering the nightclub where I had danced only hours before. To my surprise there were lots of people trying to find transport, so I slipped into a street where I guessed a calesa might trot by. My hunch was right, but for some reason the driver was unable to pull up at the spot where I was standing and stopped quite a distance further on. By this time mobs of people had appeared and were trying to board the calesa, so I just stood where I was and kept looking away down the empty street until I became aware of a great commotion amongst the crowd. The driver was refusing to let anyone board because he was doggedly holding it for me, who had hailed him first. I ran up and climbed in, fearing the enraged mob would attack me any second, and it was only when we trotted into Cawa Cawa Boulevard that I could relax, watching the vintas ghosting along a sea smooth as glass. At the end of the ride I handed over a generous payment for the driver who had managed to "get me to the church on time," hoping that some of the money might buy a more generous feed for his skinny little horse.

Rob ruefully held up his thumb. It had been infected for two days and was twice its normal size, reminding me of my infected toe when I was staying with the Reiths. Poor Rob hadn't slept for two nights with the pain, but despite this he escorted me back to the Bernado house after the service. By now it was raining thick as a waterfall, so we played Scrabble, to which I had become addicted. This was a once-only opportunity where I could take unfair advantage over Rob with his painful thumb, but despite this I won only by the smallest margin.

At midday the rain eased off, and Rob made his way back to his lodgings in Santa Maria. The maids made me lunch, and just when I decided to take a solid siesta Jun rang to see if I'd like to go swimming. I accepted in a blink! It seemed that he and the Alvarez boys had been spurred on by our adventure just a few days before, because at 2 P.M. Jun arrived in a battered old jeep, crammed not only with all the Alvarez brothers but three of the cast from *La Cadena de Amor*—a slightly overweight and cheerful soul called Hoss, a tall skinny person called Manny, and a girl called Clarita.

By "swimming" Jun meant we would once again drive to the top of Pasonanca and down the other side on the narrow jungle track that led towards the base of Pulong Bato. Somehow space was made for me and off we chugged, this time finding a track that allowed the jeep all the way through to the main river. It wasn't a track meant for vehicles, and the ancient jeep was not happy. Whenever she baulked at a slippery slope or a muddy ditch, everyone except Jun the driver needed to get out and push until the old girl reluctantly started up again, chugging across the jungle floor. Eventually, amazingly, we arrived at the main river. This time it was surging gracefully along in a much more placid mood than the mad torrent it had been two weeks before.

Espy was ecstatic—now he would be allowed to swim, albeit in the shallows. Once again, Litong seemed happy just sitting and watching. I gazed across at that small muddy ledge on the other side, the steep side of the bank. The ledge was so narrow that even if we could somehow reach it, our feet would be forced to stand sideways when we pushed off for the dive. I pointed out the ledge to Hoss and Butch, but they laughed and shook their heads. Then Clarita spoke up. "I'll try," she said. Everyone was flabbergasted. "But, can you swim across the river?" I asked dubiously. "Yes," was all she said, which gave us no choice but to take her at her word.

Jun had managed to borrow a camera, and because he wasn't exactly a water baby he made it his business to take photos while we clowned around. Every snap Jun took needed to be developed, which was not cheap, and yet he did this for me with no thought of reimbursement and with his charming buck-toothed smile.

Leaving the others on the bank or in the shallows, Hoss, Manny, Clarita and I swam out to the middle of the river where Hoss and I tried to dive for the bottom. Each time proved excruciatingly painful for our ears, but we were thankful the river was safely deep. I had never forgotten the sight of a young man in a wheelchair hauling his way along the Port Lincoln jetty. A year earlier he had dived from that jetty at low tide, breaking his neck.

The boys were kind enough to escort Clarita and me to the cliffs on the other side, because I was still unsure about how strongly she could swim. We reached the far bank, and immediately I tried to find a way up towards the ledge, seeking each toehold with great care to avoid a painful fall down the muddy stones and roots which made up the vertical surface. Hoss and Manny left us and swam back towards the other side, probably to get a better view of the spectacle to come.

I made it to the impossibly narrow ledge, stood awkwardly, and looked down. Clarita hadn't yet attempted the climb, and the river seemed a long way down. I quailed. But the crowd on the other side were lined up, watching expectantly, Jun poised with his camera. To descend back down the cliff would be far harder than the climb up, so I took a deep breath and dived.

I dive from precarious foothold: Clarita waits her turn.

It was exhilarating. Whether or not it was a neat look I'll never know, but the camera caught me in the first two seconds when my feet had left the ledge, for better or for worse. Filled with triumph I surfaced, and over the watery distance saw Hoss's grin and his thumbs up. Poor Clarita. I bet at that point she wished she had never volunteered to be my diving companion. I tensed as she clambered up to the ledge and jumped rather than dived. I tipped my invisible hat to her—a Filipina who, although she had been cosseted, showed real guts.

I lay floating on the surface, gazing up into the sky. And that's when I saw the biggest eagle I had ever seen—soaring majestically in the up currents. I yelled to the others and pointed. Jun's voice fell to an awed whisper. "It's the monkey-eating eagle!" We stood watching, until the Philippines national bird disappeared somewhere behind the Island of Rock.

That night I felt almost happy. Just because I wasn't living chez Alvarez didn't mean I couldn't spend time with them—Jun and Rob would see to that. I stood by my high bedroom window, brushing away the mozzies and watching dreamily as dusk descended over the Bernado's backyard and the sea beyond. A movement caught my eye in one of the fruit trees below. As if he could sense my gaze, the little thief looked up, his eyes meeting mine. He froze. His face was so cute, his big black eyes shining with such horror, that I couldn't help but smile. Now he pointed upwards with a questioning look. I nodded. He beamed until I thought his face would crack, and he continued gathering the guavas. I guessed where he had come from. Within plain sight of Bernado's was a line of hovels made up from bits of tin leaning up against an old wooden fence, with bags hanging down for doors and a small cooking fire nearby. These people lived in dire poverty, and although this little vignette had made me smile, it was also sad.

* * *

During the latter half of July and into August it teemed with rain almost every afternoon, and what was so unfamiliar to me was not only the density of the downfalls, but the fact that the temperature remained as warm as ever.

I had become known as "the biggest ice-cream eater in town" which spurred the DJ of DXLL (Eddie) to make a bet that I couldn't eat a half a gallon (nearly two litres!) of ice-cream in thirty minutes. The venue was, of course, Laura's Bakeshop, and the start time was set after my Spanish and English lectures in the afternoon. If I won, Eddie would be compelled to buy me a pair of sunglasses, which I needed, and if I lost I would have to buy him a wallet. I simply couldn't afford to lose, because a wallet would cost twenty pesos which I didn't have right now. I ate no food all day (in retrospect, perhaps not a good move), so, starving, I arrived at Laura's a little before 5 P.M., shaking off my umbrella. It was teeming outside.

Word had spread and a mob of friends and acquaintances had gathered, including Jo-Jo and PC Lenelle, but no sign of Artu himself or Eddie. I became suspicious that these two were sourcing an "impossible-to-eat" batch of ice-cream, kicking myself for not insisting upon plain vanilla. We milled around in the top room unsure of what to do. "Where's Nancy?" I whispered to Lenelle, and we moved to the window, peering down at the street below which was in full flood. In the middle of that stream hopped a strange figure dressed in green, shoes held high, hair clinging to her face. Lenelle and I looked at each other and grinned. In a few seconds Nancy would burst through the door, drenched from top to toe.

Still Eddie and Artu had not shown up. Meanwhile everyone began placing bets. I put on a serious face and jogged for two laps around the room—a top-class athlete preparing for the Olympic ice-cream-eating event. Suddenly the two evildoers appeared bearing a large container. Amidst cheers from those who had bet on me, I sat down. With flourish Artu opened the lid. I stared in horror. Half a gallon of chocolate fudge ice cream!

I protested, but it was too late. Someone started a stopwatch, and I began to eat. It was time to reward all those who had placed their faith in me. Spoonful by spoonful of that delicious dark creamy substance slipped down my throat, and I smiled. I had this in the bag! While my team sang "Waltzing Matilda" I jumped up and jogged around the room again, playing to the crowd. I sat down, someone theatrically wiped my face with a small towel, and off I went again, spoonful by spoonful.

Almost indiscernibly at first, my stomach began to resent the sweetness, and by halfway through it baulked at the coldness. Every now and then I needed to cough, a dry cough. Two-thirds of the way through I was *not* enjoying myself. It was hard to raise a grin when those who had bet against me loudly began to describe quantities of chocolate ice-cream, vats of it, mountains of it . . . there was still another eighth to go. My whole body started to reject what I was trying to feed it. A sharp headache began, and in between mouthfuls I felt so sick my head would slump to the tabletop. My sense of humour had evaporated.

It took me only twenty-three minutes to finish the last mouthful, not because I wanted to beat the time limit, but because if I had been sick without completing the bet all my willpower would have failed. Hearty cheers and groans issued from all sides of the room, but I ordered everyone out, except for the two PC girls who had already guessed why I wanted the males gone.

And then the strangest thing happened. I vomited quietly into the container, and undigested chocolate fudge ice-cream returned and settled just as it had looked at the very outset. The headache faded. I felt better again. With apologies for being so disgusting, I reported in a letter to my parents that the vomit could have been refrozen and served up to someone else—a delicious chocolate dessert! Fitting the lid back on, I requested Nancy to please take it downstairs and invite the rabble back up.

Upon their return they were at loggerheads as to whether I should be disqualified. No one had factored in the possibility of me vomiting up the entire tub of ice-cream, and so consequently there was dissent as to whether I had truly consumed it. The lawyer in me triumphed. "Well, just as I failed to stipulate that the ice-cream had to be vanilla, you failed to stipulate that I should keep it in my body for a certain length of time." The case was closed, with me winning. But it was at least two days before I could look ice-cream in the face—well, the choc fudge version anyway!

Two days later I came down with another kind of headache, from a kind of flu. For two full days I languished in my bed upstairs with night fevers, sore eyes and a splitting headache along with terrible homesickness made worse by the fact that no one in the Bernado house seemed to even notice I was unwell.

A letter from SJ one month later revealed that he too had suffered from the same type of virus over the same time period—a strange happening with no rational explanation.

* * *

During the segments of time Artu was studying in Manila, numerous telegrams and bouquets came almost every second day to make it impossible for me to forget him. It is only now I understand why Chito was away so long while Artu seemed to return every week. The boy from the middle class simply couldn't afford to come and go as he pleased. He wrote often, but even if he hadn't, he would have remained firmly in my heart.

Every time Artu returned to Zamboanga he took me to the movies. Halfway through the film, snacks and drinks would magically appear out of the darkness, and when we wandered outside afterwards, sometimes the red sports car would mysteriously have been replaced by the yellow Renault. I gave up asking questions, finally accepting that in the Philippines things seemed to just—happen.

One morning, after spending up until lunch time catching up on my letter writing, I rang Jo-Jo and begged him to rescue me before I turned into a vegetable. Within fifteen minutes my good knight was driving me up to Pasonanca, patiently waiting until I'd had enough of diving and swimming. Then he took me to his house, the "castle," and proceeded to show me photos of the Filipina from Manila whom he planned to marry the following year. I couldn't help smiling when comparing this glorious immaculate female posing in all sorts of alluring attitudes, to me standing there with bare feet, dripping wet and sniffing!

* * *

In late July Nancy asked me to help her clean up an old Red Cross building with the aim of making it into a homeless shelter for street kids. This was the first time I had witnessed exactly what the Peace Corps did, apart from clowning around. When I arrived at the allotted time Nancy wasn't there. I surveyed the scene, perplexed. *I should make a start, but how, and where?* Under all the spiders and cobwebs lay rubbish piled high to the ceiling, and so I got to work clearing out the junk.

At one stage I perched high up, wobbling perilously on a creaky bookshelf with two bowls of water. Cleaning the ceiling meant bending backwards, and the water from the sponge dripped all over my dusty face which became a muddy face. Three hours later my hands were red raw, and it hit me how long it had been since Princess Stefania had done any housework at all. Two Filipino social workers wandered in, wisely staying a safe distance from this strange foreigner smeared from head to toe with mud. When they praised me and the Peace Corps for doing such a great job, I got secret delight in confusing them by casually mentioning I was Australian and in no way connected with the PC. It was fun to see their jaws drop.

After I somehow put a rusty drawing pin through my thumb, the mercurial Nancy appeared—too late in the day to work. However, the following morning she drove me back to the old building, set me up with sandpaper and scraper, told me she was on a quest to persuade businesses to donate paint, and once again vanished. Two hours later she reappeared, along with brushes and many tins of paint, each a different colour. I shook my head in disbelief. Not once did it occur to Nancy that she could fail, and that's why she never did.

I went to my first jazz dance class, run by Rosie of course, who assured me I would take to it like a duck to water. "Like a duck that's for sure," I retorted, quite convinced that I detested jazz dance as much as I detested jazz music. Within minutes, however, I was addicted. It needed precise skill, and speed, and when Nancy appeared the whole experience became hilarious. Being a little overweight, and because she had never set one large foot in a formal dance studio, she caused so much mirth that I was more puffed from laughing than the dancing. Every time we were going left, Nancy would go right, and when we sprang down Nancy would jump up—I laughed so hard the tears were streaming down my face.

* * *

On 2 August an earthquake, magnitude seven, struck Manila. Chito, who was boarding with five other students in an apartment block in Quezon City, came close to becoming one of the victims. He wrote that around 4 A.M., just after he had finished writing to me, the quake struck. He and his mates jumped from their beds as their concrete building began rocking. At first they stood, tense, listening, but when they heard people shouting in the streets and the audible cracking of walls, they jumped towards the door only to find it had skewed and jammed. Luckily a wide crack appeared in the wall through which they scrambled and made for the stairwell, almost falling in their panic before making it out onto the street.

They witnessed a nearby five-floor building collapsing with 600 people in it.

From the newspapers displaying all too graphic pictures, I learnt that there were only fifty survivors in the doomed building. The examples were tragic. One girl with a fractured leg was rescued after being trapped for thirty-six hours in her tomb, and another was pulled out from under a cement wall which had pinned her down for many hours. Yet another had written his name on a piece of paper before he died. Most of the bodies were so mangled it was hard to tell male from female. Nightmarish stuff.

As daylight came and before the authorities could prevent them, Chito and his five roommates ventured back upstairs, crawled through the crack and collected what they could of their belongings. That day Chito found different lodgings, but the nightmare refused to leave his mind as he pictured being pinned down in the dark, slowly suffocating to death under a mountain of rubble.

From that moment when my dear friend's letter arrived, reassuring me he had survived, I could breathe easy again.

* * *

In the Bernado household the two young teenagers, Toti and Freddy were on a mission to beat me at Scrabble. Despite English being their second language, Toti at least always managed to throw out enough of a challenge to give me an interesting game. Mr Bernado would often rebuke Freddy for lapsing into Chavacano. It seemed that one of the reasons I had been sought as a guest was to improve the boys' English.

One night, as I lay under the netting watching my gecko pal stalking a mozzie, I heard Toti and Freddy having a conversation in the next bedroom. "Hey Freddy, dare me to court Wendy, go on, dare me!"

Freddy replied, daring Toti to court Mary Lou. I grinned, because there was only one Mary Lou in town, and this mestiza was not only feisty but at least ten years older than either of the boys.

I called out, "Freddy, I dare you to court *me*!" Stunned silence on the other side of the wall before both cracked up laughing. From that moment the boys and I enjoyed half an hour of surprisingly witty conversation, and I realized I'd grown quite fond of them.

One night, after Scrabble, we said our goodnights and headed off for bed. As usual, it was a warm night and I wasn't quite ready for sleep, so I switched on the stereo player in my room and put on a dance record. Then I wandered to the open window to make sure nobody could see me, shed my clothes, and began to dance.

This might sound weird, but it must be put into context. My family had a tradition of heading out to the rugged West Coast of South Australia for our annual holiday. In the 50s and 60s we were always able to find a campsite overlooking the Great Southern Ocean where we would not see another soul for a week. And on a pristine white beach, with the surf pounding up onto the sand, my mother and I would strip naked and perform cartwheels. Then, laughing with that heady feeling of freedom, we'd race each other into the green breakers. My father was more prudish, always keeping his bathers on and casting eyes to the clifftop to make sure no visitors had stopped by to admire the view.

It's a long-lasting regret that I, too, did not look upwards before I began to dance in the Bernado house, because I may have noticed for the first time that the wall opposite my bed stopped two feet from the ceiling! And with that information I may have deduced that the sound of music and my feet dancing on that glossy wooden floor would have aroused curiosity. Despite our conversation only a few nights previously, I had never noticed that gap and was totally unaware of the boys' wardrobe against the wall on the other side, which in this case must have beckoned like a stairway to heaven.

I was in the middle of performing an arabesque without wobbling when my concentration was broken by sniggers. I glanced up in time to see the boys' faces before they vanished, and all thoughts of freedom and dancing evaporated. I was mortified. Replaying that disgraceful scene over and over in my mind, I tossed and turned all night. Even my friend the gecko eyed me with a pitying expression. *How will I face those two young perverts in the morning?*

I remember that breakfast horribly clearly. My face felt hot, and because the servants expected me to utter the usual pleasantries I mumbled "Good morning," instantly looking down at the table. The boys too mumbled greetings, but when at last I glanced up, they too were studying the table. Suddenly I realized that Toti and Freddy were deeply fearful that I would spin some sort of story to their parents about them spying on me as I got undressed.

This incident alone would not have justified falsifying the name of my host family—it was harmless mischief from two young teenagers. But a few days after, when I was due to pack my bags to move to another Rotarian host, something more serious occurred. While none of my letters home mention the episode, I can still recall the detail with sickening clarity.

Nineteen-year-old Leo Bernado arrived home from Manila where he had been studying. One evening he asked me out, saying we would meet up with two of his friends on Cawa Cawa Boulevard for a "barbeque" (shaslik chicken). He had borrowed his father's car for the night, a very classy Mercedes Benz, and off we set with me dressed in the same pink chiffon dress which I had worn on the flight from Australia.

Just upon nightfall our car drew up at the familiar building housing the barbeque restaurant and Lucky 7 upstairs. A couple about Leo's age emerged from a parked car. While I chatted to the girl and ate barbeque, Leo and the other boy drank San Miguel beer and talked earnestly together until it was well and truly dark. Suddenly Leo opened the Merc's door, ushering me in, casually telling me we were going "somewhere else," and that the others would follow. Because my Filipino escorts had always been spontaneous about changing venues, I was only mildly curious as to where we were going.

After heading along the coast for a minute or so, I looked back. "They're not behind us."

Leo glanced in his rear-vision mirror, then looked ahead. I stared at him. Why was he not answering, and why wasn't he slowing down? In fact, he was driving faster, very fast, and soon the tyres were flicking up pebbles as we sped along the dirt road leading out towards Caragasan. "Where are we going?" I demanded, and now there was real anger and alarm in my voice. As we roared through some Muslim villages I was thinking of Charlie's warning when we had first driven me to Patalon. "You don't want to break down out here." But this night it was not Muslims I needed to fear—it was a so-called good Catholic boy from my foster family.

By the time the car slewed to a stop in the middle of pitch black, I knew I was in trouble. We sat in breathtaking silence for a few seconds. Then suddenly Leo lunged, grabbing the back of my head to pull me towards him. With the other hand he tugged at my dress, and I heard the chiffon tearing. In those first few seconds I flailed ineffectually to defend myself, but when it was clear he wasn't about to stop, my fingers curled into fists in the hope of landing an effective blow. Again and again he warded off my fists, and in a haze of panic I realized what a hopeless fighter I was. Perhaps we struggled for what may have been three minutes, and then abruptly Leo stopped, throwing himself back behind the wheel. Silence, except for our puffing. All around us was darkness. I reached around to zip up my dress and felt shreds of chiffon. Leo sat staring ahead, and I didn't need to look at him to know he was fuming. He started the car, did a screaming wheelie in the dirt, and hit the accelerator. I was in such a state of shock that I barely felt this new danger as the car reached crazy speeds, driven by a testosterone-fueled madman. And all the while—stony silence between us. I fretted about what would happen if we got home and a maid or one of the family saw me with my flustered face and dress in tatters. But one thing I knew for sure. Until I reached home in Australia, I would never tell anyone about what had happened that night. It wasn't fair to the rest of my host family, and what exactly would I achieve? My only satisfaction lay in the fact that Leo would sweat for the next few days, not knowing which way I would jump.

Somehow we reached the Bernado house without ending up mangled in a car crash. My mind and dress, however, were mangled. I managed to creep upstairs to my bedroom without anyone seeing me. Presumably Leo did the same. The following morning I did not come down for breakfast, simply asking a maid if I could have a needle and pink thread. "I will do for you ma'am," she offered. But with a tired smile I declined her offer.

For many nights after that, perched in my bedroom outside the romantic net, typing letters back home, I was plagued with mosquitoes. I was also plagued with sadness and loneliness in this household which was showering me with luxury but failing to provide me with emotional support. It had also become threatening. I wrote to SJ, "Since I've been in this house my heart hasn't been quite as light—I miss home even more." That was an understatement, given the emotional traumas of the last week, although SJ would not be told any of this, not until I was safely in his arms back home.

Two months before meeting President Ferdinand Marcos
Host family — Lopez-Vito

Mrs Lopez-Vito came to collect me in an exotic car, the family's driver behind the wheel. As we purred into the pretty suburb of Baliwasan I could feel the heaviness lifting from my heart with every mile. Then into view came the modern two-story abode of my new family, another palatial house, perhaps because it needed to accommodate twelve children, three cars, seven servants, a cook and a driver! Two of the older children were away studying in Manila, but that still left ten of all ages, which made it all the more generous that I was given a vast room all to myself. It had a double bed and an air conditioner, and there was a tin of expensive biscuits on the dressing table. I had also spotted the grand piano in the open lounge and couldn't wait to have a tinkle. As my spirits lifted further, I began to realize just how unhappy I had been at Bernados'.

Florry was my female companion, a lively girl by nature, but a typically over-protected Filipina. When she confessed to having never ridden in a jeepney, I couldn't believe it. "Don't worry," I offered, "I'll introduce you to the wild experience of jeepney riding!"

The servants, cook and driver all came from the Visayas where Chavacano was not spoken, so they understood neither pigeon-Spanish nor English. The maids always hovered near the table after they had served the food, while the three male servants were employed swishing the flies away.

The meals were luxurious, placed on a smaller inner table that rotated on top of a vast round table. This was a novelty for me which seemed at first glance to make sense when there were so many mouths to feed. Theoretically, you spied a prawn dish before hauling the central table around until prawns lay temptingly before you. You would help yourself with a serving spoon before turning the table again to bring some roast pork within reach. But in practice the lazy Susan was either a source of frustration or hilarity, depending on my mood. For example, I would patiently wait until the prawns came into view, but just as I would reach for the serving spoon they would circle to the other side, replaced by noodle salad. Now resigned to the noodles, I would pick up a load with the tongs, but before I could return the tongs to the dish the noodles would have taken off on yet another journey. The servants must have been secretly entertained during each dining event.

One morning I rose late. The dining room felt surreal—not a soul in sight. A maid peeped out from the rear kitchen, and instantly all four maids materialized. It became clear—they needed to know what ma'am would like for breakfast. "Could I have a fried egg on toast?" I asked. They looked at each other, baffled. I tried to mime a fried egg on toast, which tested my acting skills to the utmost. I did the egg-laying thing first, with lots of flapping elbows and clucking, climaxing with one huge "Claaaark" when I produced an imaginary egg from beneath me. The girls screeched with laughter but then came the much harder mime of cooking the egg and toasting the toast. The effect achieved more hilarity than clarity. I sat down, and a mug of pale lukewarm tea was brought to me, half tea, half evaporated milk. One maid stayed back to see if I was enjoying my beverage, so I made "Aaaagh" sounds of satisfaction after each sip of the revolting liquid. She beamed.

The three others proudly brought in the meal and set it down in front of me. I stared, and it was seconds before I recovered my wits. Two eggs, lightly cooked, almost raw, were sitting in a half inch of melted fat. The toast seemed to have been forgotten. All four maids stood around me, beaming. There was no way out. I mustered all my inner strength and set to work trying to balance slippery egg on my fork to reach my mouth before bits dropped noisily into the fat, which was beginning to congeal. "Mmm," I mumbled, struggling to resist vomiting onto the white linen tablecloth. My recent ice cream ordeal paled in comparison to this. Then I had a terrible thought. What if the maids concluded this was what I craved every morning?

Later that afternoon I had a quiet word with Florry, and, careful not to make any mention of fried eggs, I asked her if I could have papaya, bread and coffee every morning. "Of course," she said, puzzled at the request. And from that day onwards my breakfast consisted of exactly what I had ordered—half a papaya, a bread roll, and a mug of coffee.

The coffee was super strong, straight from the coffee plantation next door. About one hundred coffee trees offered shade to the house, and to the other mansion on the block beside it. This residence belonged to the cousins of my host family. Just as the Climacos nestled up to their Alvarez relatives in Santa Maria, so the Guingonnas and the Lopez-Vitos lived close together in the clean suburb of Baliwasan.

I had never tasted nor smelt coffee as wonderful as this, and it became my favourite beverage. Early in my stay I was lying on my stomach in my queen-sized bed, and I had just fallen to sleep when the earth began to shake beneath me. *A quake!* Wild-eyed I sat up, listening, but the night was still and silent. Tentatively I sank back down. Immediately the earthquake struck again! Once more I sat up, certain now that the whole household would be scrambling for safety. And only then did my brain begin to compute that the earthquake was not beneath me, but inside me. My heart was thumping so hard in my chest that when lying face downwards the whole bed shook. And with a jolt I remembered the big mug of coffee I had drunk not long before! For half an hour I breathed slowly, lying on my side, listening to the thumping within, waiting for the intensity to die down. Eventually my heart rate slowed, and calmed, and at long last I slid into the land of nod.

Something rustled. A creature scuttled over my face. Panting with terror, I lunged for the bedside light in time to see a fat rat running up the wall and disappearing over the other side. My heart rate leapt up a notch and I couldn't stop trembling. There was nothing I could do except to get out of bed, put on a light gown and pace the room, my eyes searching the shadows. When my addled brain could think straight, I noticed that the biscuit tin had been left open, by me, when I had treated myself while I drank the mug of bedtime coffee! I slammed the lid shut, but the light stayed on while my eyes tried hard to stay open.

I used all my willpower to ignore any rustling sounds, and about midnight I fell into a heavy sleep. One hour later there was a blackout. The reason I woke was that the air conditioner had stopped, and the room soon heated to a point where even a sheet over me was too much. Yet to throw off the sheet was to expose me to the rats. Then the mosquitoes arrived in squadrons, forcing me to pull up the top sheet until only my nose was peeping out. I began to sweat profusely, until I was lying in a pool of wetness, and that's when the rats turned up, black bodies scuttling and crisscrossing the room. There was no light to turn on, so I lay on my stomach, head to one side to allow breathing, sheet pulled up to eye level. And that's how I stayed until the first light of dawn.

As soon as I clapped eyes on Florry I told her my tale, but instead of consoling me she began to tell me (with relish) how one of her siblings, when he was a baby, had been attacked in his cradle by a rat. Only his screams had prevented him from being eaten!

Rob came to visit me that day, and side by side we sat at the piano rendering a harmonized version of "Chopsticks." Afterwards, as we sat chatting, a dark shape streaked across the floor and ran vertically up the wall before vanishing over the top. My hand flew to my throat, and I told Rob why my eyes had dark rings under them, and how I had developed a terrible fear of rats and would never be able to fall asleep in this house.

"Ah, so have you politely asked the rats to leave?" he asked. I warned him this was no joke, but Rob insisted it wasn't, asking me again whether I had asked the rats to leave. "No. I haven't," I retorted. "Not politely anyway." Rob explained that rats were super intelligent animals, and that they would never bother me again if—

"If what?" I asked.

"If in a loud voice you ask the rats, nicely, to never again enter your room."

I searched Rob's face for any sign of mischief, but he seemed dead serious. I began to doubt whether the world was round. We then had a conversation about how rats can run vertically up walls, but even Rob's super brain could not dredge up a definitive answer to that.

When night fell I shut myself in my bedroom, stood as if I were auditioning on stage, breathed deeply and hoped fervently that no one in the household could hear me. Loudly, in polite tones, I requested the rats to stay away and never bother me again.

As long as I live this will remain a mystery—for the rest of my stay, I never laid eyes on another rat in the Lopez-Vito household.

* * *

Nonong, a Filipino student at Ateneo who was one of the Lopez-Vito cousins, began driving me home after lessons. One day he offered to take me to see the San Ramon prison. Every time I had been driven out of town towards Charlie's coconut plantation, I had stared at the compound at the base of the jungle-clad mountains in the distance, wondering, *How are the conditions inside? Do prisoners ever escape?*

One Sunday morning Nonong, Rob and I drove out along the coast road to visit the prison. The red Mercedes sports parked outside the walls, and from the moment we were admitted through the gates I tried to appear no more than mildly interested, though inside I was super tense—bracing for what was to come.

This jail had once housed the very traitor ("Captain Moreno") who had been released during the Japanese occupation and had murdered most of the Reith family living at Patalon.

It was an "open" jail—high barbed-wire walls surrounding a big square, with rows of sleeping quarters in open cages, ten men to a cage. There was the usual prison platform around the perimeter from which the guards could view activity below in the courtyard. I had always imagined a prisoner of war camp looking like this. The inmates stared out at us. It felt like we were superior beings detachedly appraising caged animals, and it made me sick to the stomach. I could see Rob felt the same way.

The guard explained that some of the more trusted prisoners were allowed outside to work the coconut plantation encircling the prison, but most stayed confined. The prisoners consisted of Muslim, Moro, Catholic, and Indigenous. I consoled myself that at least the men worked and slept in the open air, rather than incarcerated in dungeons, away from sunlight.

We were shown into a shed where we had the opportunity to buy beautifully carved objects inlaid with shell, made by the prisoners.

I still possess several small pieces I purchased, and every time I look at them, I think of those prisoners who made them.

I asked the guard if we could see further into the prison. For a moment he looked dubious, then nodded. All this time I was playing it cool, and so were the boys. If we had said anything derogatory about the prison, or appeared upset, within minutes we would have been looking at the interior of Nonong's car.

Our steps clanged and clattered as we were shown up a steel stairway which led to a steel walkway. Now we had a bird's-eye view as to what was going on. I tried not to wince under the stares of the prisoners as they looked up. A stinking open sewerage canal lay below us, and a large cage near that canal served as a hospital.

A burley man in one corner of the square rang a bell and picked up a ladle. Another man stood behind two barrels, wielding a wooden spoon. Prisoners lined up, each with a tin plate and a bowl. Into the bowl was slapped a spoonful of gluggy rice, and onto the plate was dropped a ladleful of green muck. Nonong whispered that half of the money allotted by the authorities for food went straight into the pockets of the top guards.

On the drive home we stopped at Caragasan for a swim. The sun shone brightly on a clean green sea tipped by creamy foam on the crest of each wave. All three of us dived again and again in a vain effort to wash away the dirty images we had just experienced at San Ramon.

* * *

A few days later Nonong arrived to take me to a beach called Talisayan, a long way past the prison on the coast road. This kind of outing occurred often enough, but something happened on this particular day which etched itself into my memory. The beach itself was vast and wide, and the day was super sunny. After we had swum, I lay front up on my towel to sunbake. Nonong hung back somewhere under the coconut palms with the opposite motive—to shade himself so that he would look fashionably whiter.

There I was, lying almost asleep in my bikinis and all alone on that wide beach, when a small plane buzzed high above. Lazily I looked up, then went back to snoozing again. The engine noise seemed to increase, and I turned my head to one side. To my horror the plane was flying towards me, maybe twelve feet above the beach, heading straight for me! I screamed, hugging the sand. The plane roared over the top of me. Scrambling to my feet, I saw Nonong peering in disbelief from the shade of the palms. He ran forwards, but before he could reach me the plane approached from the opposite direction, flying so low that both of us had no choice but to fling ourselves face down onto the sand. As it banked and aimed at me for the third time, Nonong yelled that he was going to get his gun from the car, which was several hundred yards away. As he headed back towards the palms I struggled up and ran for the closest cover, into the water. As the plane zoomed in I dived, but upon surfacing, when I saw that yet again it was performing a tight turn, I felt a surge of anger. The pilot was playing a game to scare me, no doubt killing himself laughing.

As Nonong appeared from the palms waving his pistol, and as the plane lined up again, I stood in the shallows, hands on hips, bracing every muscle to stand motionless, staring straight at the cockpit as the plane roared over. It seemed to miss the top of my head by inches. This was the last run the plane made, and seconds later Nonong and I stood side by side watching the small plane disappear inland, up and over the jungle.

Just as I had picked up my towel and was walking with Nonong back to the car, a nice-looking man appeared from the palms with a camera. "Do you mind very much if I take your photo?" Before I could reply he was snapping away, even when I turned my back on him. Poor Nonong didn't know what to do—it wasn't behaviour bad enough to warrant death by gunshot, but it was intrusive and insensitive. I covered myself with my towel as best I could and told him I wasn't interested. "I will show you the photos once they are developed," he said, all innocence. Without a word I walked to Nonong's car and we drove away.

Perhaps wary of parental overreaction, I made light of the two incidents in the letter home. "I've never been paid so much attention in one morning!"

* * *

Jun had written another serial play for DXJW. *Ray Santander* featured a fictional Filipino hero who was a Philippine Intelligence agent. Rob was cast as a Russian spy, while I was Heidi, a German CIA agent skilled in sharpshooting and all the martial arts. And my mission? To kill the Russian spy. Although the plot was exciting, rehearsals involved many hours sitting in the soundless (and airless!) studio. I was perched on a stool watching Jun hard at work behind the glass, waiting for the "stand by" and "on air" lights to appear. After four hours my concentration began to wane, and as if Rob sensed this he began to act melodramatically, making me shake with laughter that was agony to hold in. The strange thing was, on the airwaves Rob's voice and accent seemed restrained and perfect. I wrote home that despite the tediousness of some of the recording, the whole experience was "still loads of fun" adding carelessly, "I kill Rob Saturday night."

By this time, I was known by almost everyone in town, for better and for worse. The jeepney drivers knew exactly where to drop me off, whether it was at the pool or the Lopez-Vito home or Ateneo, without me having to call out "Aqui lang!" And as I walked through the town I heard comments like "There goes Miss Australia," or "That's Stiffy," and the one that always made me smile, "There goes Heidi!"

Jun loved me deeply. Trying to thank me for adding some prestige to his radio plays, he took it upon himself to borrow the Alvarez jeep every Sunday and take me and any other friends off to the big river at the base of Pulong Bato. One Sunday Rob came too, and before we plunged into the jungle valley, we bought wooden skewers of fried bananas as snacks for when we reached the river.

I got changed behind a big tree trunk and wandered into the water, a wooden skewer in each hand. Rob's lanky body appeared on the bank. Now in over my depth, I was treading water and chewing away on the bananas. And then he got me laughing. I laughed so hard that I went under, bananas and all!

After the fun at the river, we went on a short walk in the jungle, and that is when we arrived at an unlovely village. The huts were positioned facing each other along three sides of a dusty, barren area. Barren that is, except for a primitive cage set in the centre of the square, and in that cage was confined that most rare and awe-inspiring bird—the monkey-eating eagle. The three of us were drawn towards the cage, our hearts sickened by the sight of a huge bird confined so cruelly it could not spread its wings. My eyes searched for the latch on the cage door. Rob guessed my thoughts and warned me under his breath. Some raggedy boys appeared, and for our further entertainment they began to prod the eagle with sticks. I turned away, hot with anger, and almost ran back along the track with Rob and Jun close behind me.

Usually after our river adventures I felt so happy, but that night I wept.

* * *

In this hot and humid climate, I dreaded "that time of the month" for obvious reasons. Tampons had been available since the 50s, but all through the preceding years, and perhaps even in 1968, I was still supplementing tampons using homemade pads made from old towels, which of course needed to be washed and dried before reusing. One afternoon at Ateneo, in the middle of my period, I felt unbearably hot and sweaty. I was haunted by the fact that anyone who approached me might find my smell offensive, and so in the hour between classes I roared back to the home of my Spanish teacher, Señora Araneta, in a sidecar, freshened up with a shower, then returned to the afternoon lessons.

Usually, a female gets some warning that her period is on its way, but one day, with no tell-tale signs, I set off with Jun and the Alvarez brothers to a large party, happily wearing my white cotton dress. As I entered the marquee I walked between the tables, stopping every few feet to chat to friends and acquaintances. Making my way to the head table I was talking to the hostess when an Alvarez brother whispered in my ear

"There is blood on your dress." My cheeks burned with embarrassment. Excusing myself, and with the boys gathered close behind me, I made my way back down through the tables, looking straight ahead so that no one could catch my eye and postpone my exit. I was hugely grateful to my male escorts, marveling at their quick-thinking and protectiveness.

* * *

In my spare time I wrote articles, usually about social issues, in the *Beacon* office. One day I was so engrossed tapping away at the typewriter that I forgot to keep an eye on the clock. I was late for my history lesson! I grabbed up my bag which felt too light, and instantly I guessed my textbook wasn't inside. Editor Vic Solis asked what I was searching for.

"My history book has gone missing," I told him, rummaging in some drawers. "You must have stolen it!" I grabbed up my bag and flew out the door, too rushed to notice that Vic had not laughed.

The following day I returned to finish my article. After a few moments it seemed clear that Vic was not his usual cheerful self. "Are you okay Vic?"

He nodded glumly. I went back to work, but whenever I looked up with a comment, he avoided my eyes and mumbled. I rose from my chair and approached him, whispering, "Vic, there *is* something wrong. You must tell me."

After a long pause he whispered back, "You said I stole your history book."

I was incredulous. "Yes, but that was just a joke."

Vic looked baffled. "But how can it be a joke? You accused me of stealing your history book."

My heart sank. How could I explain to him that the more an Aussie knows and likes someone, the more she is likely to say the opposite of what she really means, and the recipient would understand the joke instantly.

"Vic," I said, "you know how I've often said that history is the most boring lesson I've ever experienced?" He nodded. "And have you heard me say that the *History of the Philippines* is the most boring book of all time?" Still looking martyred, he nodded again. "Well, why would you or anyone want to steal the most boring book of all time?"

Now Vic looked genuinely perplexed. "Exactly," he replied, "so why did you think I would want to steal the book?"

I gave up trying to describe Aussie humour, simply asking him to trust me that it was a joke, and to accept my humble apologies for offending him. I was relieved when he brightened up, but although we got on smoothly after that, I never again assumed that different cultures would have a similar sense of humour.

* * *

It was as if some unseen force was trying to make my history lessons more exciting. A month before there had been that blackout in the middle of a test, and the mad stampede for the exit door. Then, one hot night as our teacher was reading from that boring book, the fire alarm sounded throughout the building. All heads swung to the window, and although we were two floors up we could see a red glow outside. While the teacher urged us to remain calm, his voice could not disguise his panic.

Now we could smell smoke, and that did it. Students in their hundreds poured out of every classroom on the top floor and practically fell down the stairs in their efforts to escape. In a surge of frantic bodies, I finally reached ground level where I heard glass cracking and saw the laboratory was alight, flames licking out of its windows. In itself this did not overly alarm me, but now we could smell sickening chemical fumes. Holding my breath I ran outside with a tangle of students, and word quickly spread that a bottle of acid had exploded in the lab. We held handkerchiefs over our noses as two fire engines screamed into view. Soon torrents of water were aimed at the flames.

Nonong drove me back to the Lopez-Vitos', both of us laughing about our narrow escape from death! Only two nights later I was back at Ateneo, this time dressed up to the nines in my fuchsia pink dress which simply served to enhance the rosy glow on my sunburnt face. The college ball took place in the assembly hall, a large space which contained no less than four combos (bands), and I danced every dance in high silver sandals until around midnight when my feet felt like cooked cabbage. Yet again I starred in the *Zambo Times* society page: "Gracing the dance floor in a floor-length red ball gown was Miss S. Wicks, Rotary Exchange scholar..."

* * *

One evening after Rob and I had dined at Hotel Byot, we took a stroll along the grassy shoreline towards Fort Pilar. The sea was silver-grey glass, and the silhouette of an enormous vinta seemed for all the world like a Spanish galleon. The Greco-Roman pillars of the former barracks were classic black shapes against a star-lit sky. In that romantic atmosphere we sat side by side on a tiny ribbon of shoreline, me hoping Rob would not kiss me or do anything that might ruin our friendship.

In that fateful moment we spied headlights approaching. As they got closer we identified the city police patrolling in their battered old car. They cruised past, each head turned towards us, and that's probably why the car skewed into a ditch. Trying to suppress sniggers, Rob and I got to our feet. Humiliated, the police clambered from the car as it lay drunkenly on its side, and proceeded to lecture us about how dangerous it was in this area with thieves ever on the look-out, and that it would be wise to return to the town proper. This we did, leaving the three policemen to manually heave the car from the ditch under the walls of the great fort.

In mid-August Chito wrote me another love letter, this one even more heart-wrenching than the last. Over and over he wrote "I really love you Stephie!" before admitting that although I had forbidden him to fall in love with me, no matter what I said it didn't change the fact that "I love you, and will always love you." He explained that he had tried to form a relationship with one of his female classmates, but through every day and night he saw only my image and heard only my voice. He finished his three-page letter with the worrying comment, "if God choose, I shall but love thee better after death."

* * *

One Saturday morning at Pasonanca I found a lady waiting for me by the pool. She seemed unusually urgent in her request that I teach her three young children, then explained why. A week earlier her husband, an American, had been travelling in a light plane with three others when a massive storm hit and they ditched into the sea. The pilot couldn't swim, and if it hadn't been for the others holding him up, he would have drowned. "My husband is still in hospital with his injuries, but my children need to be taught to swim." Quickly I agreed, and the children were delightful. This lesson was all the happier given the eight little Lopez-Vitos also seemed keen to learn and even asked intelligent questions.

In the afternoon Rob, Jun and I found ourselves standing on the carpet of natural grass on the crest of Pasonanca Park, gazing at the beauty of the valley below and the impressive dome of the Island of Rock rising out of that vast carpet of jungle. There on that grass the three of us went a little mad, competing at long jumps and balancing on the edge of the ridge-top. At one stage Jun and I were so weak from laughing we collapsed onto a log while long lanky Rob clambered on all fours up a grassy bank, leaping and springing like the brown toads hopping all about him.

That night Rob took Jun and me out to dinner at the Hotel Byot. When the three of us were sitting out on the balcony with no other guests in sight, I had just finished a delicious meal of "Brain of Cow" when Jun leaned over and took my hand and kissed me on the cheek. With a wicked grin he said, "You see how Steffie is now my girlfriend Rob, so are you jealous?" Rob growled, "Yaaah, I'm jealous," and he kept up a ridiculous deep-throated growling as he drank and gurgled a bottle of Seven-up, squeezing the bottle with his large hands, then banging it on the table and magically making his eyes protrude from their sockets. Once again Jun and I became helpless with laughter. However, as I laughed and danced, I felt a pang of dread. A gremlin inside kept nagging me that the day could never be replicated again, and that Rob and Jun, all too soon, would disappear from my life.

In one of his letters years later Jun recalled every detail of that wonderful Saturday, finishing with "How I wish we could relive all those beautiful moments together ... but sadly we can't. All we can do is to relive them in our hearts and minds."

* * *

Rob had asked me to accompany him on a weeklong malaria survey in the remote logging village of Lituban on the west coast of Mindanao. Naturally I was keen to go, but there were obstacles to be overcome. Both of us fronted Doc Marasigan, describing what the week away would entail and hoping for his permission to let me go. "Will you be taking a female chaperone?" he asked, and we were able to assure him that Jun's sister Claro was happy to join us. This remarkable woman was thirty-one years old but looked twenty-four, and was kind, gutsy and reliable. Rob had tried to arrange for a jeep to take us on logging tracks all the way to Lituban, but while the distance wasn't far, the terrain was so rough and unmapped that this plan was scrapped. There was no other way to get there except by sea, so the first part of our trip would involve a cargo boat which would offload us at the coastal town of Siocon. Doc's main concern seemed to be where we would be staying each night. Rob explained that in the hills above Siocon lived an American missionary couple, Mr and Mrs Hall, who would be our hosts.

It would have been easier for Doc to deny me this trip, and I hugely appreciated the risk he was prepared to take so that I could experience various adventures in his country. The dear man gave us the go-ahead.

A few hours afterwards, from the shelter of Lantaka on Cawa Cawa Boulevard, Artu and I sat sipping our drinks and peering along the coast towards the south. Through rain thick as a curtain we saw nothing but a heavy blue-blackness, with bolts of lightning stabbing into an angry sea where the swells were growing higher by the minute. When we later discovered that a cargo boat had capsized with numerous fatalities near Caragasan, I silently prayed that Doc would not reverse his decision. *After all, if our cargo boat capsized, the Mighty Malaria Trio could just swim to shore, couldn't we?*

Our mission was to visit as many huts as was possible within Lituban, ascertaining how prevalent Malaria was in this area, where people were mainly illiterate and uneducated and rarely came face-to-face with white foreigners or a doctor. They spoke a dialect called Cebuano, which Rob had learnt in his six-month training course in Hawaii. I wrote to a friend, "Rob will prick their fingers (if they don't shoot us first) and my job is to take the blood and prepare a smear on a slide, while Claro will number the slides and cope with taking down their names, which is no easy task."

One month before meeting President Ferdinand Marcos
Location: Tetuan, Zamboanga
Host family — Araneta

I had just packed a carry bag for the week's expedition when Rob rang to tell me that the weather was too bad for the boat to sail, so we would be delayed until the tempest abated. The next few days the weather was appalling. Rain gusted down in sheets and the air became uncharacteristically cold at times. Nevertheless, I had rarely been so busy. Straight after Rob rang to cancel, my host mother Mrs Lopez-Vito gave me the generous gift of forty pesos, and almost before I could say "gracias" I was on my way to the Araneta's for my next stay.

Señora Araneta urged me to call her Hilda, even though she was my Spanish teacher as well as my foster mum. Vivacious, kind and motherly, Hilda rolled her *r*'s in the classic Spanish manner. Her two young daughters were four and five, and her husband, Po Araneta, was a broad-minded attorney. Despite the couple having jobs which in Australian society would mean they were affluent, Hilda and Po owned a modest house with two maids. Nevertheless, I was given a tiny bedroom all to myself, and the bathroom was neat and clean. It was strange to go from a vast eating table with at least twelve ravenous Lopez-Vitos, to a small square table with only Po, Hilda and her father (Poppa) as fellow diners. (The little girls were regularly fed beforehand.) The meals were simple but good, and quickly I felt at home.

The Aranetas had a driver whose main job was to deliver Hilda to and pick her up from Ateneo every day. Living nearby were three tricycle drivers whom the Aranetas employed in a little business to bring in more money for the family. One of these drove me and the two little girls around the suburb of Tetuan so that I could get my bearings. The small girls only spoke Chavacano or pure Spanish, so they were hard for me to understand, but there was no mistaking their excitement when I gave each of them a tiny brass kangaroo.

Hilda's father was an old Spaniard, a man of few words. Poppa had worked at many different jobs in his life. He would ride on horseback 27 km into the mountains to check on his mines and was a serious hunter and fisherman. When I breezily suggested that he take me on one of his hunting trips he quickly offered to take me on Monday by boat to the West Visayas called Panay, and there we could hunt for bats before returning the following Sunday! Casually he remarked that his prey was the Giant Golden-Crowned flying fox, the biggest bat in the world, which he wanted for its meat and its pelt.

I back-pedalled fast. Not only did I have no wish to get up close and personal to giant bats, but I was off on an important malaria survey just as soon as the weather cleared.

* * *

Although the weather remained abysmal, Rob received the second go-ahead, and on the evening of 24 September Claro, Rob and I met down at the wharf. Jun, who had accompanied his sister to wish us farewell, lingered on the wharf. In a howling wind we boarded the boat which was rocking savagely from side to side. Loading our baggage below, we joined the fifteen passengers squatting on the deck or roof, occasionally throwing up a comment to Jun on the wharf. After half an hour the captain appeared, informing everyone that he would not sail in these conditions and that he had just heard that the weather was even worse up at Siocon. Stunned at first, we eventually struggled back onto the wharf amongst the motley crowd with our goods and chattels. I turned to our big white chief Rob. "Now what do we do?" Claro spoke up. "We could go to the Plaza Theatre. There are two movies on in half an hour." We looked at each other. Why not?

We sat through *Bonnie and Clyde*, and *Giant*, two of the longest movies ever made. Well, to me they seemed interminable, although perhaps this was because my left ear was beginning to hurt, yet again. After the show Jun saw his sister back to Santa Maria while Rob escorted me back to Tetuan, by which time the pain in my ear was truly worrying. Rob didn't say anything, but both of us knew that fate had been kind. Had we sailed that night for Siocon, where there was no medical help, not only would I have been a hindrance to the survey, but my left ear would have suffered irreparable damage. We chatted on the front porch until after midnight, when a worried Rob left for his boarding house in Santa Maria while I staggered off to bed.

Not a wink of sleep did I enjoy all night. First thing in the morning I headed downtown to Dr Reyes's clinic. The doctor raised his eyebrows—here I was again! As he looked deeply into my ear he murmured his usual warnings about the perils of diving. This time he found an abscess cooking up close to the eardrum. After two injections and a swag of pills, he delivered the bombshell. "You must come back for the next three days to receive treatment." I stared at him in disbelief. *Is some dark force preventing me from going to Siocon?*

By nature I am a mild-mannered person, but by now, maddened with pain and frustration, my temper had reached boiling point. After I reached Tetuan by tricycle, the driver charged me way too much because I was a foreigner, knowing he could get away with it. Enraged, I handed over my precious centavos hoping that the driver sensed he was lucky not to get a biff on the nose.

Mrs Araneta gave me a tiny waterbag to place on my ear as I lay in bed, but the ear throbbed on and on. Anything was better than this, so I threw aside the bag and asked Hilda if I could commandeer the driver of their tricycle to take me to see Rob. I wanted to give him the bad news in person. Rob listened gravely, saying reluctantly, "I can't go any later than this Friday." That left me with two and a half days to get better. Fighting back the tears, exhausted from pain and lack of sleep, I vowed, "If the boat leaves on Friday, I'll be on it."

In the early afternoon at the Araneta's I wrote a letter to my family, describing the sorry saga. "I'm so tired that I can hardly hold the pen." To add to my misery, there had been no correspondence from Australia for over two weeks.

I woke at 5 P.M. after three hours' sleep. The pain had miraculously faded and so had my bad temper. Later that day I even turned up to a lecture at Ateneo. Afterwards, as I stood talking to friends, Rob, Jun, and the Alvarez brothers rumbled up in the old jeep. Expecting to find me on my bed of pain the dear things had gone to the Araneta's armed with comforting ice cream and the stories of Edgar Allen Poe. I presume that Rob meant to sit by my bed and read to me, with Jun and the brothers listening respectfully. We dropped the Alvarez brothers home and continued in drenching rain back to the Araneta's. When my lovely foster family invited Rob and Jun in for a feed, I almost felt as if I were in my real home back in Oz. Oh, except for the meal which included pancit noodles and sweet and sour fish, dishes never experienced in the Wicks household.

The little girls stood back with big brown eyes, watching every move made by the giant "Americano." After the main course I asked if anyone fancied some special rice pudding for dessert. Both adults and children looked puzzled. I asked the maid if she'd be kind enough to bring me a can of Evaporated milk and several bowls. Into each of these I put a big spoonful of cooked white rice which had not yet been cleared away from the table, and on top of this I poured some evaporated milk, stirred the mixture, then topped it with sugar. Rob played along and ate his with much relish, pretending he had never eaten such a wonderful delicacy. Everyone else eventually joined in, including Poppa and the children who eyed their "pudding" suspiciously at first, before gasping with genuine surprise and cleaning their plates!

Jun, Rob and I sat up talking until midnight. When the boys left I went to bed feeling mentally and physically good. The antibiotics were doing their job. I woke at 8 A.M. refreshed and ready for action, soon heading downtown to the doctor's surgery for a top-up of antibiotics. The day was Thursday, and things were looking promising. My ear seemed to be clearing up, and so too was the bad weather. Perhaps my Siocon adventure would happen after all.

Two weeks before meeting President Ferdinand Marcos
Location: Siocon

On Friday afternoon I finished classes at Ateneo and rushed home to gulp down some tea before Rob and Claro roared up in a Peace Corp jeep. I grabbed up my bag and farewelled the Araneta family. At the wharf the market was thronging with people, but when we looked towards the boat we were pleased to see it wasn't too crowded. Because there had been no vessels sailing for three weeks, we played safe by boarding the boat rather than dallying at the market. And just as well we did, because as we stepped onto the deck we were shepherded to the starboard side where we had to lower ourselves down onto a much smaller boat tied up alongside. To our dismay this smaller vessel was literally overflowing with people! We squeezed in amongst a mass of humanity on top of the cargo, which consisted of a mound of sacks stuffed hard with rice. We tried to make pleasant conversation, Rob with faltering Cebuano and me with my even more faltering Chavacano, but it seemed that our fellow passengers were in no mood for pleasantries. It began to get dark, and during the two hours of waiting Claro got off the boat and disappeared into the market, returning with a thermos of hot coffee.

To my astonishment, at 8 P.M. exactly we were chugging away from the wharf under a black sky and drizzling rain. *Punctuality? In the Philippines?* But the pleasant surprise was short-lived. Five minutes later we stopped at another smaller wharf where we sat for two hours. No extra cargo was taken aboard, and everyone was baffled. We also knew it was useless to query the delay, so there we were cramped up in the drizzling rain and darkness, with the boat pitching fretfully up and down. Every one of us was thinking the same thing. *What if the weather worsens and once again the trip is cancelled?*

At long last and to our huge relief the boat set off for the open sea, heading south towards the tip of the peninsula. The three of us had a blanket, and we tried to find a place to lie down, but the boat was rolling so badly we knew if we fell asleep, we would fall overboard. As the cumbersome craft rounded the tip of the peninsula and headed north up the west coast of Mindanao, the crests of the waves dumped on us, keeping us slightly cold, wet, and miserable. Most of the night I stared fascinated at each dark watery mountain rising from the sea, wondering how I should react if one of these crashed down upon us and turned the boat over. I was beginning to realize that no amount of swimming skills or youthful energy would be able to overcome hundreds of floundering bodies and debris set loose in the pitch black from a sinking boat amongst those fearsome waves.

Lights twinkled from the dark shoreline, and the boat headed for a wharf attached to a tiny hamlet which only existed to export the lumber from the old forests in the mountainous hinterland. To my amazement, our boat efficiently offloaded supplies and was heading back out to sea in minutes. Now the swell became more perilous than ever, the boat sliding down into the troughs and climbing with great effort up the side of each monstrous wave before surging down again.

As dawn slowly offered up the light, I spied a great swordfish leaping from the water in a silvery arc. Dolphins began to play alongside the bow as the boat cut through the water, reminding me of all those boat trips I had enjoyed out of Port Lincoln where even the grown-ups seemed excited whenever the dolphins decided to join us.

Abruptly we crossed from deep blue onto a pale green churned-up sea, and one mile later as the sun rose above the mountains, I made out the estuary of the great Siocon river. Many native vintas were negotiating the violent surf to fish, and I watched, fascinated, as each boatman played cat and mouse with the waves, trying to "outwit" them head-on, then choosing the exact moment to steer their craft through the foaming crests.

Our cumbersome cargo boat, having no chance of safely riding through that surf, dropped anchor with a rumble of chain when we were still way beyond the breakers. Then a small vinta headed for us, propelled by a quaint inboard motor fed by an upside-down bottle of petrol connected to the engine by a siphoning tube. As the vinta got closer we began to comprehend the extent of the challenge facing its skipper. In this steep swell, if he brought his little sailing boat too close to the cargo boat, he risked that hull crashing down and smashing his boat to matchsticks. Yet if he didn't get close enough, a passenger could miss the step down to the boat and slip in between the two hulls.

Only the Mighty Malaria Trio, it seemed, were disembarking at Siocon. I was ordered to go first. Steadying myself on the gunnel, trying to assess when the vinta rose to its greatest height on the crest of the swell, I jumped, and with the boatman's hand to steady me, I made it onto the sharp prow and almost fell into the hollow of the vinta where I crouched. It was Rob's turn. It must have been his large body that worked against his agility, because he misjudged, slipping quite badly from the vinta. If it hadn't been for the extraordinary speed shown by the Moro helmsman in grabbing and hauling him aboard, he could have died right there in front of us. All this time the huge hull of the cargo boat kept rearing up and over our heads. Then it was Claro's turn, but now she had the outstretched hands of Rob and me to steady her, and without drama she slipped into the last remaining hollow of the boat. Our bags were thrown down to us, and in seconds the boatman turned the vinta for the estuary, which was literally foaming at the mouth.

For the next half hour or so our lives were in that boatman's hands. The vinta needed to go fast and slow alternately as it rode straight on and then sideways to the waves. One mistake meant a headlong pitch into the surf.

We made it safely through the mouth. The chaos ceased, our boat skimming on a river towards Siocon's small settlement of huts strung out along the bank. Each hut was on stilts, half over the water and half over land, giving refuge to vintas on the river, and to workshops or storage facilities on the landward side. There were no cars.

The vinta pulled up as close as it could to the water's edge, and we paid that brave boatman what he asked for—one peso, and a few centavos extra. Grabbing our bags we stepped off into knee-deep mud and waded to solid ground, walking through a cluster of huts and out onto a muddy track. It wasn't long before a lone vehicle appeared. The hybrid monster was a vintage motorbike to which was attached a sidecar so capacious that it somehow managed to accommodate the three of us plus luggage.

We were driven along the muddy track, huts on our left along the riverbank interspersed with marshlands. We arrived at a ramshackle marketplace with few people buying—on offer was hanging dried fish, fruits, and imported basics like soap and flip-flops. In Chavacano Claro asked directions to the Lituban sawmill, and we were told to continue up the track heading towards the mountains. Under the blazing sun we rode in the side car, eventually stopping at a mini general store which was as far as the motorbike could go. We had been travelling sedately across the river plain, but from now on the terrain was steep and the track rutted with deep potholes. By now we were hot, tired, and had attracted the usual crowd of urchins who were fascinated by Rob and me, the "Canos" (Americanos). We bought a soft drink at the store, all the while hoping for a logging truck to come to our rescue. An hour passed before a truck appeared, and the driver welcomed us aboard.

All signs of habitation disappeared behind us as we clattered over the rough track higher and higher, on one side a sheer mountain wall covered with foliage, on the other a steep drop to the palms and rice paddies far below on the plains. Quite soon we were totally immersed in dense jungle as we rumbled along, and only once did we pull over as far as was possible to allow the passage of a barefooted man walking with a carabao hitched to a cart. We were in an area where the natives were called Subanan, a semi-Muslim group of small communities existing way below the poverty line.

Eventually we crested a hill. The valley of Lituban lay before us, filled with workmen's huts and the lumber mill. On the plains in the far distance the great Siocon river glinted like a satin ribbon in the sunlight, and then we were rumbling down towards the mill. The green mountains encircled us, and despite my fatigue I managed to appreciate the exquisite beauty of our surroundings. Slowly we climbed up the other side of the valley, over the crest and into the much smaller Lisukan valley where stood a hut on stilts inhabited by missionaries Bill and Leigh Hall. Their raised home served as insurance against a river which flowed 500 yards from their door at the bottom of a gentle slope.

Unlike the vinta boatman, the truck driver demanded a hefty sum for his trouble, which explained why he had been so willing to take us aboard. But by now we were too exhausted to argue. With our baggage we walked to the hut, thatched with nipa palm and primitively constructed of bamboo and lightweight wood. We climbed up the stairs to a porch where two Subanan natives squatted on their haunches, in discussion with Bill. It was hard not to recoil when I walked near one of them. An ulcer on his neck gaped open, about two inches in diameter. Leigh, a nurse, tended to the man's wound a few minutes after she had shown Claro and me to our sleeping quarters, a mezzanine floor overlooking the main open space of the hut. In a tiny room downstairs, under the main floor, Rob would somehow have to sleep amongst the Hall's three children, and I couldn't imagine for the life of me any remaining square inch where Leigh and Bill could have slept. There were no mattresses or pillows, and so for the first time I faced the hard reality of sleeping on a bamboo mat on a wooden floor.

The main area of the hut served as a kitchen and eating space, but against one of the walls a sick Subanan woman lay on matting. Leigh, who tended to the woman the entire time of our stay, was inspirational. She had no refrigerator, no electricity, and she cooked for the family and native patients on a small gas burner with two flames. With a baby and two small children to care for, she also tended numerous natives with serious medical complaints who fronted up every day. Throughout all this Bill and Leigh worked to translate the Bible into a meaningful version for the educated Subanan to read, and the illiterate majority to hear. The American couple had been in this place for five years, learning the language and earning the trust of the natives. Many children in the district would wander over on Sundays and sit in the porch to hear Bible stories—a makeshift sort of Sunday School in the jungle.

The Halls did all of this on a shoestring. I guessed that occasionally grateful Subanan natives brought some fruit they had grown or fish they had caught, as payment in kind.

Arriving just before midday, all three of us collapsed on our bamboo mats and slept like the dead for an hour. My only concession to comfort was a jacket I rolled up to serve as a pillow. At 1 P.M. I helped Leigh prepare a simple lunch of rice, fish, and a few beans. We sat in a circle on the floor, helping ourselves to food placed in dishes on a bamboo mat in the middle. Much as I enjoyed the meal, I could easily have consumed twice as much. Even the dish of rice was small, and every time I leaned forward to take a spoonful of food I was sharply aware that these three dishes needed to be shared amongst the five of us. I noticed that the six-foot-six Rob was careful to take portions even smaller than mine, so I steeled myself to take less than he did over the coming days.

We cleaned our teeth with water lugged from the river, which from now on would serve as our bathroom. Then it was time to work. Having hurt his leg when he slipped from the cargo boat in the botched transfer to the vinta, Rob accepted Bill's offer of a ride as a pillion passenger on his scooter while Claro and I took a short cut, trekking along a narrow track through the jungle. Claro wore flip-flops, but because I had developed a bad blister between two toes, I opted to go barefoot. My feet, though tough, were not tough enough as time would prove.

Over the mountain from Lisukan we climbed, then headed down to the cluster of huts that was Lituban. The four of us reached the mill and found the manager's hut, but then our luck ran out. The foreman told us that only the manager could make such a decision concerning the survey, and he was in Zamboanga. However, he'd be back by Monday morning, so maybe we could start then? As usual Rob kept calm, agreeing to return on Monday.

The two men jumped on the motorbike again, while Claro and I backtracked through the jungle, arriving at the Hall's hut hot and sweaty and needing a wash. Leigh, her baby on her hip with the two small kids in tow, led us upstream for a kilometre through a fairyland of jungle palms to a small clearing where the river offered up deep ponds and bouncy waterfalls. The environment was picture-perfect, and we had it all to ourselves. This natural bathroom allowed us to frolic and wash in cool, crystal-clear water. Leigh headed back with the baby, while four-year-old Todd and two-year-old Tammy were left in our care. These were two of the gutsiest, unspoiled and delightful kids I had ever encountered. Todd swam like a fish and slipped easily over rocks and mini rapids, while Tammy dog paddled and giggled and had a whale of a time.

Refreshed, we backtracked to the hut, where Bill told us that if we could be at Siocon by nine the following morning (Sunday), a Muslim friend of his would take us in his vinta further up the west coast to the remains of a small Spanish settlement called Santa Maria, not to be confused with the suburb in Zamboanga. No dinner materialized that night, so I assumed the Halls ate only two meals a day.

Darkness came early. Because there was no power and candles were a luxury, we headed for our bed mats. Sleep came quickly despite the hard floor and my hunger. The three of us roused ourselves at 5 A.M., ate a quick breakfast of rice, fish and buns Bill had bought from Siocon, and then headed off at a great rate for the sawmill, Rob once more on the back of Bill's scooter and Claro and I jogging at a half-run. There being no logging truck scheduled to go down the mountain, we had no choice but to keep going, all the way down that steep rutted logging track to that tiny store on the plains. With luck we would coincide with one of the cumbersome sidecars so that Claro and I could be transported from the store to the river mouth.

We got lucky, and just after 9 A.M. a motorbike delivered us to the river's edge at Siocon. Relieved to see the vinta still waiting, we trudged out through the reeds and clambered aboard. The boatman set sail, tacking out through the surf before heading north in very rough seas. In less than an hour we spied a serene inlet with three huts making up the hamlet of Santa Maria. This time we stepped off onto floating logs, balancing our way to the marshes where we sank into black mud. I looked up to see several Muslim men, agog as they stared at Rob, Bill, Claro, and me. I wondered how many white Anglos they had seen. It seemed this was a rare sight for most of them—even rarer to see a white female, especially one barefooted and up to her knees in mud! I yearned to meet the women who were forbidden to leave their huts and were certain to be spying on us through the gaps in the walls. The chief, a handsome specimen of manhood with a glorious physique, a chain around his neck and batik wrapping his waist in a long skirt, began conversing with the Muslim boatman. In their language they were advised we wanted to see the old Spanish fort.

About three minutes later the entire male population of Santa Maria plus our skipper were toiling alongside us up the hill to the promontory where lay the remains of the fort. The air was hot and muggy, the soil dry and crumbly underfoot, and the hill was massive. It took us two hours to reach the top, and all of us (except for the locals) were puffing and exhausted. Rob's stoicism was impressive. If his knee was hurting he didn't mention it.

We reached the crest and looked around. Inland the mountains reared over us, the ocean stretched far below us, and the surrounding ground was covered in knee-high grass. *But where are the remnants of the great stone walls?* The chief beckoned us to where he was standing next to an ancient tree gnarled by the ocean winds, so we wandered through the grass until we could see that the trunk of the tree was walled up with stone. Another man indicated that I should look down into the stunted trunk, and to my astonishment I discovered that the outer part of the tree enclosed a chasm that disappeared far below with no bottom in sight. Then in amongst the grass, in a straight line from the tree, I began to walk on what proved to be the top of a wall, rather than foundation stone. Either the fort had been filled in purposely, or nature had overwhelmed it over the centuries. Rob pounced upon a small shard of glazed pottery, and we tried to imagine how the would-be "conquistadors" would have lived at Fort Santa Maria.

I really did feel as if history had come back to life. In the otherwise boring *History of the Philippines* I had found one interesting section on the Moro wars that covered the sixteenth and seventeenth century battles between the Moros and the Spanish colonizers. In a series of raids and in several notable full-on battles, the Spanish had fought mainly with gun and cannon while the Moros faced them wielding the wicked jagged-bladed kris. Their bravery was legendary, and it was even said that their women fought in the second rank, often with babies on their backs. The book claims that if the Moro warriors sensed they had lost the battle they would turn and quickly dispatch their women and children before killing themselves.

I looked at the Moro men around me, wondering if their ancestors had once fought the Spanish. But all historic musings vanished as I became uncomfortably aware that I was parched. I asked Bill if we could get a drink of water, but he explained that water here could be polluted, and that we'd need to wait until we got back to Siocon.

The return trip was rougher than ever, the outriggers leaping clear out of the water and thumping back to the surface with such force that each jolt threatened to catapult us from the boat. We were sopping wet from the waves breaking over us, but we were so hot and thirsty it felt better to be wet.

In Siocon we visited a tiny wooden store under one of the huts and bought some soft drinks which we rapidly sculled. And lo and behold, up drove a logging truck. Once again Bill rode his scooter with Rob seated behind, and Claro and I were relieved to be able to ride with the driver in the cabin of the truck as far as the mill. From there we girls had to use our legs to transport us over the crest to the Halls' hut nestled in the Lisukan valley, and almost immediately we headed for our river bathroom to relax and wash away the sweat and mud. Anticipating our hunger Leigh had prepared a meal of dried fish, rice, and beans, and it presented a huge mental challenge for me to reach out but take only a small piece of fish, a spoonful of rice, and four beans. The usual role model, Rob took no more food than I did, but he must have been ravenous. Claro, of course, behaved impeccably as she always did, never complaining even when just the two of us lay side by side on our mats, whispering about the day's events. Once more we were fast asleep by nightfall, grateful just to have somewhere to lie down.

The next day was arguably the most physically taxing of my life. We awoke at 5 A.M. to pouring rain, gobbled down a bun for breakfast, and headed off in the usual way to the Lituban sawmill, Bill donkeying Rob on scooter while Claro and I walked fast to reach our destination by 6 A.M. Bill had found us a wonderful helper who could speak Subanan and Cebuano with ease, and he was waiting at the sawmill for us. Around the vast valley there were about forty nipa huts and precisely 181 people. Our translator set to work making each adult understand why it would be in their long-term interest to give their blood.

Stepping ankle-deep in mud and drenched with relentless rain we trudged from hut to hut, carrying our equipment with great care and climbing up each wooden staircase to the shelter of the porch above. Claro liaised with the translator to find out the names of each occupant, while Rob and I set up equipment as fast as possible, me cleaning each slide, handing him the "pricker" and cotton wool and antiseptic. As soon as he had pricked the finger, I would take the slide with its bloody smear, wait for it to dry enough so that I could scratch in the date and number, and wrap it in order. The mental strain was huge. Rob had warned that if we made one mistake with the names and numbers, the whole survey would be useless. He had his fair share of strain too. The children tended to scream when the needle pricked their tiny fingers, and he needed to calm them in Cebuano.

There was so much moisture in the air that each smear took several minutes to dry and therefore could not be recorded and wrapped instantly. This meant that in the pouring rain I often had to balance the storing boxes from hut to hut, my brain scrambling to remember the correct order of naming and numbering.

At midday, still in drenching rain, we made our way back to the Hall's for a quick (and meagre!) lunch, returning to Lituban and continuing where we left off. Halfway through the afternoon we began to run out of slides, so because I was the quickest, even with bare feet, I was given the task of jog-trotting all the way back to Lisukan. I grabbed up a box of slides, hugely grateful when Bill offered me a "donkey" back to the sawmill on his scooter.

Night fell, and still we worked on. Everything became a blur of darkness, mud, and water as we trudged from porch to porch, with only candlelight to work by. At 9 P.M. we finished, and in pitch black we hiked over into the Lisukan valley. Somehow we found the strength to wash most of the mud from our bodies using a basin of water, and although Leigh supplied us with another tiny meal of fish and rice, I was almost too tired to eat. The Mighty Malaria Trio fell onto our sleeping mats and slept like the dead until 7 A.M.

After breakfast the faithful Bill hopped on his scooter and drove all the way down to Siocon with the express task of learning the exact time we needed to board the cargo ferry. We used the morning to frolic in our natural bathroom upriver, splashing around with the kids, washing our tiredness and aches away.

At lunchtime Bill roared back at top speed with the news that we needed to be at the river mouth at Siocon by 2 P.M.! With no time to eat, we threw our possessions into our bags, gave our hosts a set of new towels as a thank you, and headed for the sawmill at a run alongside Bill, who was carrying most of our luggage on his scooter.

No logging truck came to the rescue, and the blister between my toes and my ravaged feet meant that by now I was in trouble. Time was running out, so I needed to limp fast, and halfway down the mountain Bill sped up, abandoning us to try to find some sort of transport willing to come out and get us. By three-quarters of the way to Siocon, as we descended to the plains, Bill returned with the news that no tricycle driver would agree to coming this far out in the mud. Rob ordered me to take his place on the scooter, assuring me that his knee was much better (liar, liar!). For the greater good of all of us arriving in time to catch the boat, I accepted the ride on Bill's scooter, my entire body overwhelmed with luggage. Luckily, as the first of the stilted huts on the riverside came into view, a tricycle approached. Gratefully Rob, Claro and I climbed into the enormous cavity of the sidecar together with our luggage, and with Bill driving freely behind we made it to the river mouth. But it was 2.30 P.M., and no boat was visible out in the ocean. It had sailed. We stood there, pictures of misery. Then Bill got talking in Subanan to a man who informed us that yes, the boat had sailed from Siocon, but had headed further north to collect a load of lumber and would return around 5 P.M.!

We looked at each other, laughing hysterically. It was such a Filipino thing, so why had we never got used to it? With hugs and handshakes we thanked Bill, watching him putter away towards the mountains. We asked the general store lady if we could wait inside out of the sun, and she nodded. Claro followed her to the rear of the room and they chatted while Rob and I read macabre Edgar Allen Poe stories to an attentive audience of at least forty Muslim children standing wide-eyed from every corner. They filled the doorway, and did not understand a word. They studied every move we made, and when Rob or I laughed at something in the story, they would laugh too. The store owner approached and offered us a meal. There are no prizes for guessing whether we accepted her super kind gesture.

As Rob and I rose from our seats the kids screamed in mock-fear and scattered in all directions, which amused us immensely. We joined Claro and the store owner for a poor man's meal of noodles and sweet and sour fish, but there was plenty of it and my tummy felt satisfied for the first time in many days.

Darkness fell, and there were more surprises to come. The captain of the boat strode in unannounced, telling us that a vinta was waiting in the shallows to ferry us out to the bigger vessel. We were flummoxed. *How did he know that we, the passengers, were waiting in this little store?*

Clouds curtained the moon so that we could see only the white luminescence of surf as we sailed in a vinta out through the breakers, heading for the ship. This time it was me who misjudged the jump from vinta to boat, and once again it was the quick action of the boatman who saved me. This cargo boat was only thirty feet long, and to our concern the decks were packed with people. For the hour it took to reach the logging town of Sarawai, we could not find a place to lie, until Rob suggested we should climb atop the piled-up cargo. No sooner had we lain down than a heavily loaded punt, battling the heaving swell, pulled up alongside and we were asked to move from the cargo. First the punt offloaded several more Moro passengers, then great sacks of copra, and lastly many crates of empty bottles onto the decks. It was now 11 P.M., and only standing room remained. Being wedged in between all those bodies at least stopped me from being pitched overboard.

It was dawn when we docked, not at a Zambo wharf, but at the suburb of Baliwasan. I couldn't help but question this, and this time to my surprise I received a credible answer. This ship was smuggling cigarettes, and because it was now daylight the customs officers would be well and truly awake and patrolling the city wharves. In a throng of passengers we clambered off the boat. Eventually Rob and Claro found a tricycle heading for their suburb of Santa Maria, while I managed to hail another to take me to Tetuan.

Tired through to my bones, I staggered into the Araneta home with my bags and slumped into a chair. After the maids fed me a veritable feast of a breakfast, I fell into my beautiful, comfortable bed with my supersoft pillow and slept soundly until early afternoon.

One week before meeting President Ferdinand Marcos

After lessons at Ateneo I was swept up by two hefty boy journalists from the *Beacon* and driven downtown to experience a "rally for Sabah" (British North Borneo) by hundreds of students. Even the city's high school students had been required to attend. The two lads escorted me through the crowds and up onto a balcony overlooking Madrid Street and the plaza. From there we could overlook the vast throngs parading along the streets leading into the square where leaders were waiting with loud-speakers and microphones. The Philippine government had again raised the contentious issue of its sovereignty over Sabah, this quickly inflaming the ongoing dispute with Malaysia about who owned this province, which was located just a few hours south of Zamboanga in a fast boat. Sabah had been controlled by the Tunku Abdul Rahman ever since 1963, but now President Marcos had decided to dispute the claim.

Only a year earlier, at the ASEAN summit, Marcos announced that the Philippines would make no further claim to Sabah, but few, including me, knew this. Also, it seems a fair assumption that few if any in the rally were aware of the Jabidah massacre which had occurred in March 1968, only days after I began living in Zamboanga. Marcos had ordered a crack commando unit to secretly infiltrate Sabah and create havoc in the region so that he could justify taking control and ownership. But his plot went awry when several Muslim troops refused to participate, so in a desperate attempt to avoid the story leaking to the public, at least twenty were shot.

One victim escaped to tell the tale, but it would be years after Marcos had won his second term in office and imposed martial law before the horrendous story came to light.

A few days before the rally, Malaysian students had reacted to the Philippines' claim by burning the Filipino flag and sacking the Philippine embassy in Kuala Lumpur. The Malays had lit the fire, and now the Filipinos were determined to stoke it. An effigy of the Tunku swayed high above the crowd, and the slogans on the placards varied wildly from "Open Season for Malaysian heads!" to "Down with riots, Up with reason!" The latter one was raised above the Atenean College contingent, which was good to see, but at that point some Ateneans came onto the verandah holding up a placard upon which was written "Britons and Aussies, lay off!" When they asked me to carry it amongst the crowd I was horrified, slow to twig they were joking. However, I learned that Britain, America, and Australia had not backed Marcos on this issue, and that Aussie gunboats had been patrolling the area. Whether or not Australia and Americans had sent gunboats to Sabah deliberately to send a clear message to the Philippines, or to simply service the war with North Vietnam, I had no way of knowing. However, the more I saw and heard at the rally the more uneasy I became. So far I had always been treated as an individual, but suddenly I felt vulnerable, even threatened. I was Australian, and therefore the enemy. Fortunately my two strong Filipino minders were there to protect me should that feeling translate into any physical attack.

As I listened to the speeches, I concluded that most of the mob had absolutely no idea of the dispute between their country and Malaysia, one of their closest neighbours. Placards varied between "Whose is Sabah? Let the world court decide!" to "Down with British Imperialism!" and speakers were shrieking into a microphone "To hell with the Malaysians!" The crowd was quickly morphing into a rabble that wanted blood. They began singing patriotic songs, and behind me a fight broke out that was quickly quelled by the police. Just when I was tempted to sneak away with my escorts, some Ateneo leaders stepped up to the mic and began to reason in a way that made me proud of my colleagues. Refusing to rouse the mob as the others had done, they urged everyone to look at the facts and to behave more maturely than the Malaysian students had done. "We must not condemn America for refusing to back us. This is our affair and ours alone!" they called. A local councillor rose to his feet and requested the crowd refrain from burning the Tunku's effigy, but people knew the Malaysian PM had already been symbolically hanged and the damage was done. Gradually the ambience became less frightening, but the whole experience rocked me. Never had I witnessed a mob that collectively forgot that I was an individual, wishing me harm because of the country I represented.

The two escorts flanked me as we returned to Ateneo via the concrete path towards the *Beacon* office. Then something occurred which had a profound and lasting effect on me. A stranger approached, his eyes sparking fire, and shouted "What about the White Australia Policy?" I was stunned, not so much from this unexpected aggression, but the fact that I had never questioned the White Australia Policy and certainly didn't consider it controversial. My escorts immediately moved to protect me, and I could see how embarrassed they were at their countryman's blatant rudeness. However, I needed to talk further to this wild-eyed boy. "What exactly are you meaning to say?"

"Why won't Australia allow Filipinos into your country? Why do we have to be white?"

I flushed hot with embarrassment. Put like that, the policy sounded abhorrent, like Australia was maintaining some sort of white supremacy. My brain spun, and the answer I gave may have sounded lame but at least it seemed to mollify the stranger, and there is a grain of truth in what I replied. "I think it's to do with wanting similar cultures in our country," I explained.

"What's so different about our culture from yours?" he demanded.

At this point I floundered. "Well, we eat bread, you eat rice, you chaperone your girls, we don't, that sort of thing I guess."

The boy was still breathing heavily, but because I had answered to the best of my ability the fire in him waned, and he seemed deflated. I managed to stammer, "I'm sorry, it's my government, not me. I have so many close Filipino friends."

He sidled away, clearly unsatisfied. The boys and I continued on, with them apologizing and me feeling uncomfortably small. That night I berated myself for not giving much better examples of cultural differences, such as the Philippines being influenced both politically and in behaviour by Spain and more recently by America, while Oz had strong ties to everything British and to a lesser extent, Western Europe. But no matter what I might have said, nothing justified calling the policy by a skin colour. Nothing.

Back in the office, editor Vic Solis and I discussed the Sabah rally. What if the Tunku kept refusing to take this matter to the World Court? Would Filipinos be content to lose face by standing back forever and saying "Peace, not war?" We pondered who would attack first, and when war between the two nations might break out. We discussed the angle I might take for my article on the Sabah question, which would be given top billing in the next print of the *Beacon*. "Wouldn't it be fantastic to discuss Sabah with the president himself?" I mused, smiling at the absurdity of such a dream.

Five days before meeting President Ferdinand Marcos

On Saturday 5 October I joined the Ateneo softball team in a collegiate match. When I arrived, I was astonished to see such a big student audience. At Woodlands I had only ever reached the dizzying heights of B-grade softball, yet the expectation of this crowd became clear—Australia was a great sporting nation, and that meant the Aussie girl was sure to be a star player.

Normally I performed hopelessly under pressure, but perhaps because I was amongst friends I tried to encourage a mind-set of simply having fun. Under that hot tropical sun I could feel myself frying. A member of our team was missing and so I was forced to fill in the gaps for right and left outfield which meant covering a big swathe of the field. The adrenalin was running high. While I managed to catch all the balls batted far to the left and right, at one stage I panicked and threw the ball to the wrong base. Then it was our turn to bat, and amazingly I managed to hit every ball and get a run.

Our win seemed to be celebrated by the Gods as thunder rumbled, lightning flashed and rain dropped in torrents. Jun, Rob, Butch Alvarez, and a man who had played the part of Ray Santander in Jun's radio series, rocked up in the battered Alvarez jeep, abducting me for one glorious hour to Caragasan where I floated happily in a green ocean pricked by warm rain.

Exhausted, I arrived back at the Araneta household to find the little girls clamoring to go swimming at Pasonanca. My one-piece white bathers having finally disintegrated, I donned a sleeveless cotton shirt covering my bras and tied in a knot at the waist, before the tricycle driver drove us to the pool where the little girls screamed and squealed and had a wonderful splashy time.

Wielding the baseball bat at Ateneo.

That evening when I returned to my room I stared at the dressing table. Something was missing. My gold pendant on a chain. Of all my possessions in the world, this rated high, not just because my grandmother had given it to me, but because it was unique. The pendant was a tiny "casket," topped with an enameled picture of a robed man on a camel with a pyramid in the background, and the whole unclipped to reveal a golden naked baby asleep on green felt. I had never worked out whether the baby was meant to be Jesus or Moses, but the piece was rare and exquisite.

I searched every inch of that room, but my necklet was gone. This was a horrible situation. I guessed it was one of the maids, but how could I risk ruining the serenity of the Araneta household? Then again, I had to say something, so I told Hilda. A broader search ensued but to no avail. I needed to let the matter drop. I was comforted by the memory of me as a small child running up and down the passageway with the family dog in the home of my grandparents. The husky was bounding back and forth with me, and at some point a precious ornament flew from a shelf to the floor where it smashed into pieces. I looked up, saw the stricken face of my grandmother and burst into desperate tears. Instantly "Gay" rushed to my side, sat on the carpet, and hugged me close. "Stephie," she said sternly, "you are not to cry, not one tear, do you hear me? That is just a thing, a thing!" And after that, whenever I lost or broke something, that wise counseling always sustained me. It was just a thing.

The next day Hilda fronted up with a gorgeous piece of Batik cloth, and it was mutually understood that this sweet gesture was her effort to compensate me.

Two days before meeting President Ferdinand Marcos

By Tuesday 8 October my article on Sabah was almost ready to go to print, but I felt I should read more articles in other Philippine papers before I committed. I was just about to leave the *Beacon* office when editor Vic Solis burst in with news that the president had decided to visit Zamboanga in two days' time to win over the Muslim vote—the first president ever to do so! Vic looked me in the eye, telling me that because I was a foreigner I would have more chance of an interview with President Marcos than any of the Filipino journalists. "So, just how is that supposed to happen?" I laughed.

Vic frowned. "Maybe you could ask around... Rotary or something?" It was clear Vic had no more idea than I did, so I scooped up the newspapers and returned to the Araneta household for dinner.

It was like an answer to a prayer. After having dinner with Hilda, Poppa and Po, I retired to the lounge area to peruse the articles on Sabah written by more seasoned journalists. Barely had I unfolded the first one when a man entered the room and introduced himself as During Araneta, Po's brother. He had flown down from Manila that afternoon because, as a politician, he obviously felt he could make political mileage by being present at the biggest show on earth about to unfold. Asking about my journalism, During seemed impressed by my views and enthusiasm. He left to go to his room, but when he was halfway up the stairs he stopped and turned, asking casually, "How would you like to meet the president?" My mouth fell open. I stammered that this would be an incredible opportunity for me as a student journalist as well as an Australian.

During said that while he would do his best, there were no guarantees. As I'd heard that a face-to-face meeting with the president of the Philippines was about as easy to get as a tete-a-tete with the Queen, I got the message loud and clear—*don't get your hopes up.*

One day before meeting President Ferdinand Marcos

All throughout Wednesday I attended lessons at Ateneo and made some adjustments to the Sabah article, but mostly I was wondering how I would behave if I were lucky enough to get three minutes with El Presidente. Vic Solis turned up at the office, and while he was encouraged to hear that an MP was trying to arrange an interview, he voiced his cynicism. "You'll never get to actually talk to him," he said. "Not in a million years."

"Don't worry, I'll get you direct quotes from the president!" I said, immediately wishing I hadn't, especially when Vic roared with laughter. That was the kind of joke he understood!

From Ateneo I walked across the road for a manicure and hair-set, gratis thanks to Mrs Ebby's children still turning up for swimming lessons. Back at the Araneta house Po had a message for me. "Be on the rooftop of the Zambo Hotel for breakfast at 8 A.M.," he said.

"Will the president be there?" I asked. But Po shrugged. He had simply relayed a message from his politician brother During.

My brain churned all night. If a miracle occurred and I found myself face-to-face with Ferdinand Marcos, what would I ask and in what order? The first question should not be too confrontational, surely, perhaps something about infrastructure? *Oh, and how does one address the President of the Philippines?*

* * *

By 8 A.M. on Thursday 10 October, in my white cotton dress, I was standing alongside During Araneta on the rooftop of the Zambo Hotel amongst a crowd of congressmen and provincial governors. All the men wore crisp barong Tagalog shirts and tailored trousers, and roughly half wore small brimless hats (kufis) indicating they were Muslim. Round tables were set up amongst the bright bougainvillea and fragrant frangipani, and one long VIP table bristled with microphones.

Naturally I imagined myself sitting alongside During at one of the smaller tables, but for some inexplicable reason I was ushered up to the long table and seated next to the chairman. From my handbag I whipped out my notebook and tried to look businesslike, as if I did this sort of thing every day, and the discussion got underway. *But—where is the president?* Between bites of toast and sips of coffee I scribbled away in my notebook. It became clear that most of the governors were from the southern provinces of the Philippines and had come to air their grievances. Some spoke heatedly, often about problems pertaining to their districts. Most complained that Mindanao had always got a worse deal than the Visayas and Luzon, so they were demanding a change in attitude from the main power base in Manila. They were also desperate for the Maharlika Highway to reach Mindanao, the project involving a 3,517 km network of roads, bridges and ferries linking the three main islands. Under Marcos's watch, and with many millions of American dollars given to the Philippines in gratitude for its support in the Vietnam war, building of the highway had already begun in Luzon but had not yet crept further south.

With the Jabidah massacre remaining under the public radar at this time, the Muslim leaders chose to express little more than frustration with their national government.

At about 10 A.M. the meeting finished. In a rush downstairs I saw VIP cars lined up and ready to go, and I found myself jammed into a car with several congressmen proceeding to the Zamboanga airport. I was escorted to the VIP dais through thousands of standing adults and uniformed students crammed onto every square inch of the airport grounds. Some waved placards offering support for their president's "peaceful" claim to Sabah. The complexity of the organization behind this rally had included rescheduling all flights, and a student leader from Manila had spent the last week in Zamboanga visiting every college and school to arrange the pro-Marcos placards.

On the dais sat about thirty people, including and to my delight, a foreign correspondent from Melbourne who worked freelance for *The Advertiser*, South Australia's main newspaper. I was hungry to talk to a fellow Australian, and he was keen to know my observations about Zamboanga as well as the Sabah issue.

It seemed an age before the president arrived. He inspected the troops before at last appearing at the back of the dais, striding down the centre aisle, everyone on their feet clapping. He passed close by without even glancing in my direction, and from then on I only saw the back of his head as he was seated in the front row. A bulky Muslim congressman rose to speak about how fervently he and his people supported the president's policies. A provincial governor rose and made a less fiery speech, but the general gist was his people's unreserved support for Marcos.

Then the great man himself stepped up to the microphone, and in seconds I was witnessing the performance of a master orator. He began by enthusing about his grand plans for "rice, roads, and school buildings," and of course made promises about completing the Maharlika Highway. I tried to distance myself from the masses who went mad with adoration as he used both humour and emotional hooks to win their hearts. Then came the build-up towards the climax, so brilliant that the gist of it etched deep into my memory.

He described his role as an officer in World War II as he fought to hold back the Japanese on the Bataan Peninsula. "We had been fighting for many days, when suddenly I felt a searing pain—I had been shot in the back." A low moan of sympathy spread across the grounds, and he paused for the horror to sink in, the vast mob now holding its collective breath. "I fell to the ground, thinking I had been mortally wounded!" His voice rose. "And then—another burst of gunfire and one of our brave soldiers fell beside me!" The silence was intense, as if everyone sensed the magnificent punchline to come. Marcos slowly ramped up the passion. "I saw my blood flowing out like a stream on that jungle floor, and our two streams of blood merged together to make one river!" A buzz of excitement thrilled the crowd. "And do you know something?" thundered Marcos. "The blood from my *Muslim brother* was as red as mine!"

The crowd erupted, and even I, who had vowed to keep objective, found myself enthusiastically clapping and nodding to individuals around me. The entire speech was nothing short of genius. He had flattered the Muslim population of his country, at the same time elevating himself to hero status and thus securing the votes of both Muslim and Christian for himself in the forthcoming election.

With that masterstroke Marcos had gone a long way towards uniting his people. This is both tragic and infuriating given that only a few years later he would deliberately capitalize on the age-old antagonism between Muslim and Christian in his secret ploy to destabilize the country—to justify the imposition of martial law. And the thousands of Filipinos and we few foreigners at the airport on 10 October 1968 were unaware of the Jabidah plot, the consequent massacre, and the two faces of their president.

While the crowd still madly cheered, Marcos returned down the aisle without looking to the right or left. It seemed probable that the great man had not noticed me. Several journalists were in a rush to get to a briefing session. Deducing that Himself would be there I jumped in one of the cars and within five minutes found myself in a shed at the air force base surrounded by foreign correspondents. Disappointingly, only the president's secretary and press agents turned up to give well-rehearsed speeches that droned on about the increase of smuggling in the south, the rise in banditry, and the (unsubstantiated) suspicion of "Malaysian spies." I had no option but to sit and look interested, all the while churning with frustration.

The foreign correspondents threw out the casual invitation that I join them for lunch, and because the president's secretary was joining us my hopes rose again for a meeting with the man who had thrilled me with his oratory just hours before. Lunch on the Zamboanga Hotel rooftop was much less formal than breakfast, and this time, as the only "native" of Zamboanga present, I was given the honour of ordering the meal.

Lunch finished and still no president. It looked as though Vic Solis's prediction would come true. "Not in a million years" kept ringing in my ears.

After the banquet I wondered where I might go to maximize my chances of interviewing the man at the top. Marcos was scheduled to play a round of golf that afternoon, but while I would certainly get to see him at the golf club, during the game he would hardly be keen to engage in an interview. Also, the idea of trudging around in the hot sun and clapping politely whenever Marcos hit the ball, did not appeal. However, I had heard that there would be a press conference at 7 P.M. that night on the "royal yacht," which had been the president's mode of transport from Manila to Zamboanga. I made the decision to go home, take a siesta, and be at the docks by 7 P.M., fresh and fired up.

My first meeting with President Ferdinand Marcos

When I awoke at 4 P.M. and came down to the lounge room, During Araneta was sitting with Po and Hilda in the lounge. I told them that I still hadn't managed to have a word with the president, and that I was off to the main wharf for the press conference in a couple of hours. During informed me he was flying back to Manila at 5.30, but that I might have more luck at the mayor's house, where the president was due to arrive for dinner. My brain was racing. If I attended the press conference, I could definitely ask a question along with the other correspondents. But one only, and that would be that. If I attended the dinner, however, it might just be possible for me to have three minutes with him before he sat down. "I can arrange for your invitation," added During.

I made my decision. It would be the mayor's house—my last chance.

Turning my attention to looking my best, I chose my pink dress with the draped low back (the one I had mended after being assaulted nearly two months ago) and Hilda loaned me her pearl bracelet, necklace and brooch. I felt like a million dollars.

Mayor Enriquez's house was vast and open, with party lights twinkling all over the garden and a long table set inside lavishly for everyone to see. At least sixty people were milling around, most of whom I didn't know and were older than me. There was nowhere to sit, except at the table which was forbidden until the arrival of the president. I felt out of place—lost.

By 8.30 P.M. I was worried, especially when by 9 P.M. rumors circulated that "he" wasn't coming. Someone added that the mayor was from the opposition party, and that's when I lost hope completely. Many people seemed to be leaving. With the image of Vic Solis laughing at me, I was on the brink of slipping out into the darkness to catch transport back to the Aranetas' when a dignified lady stepped towards me. She introduced herself as the only female governor in the Philippines. As we chatted, I lamented the fact that it seemed the president had decided not to come. After all, it was now 9.30 P.M. In a low voice she confided that, knowing the president as she did, he would wait until a few people had given up and gone home before he made his appearance.

With that tiny flicker of hope, I continued to wait. And wait.

Abruptly the silence of the night was shattered. Throbbing motorbikes were revving out in the street, and in seconds the entire property was thronging with excited guests. "It's his entourage!" exclaimed someone. "They say he has a bigger cavalcade than the president of the United States!" I edged from the garden into the living room so that the long table was in sight, but the crowd swelled until I was pushed back against a wall and could see nothing except the backs of the guests.

The engines cut, leaving the chitter chatter of the crowd who were beside themselves with anticipation. For at least five minutes I had no idea whether Marcos was even in the room. But then—something occurred which made me feel for the rest of the night as though I were in some fantastic fairytale.

"The Australiana! The Australiana!" came the shout, and the crowd before me parted like the Red Sea. There he was, standing just in front of his minders, about ten paces across the room. All the words I had rehearsed vanished from my mind. Acting as naturally as possible I walked across the room, smiled, and offered my hand which he shook warmly. "Good evening Mr President," I said, and a few pleasantries followed before I picked up courage to ask the questions that Vic and I had cooked up. "Mr President, as a journalist for my college of Ateneo, could I ask you a few questions about—?"

"Later my dear," said the president, "would you like to sit next to me at dinner?"

"That would be—wonderful," I replied, and he shepherded me to the long table. I was vaguely conscious of Mayor Enriquez and his wife bustling around, and most of the crowd standing back gawking. Within seconds a minder had pulled out a chair for me, then to my astonishment

I was seated to the left of Marcos, with Mayor Enriquez to his right. *But where is Mrs Enriquez?* There she was, sitting on my left, while I was uncomfortably aware she should have been seated where I was.

All eyes were upon me. Then—something else awkward—Marcos turned his back on the mayor and began an animated conversation with me throughout the entire dinner. There were at least ten other people seated at the table, and if they talked at all it was muted, while the bulk of the crowd stood by respectfully, no doubt straining to hear every word between me and the president. There's the saying that you could cut the air with a knife, but I knew I needed to forget that for now and focus on what Mr Marcos was saying.

For more than an hour he talked to no one else but me, and the only small interruptions were the clicking of cameras or a meal set down in front of us. In the first part of the conversation the president and I discussed what we had in common. Both of us liked uncomplicated food and relished good ice cream, and he mentioned his stables of Arab horses.

The President turns his back on Mayor Enriquez, and talks to me.

I described my mother's Arab mare Silver Dash, the grey beauty that had carried Mum safely over countless jumps and cantered so slowly for me during Musical Chairs at shows. We shared a love of poetry, and he was delighted to hear I genuinely admired a poem he had written for his wife Imelda. And it was then he invited me to "look us up at the palace" when I next visited Manila. I grinned, asking him how one is supposed to "look up" the president of the Philippines.

He chuckled, and we chatted on, about how we both liked water skiing and swimming. "I hear that you have been teaching Filipino children how to swim," he said. "Perhaps one day you could teach me."

Inside I laughed as I pictured my hand balancing him under the tummy while he kicked and splashed up and down Pasonanca Pool. Then (perhaps it was the mention of water that reminded him) he said how sad he was to hear about Mr Holt, the Australian PM who had disappeared from Cheviot Beach the previous December, never to be seen again. "I was good friends with Mr and Mrs Holt," he told me. "When they stayed with us at Malacañang we agreed that we need to improve understanding between the two countries." I wondered whether the two leaders had discussed the White Australia Policy, for which I now felt almost personally guilty. At the same time I realized that over the past nine months I had rarely given Harold Holt a thought, and when I did it was all about the mystery of his disappearance. *Did a monster shark swallow him whole? Had he faked his own death and been picked up by a Chinese submarine?* The rumors were unstoppable.

Marcos seemed keen to hear about my childhood in Port Lincoln: how my dad had been a country GP and was now an eye specialist, how he loved sailing, how my mum was a champion horse rider and a skillful actress, etcetera, etcetera. At some stage I remember him saying, "I'm old enough to be your father," and it was phrases like these that put me (still so naïve!) increasingly at ease. I was genuinely enjoying conversing with this man, and during one bout of merriment Mr Marcos asked me if I'd ever properly seen his lovely island of Luzon. I replied that while I had stayed in San Lorenzo Village for two weeks before flying down to Zamboanga, I had never toured further than Manila. Marcos caught the eye of a well-built man waiting nearby. "Colonel Ver," he said. The big man immediately strode forward and stood attentively to one side. "Make out a plane ticket for this young lady. She shall come to stay with us at the palace, and she shall be taken to all the provinces around Luzon. She shall see the Philippines and write about it and remember me and my country with fondness."

Shocked, I blurted out, "That is so kind. Would next week be all right?"

President Marcos smiled. "Of course. My secretary and my chief security guard will be there to meet you, and the ticket will be sent to you as soon as possible." Colonel Ver was jotting something down in a notepad, and he asked me a few questions such as my current address, but everything was a blur after that. Marcos left with his entourage, and I stood by the table feeling dizzy with shock. Many wide-eyed people approached me with congratulations, but I sensed that for all the well-wishers there were just as many furious with understandable jealousy and resentment, including the mayor and his wife. I tried not to feel bad about this. It wasn't me who had manipulated the situation.

I don't know how I got home. Struggling to come to grips with the reality of what had just occurred, I had a restless night. One thing that did make me smile wryly was the realization that while the president and I had talked about a great variety of subjects, I had failed to ask one single question for the *Beacon*.

* * *

News of the meeting spread like the proverbial wildfire, and students from Ateneo were agog, including Vic Solis and the other *Beacon* journalists. I tried to reassure Vic that I would ask the vital questions about Sabah and the Maharlika Highway when I met with the president again in just a week or so, and this time there was no mocking laughter from anyone.

When I told Rob Park he sat down and frowned. I was taken aback. *Why isn't he overjoyed for me?* Then he said in his deep voice and thoughtful way, "I guess there's nothing much that could go wrong."

I felt a stab of annoyance. "What do you mean?"

"Well, you must be very careful at the palace."

"Careful? Why?"

I could see Rob's big brain working overtime. "I don't know. Maybe some of the younger male staffers might put something in your drink and take advantage of you in some way."

While this gave me food for thought, I really did think my American friend was overreacting. "Oh, well, I'll watch out for big bad wolves then." I grinned, but Rob did not return the smile. It was as though he had a strong premonition that my forthcoming visit would somehow bring me harm.

He accompanied me to see Father McNally, principal of Ateneo, to discuss the invitation. Even though the news had preceded me, McNally looked out of his depth. Like Rob, he was taking the matter seriously, but he had little to say except, "You'll be in Luzon for two weeks?" and when I nodded, he simply added, "Go with God Stephanie."

That night I woke from some vague nightmare which left me feeling sick with terror, and I was unable to rid myself of it. Eventually I gave myself a stern talking to about being irrational and scared for no good reason.

The plane ticket arrived at the Araneta house on Saturday 12 October, showing that departure would be exactly a week from that day. I stared as if it were a winning lottery ticket. The only person who needed to be notified now was my beloved Doc Marasigan, so Rob and I went to see him that afternoon.

My main guardian looked as concerned as Rob and McNally had done. I was getting a bit impatient at what I saw as an overreaction. Was nobody thrilled for me? When Rob reiterated to the doctor his fears about male staff at the palace, I reassured Doc that I would be exceptionally alert to any funny business, and that anyway, most of every day I would be out touring Luzon.

I feel very sorry for Dr Marasigan, whose president had invited his "charge" for the trip of a lifetime. The situation was unprecedented, and he was put in an impossible position. After all, if he barred me from going, people would want to know why, and if he expressed any concerns about the morality of the president or his staffers, the repercussions may have been unpleasant to say the least.

At no time during the week before I left Zamboanga did it occur to me that it might be the president himself who posed the danger. After all, he had confirmed that he was old enough to be my father, and he had presented himself as so kind, so generous, and one of the most interesting human beings I had ever met. I imagined myself having morning tea with the First Lady Imelda, and the kids frolicking around us, and how we would chat together about anything and everything. In fact, he had been so charming that in the excitement of the moment I completely forgot that he had once been accused of cold-blooded murder.

Tony Mas, soon to be my foster father and now president of the Zambo Rotary Club (Charlie had resigned before his overseas holiday), rang me to say that he would look around for a female chaperone for the trip, and this put my mind totally at rest. Even better, he said he would be in Manila next Saturday on business, and that he would meet me at the airport. As if that were not enough, Po Araneta assured me that his brother During would also be amongst the welcoming party.

Surely the necessary checks and balances were now in place. All I had to do now was to relax and enjoy the experience of a lifetime.

* * *

At 8 A.M. on Saturday 19 October I stood next to Rob waiting for the signal to board the plane to Manila. I had already checked in my suitcase full of clothes along with my book of poems should the president express an interest in reading them. The plane was delayed—*surprise surprise!*—so Rob and I waited for at least an hour, he looking quite unhappy while I was high with anticipation and nervous energy. In the minutes before boarding Rob removed the gold chain with the crucifix he always wore around his neck. "Wear this for me," he said. "It will protect you from harm." I knew how much Rob valued this icon, but before I could refuse he placed it around my neck. "For my sake," he insisted, so I had no choice but to thank him and give him a hug goodbye.

Waiting for me at the Manila airport was a young man called Lim from Manila Tours alongside an officious man who never did introduce himself. The official had a short but earnest conversation with Lim in Tagalog and promptly disappeared. I looked around for Tony Mas or During Araneta, but neither was to be seen. As Lim carried my case out to a very new Toyota, he apologized that his mother, who owned Manila Tours, had needed to attend another appointment because of the delay. I reassured myself that this was the same reason Tony and During were not there, and that they would contact me soon after I reached the palace.

As Lim stashed my case in the trunk I told him how much I looked forward to staying at Malacañang. Lim hesitated. "My mother has told me to show you VIP treatment, and not to ask any questions." Puzzled, I opened my mouth to mention the palace again, but Lim added quickly "We have a tour planned for you now."

The day was hot and humid, and I would have relished a shower to freshen up. However, not wanting to be discourteous I settled back to enjoy the tour. As we chatted I found out that Lim was married and twenty-one years old. He never once asked about my life, but I assumed that prying must be a no-no in tour guide ethics. After ten minutes the choking traffic thinned, and quite soon we reached a satellite city south of Manila called Las Piñas. Lim stopped the car outside a substantial stone church and rushed around to open the door for me. "St Joseph's Parish is famous for its bamboo organ," he told me, and he led me up a flight of narrow stone steps on the outside of one wall before entering a mezzanine space overlooking the interior of the church. There before us was a magnificent organ, constructed of almost a thousand different-sized pieces of bamboo over a period of two years by a Spanish priest in the 1700s. A waiting organist began to play, the church filling with the most ghostly and uplifting sound, like a thousand pan flutes.

Back in the Toyota we headed out on flat land through rice paddies, various fruit plantations, and ramshackle poverty-stricken towns. Heavy rain began to fall as we ascended into mountainous terrain, and soon we arrived at a resort perched close to the edge of an enormous crater. Like Russian dolls, within that crater was a vast lake, and in the middle of that lake was a smoking island volcano, and within that was another lake. It was mesmerising, even when Lim informed me that the last Taal eruption had claimed hundreds of lives. "How long ago did Taal erupt?" I asked, shocked to hear the reply—"last January." I pictured the scene in the Adelaide Hills, last January, when my friends and family had rushed to fight the bushfire in the valley below our property. Nine months ago, but it might as well have been nine hundred years ago, and on another planet.

The restaurant at the resort was five-star. Being urged by Lim to order anything my heart desired, I ate one of the yummiest meals of my life—lobster with salad, the whole presented like a piece of art. Gazing dreamily at the strange landscape before me, I was rudely interrupted by a swarm of loud-mouthed American tourists pushing through the main doors. Many of them acted like the "Ugly American" I had heard about but never witnessed personally, just as the Bacolod exchange student John had behaved at the time—the "Ugly Australian." The men had cameras slung around their necks and loud palm-leaf design shirts buttoned tight over big bellies, while the women were obese with impatient, drawling voices. "Frank? Where's my bag?" "In the goddam bus where you left it!" "So damn hot!" and "You gotta expect this kinda thing in the tropics!" All I could do was to sit there and hope that no one here imagined me to be an American. I was also certain that Rob Park would have winced at these brash, bigmouthed countrymen.

At about 2.00 P.M. we headed back to Manila, but this time we got stuck in frequent traffic jams. Even though the car was air-conditioned, I looked forward to that beautiful shower I would have at Malacañang. Lim looked hot under the collar too, but the reason seemed to be that we were running late for something. It was 3 P.M. before we reached Forbes Park, entering the same gated estate I recognized from my visit there with Charlie back in March. I stiffened, a trifle anxious. "But—the palace isn't in Forbes Park, is it?"

"No" replied Lim. "We will swap cars now, in Memorial Park." I relaxed again, believing I would soon be on my way to Malacañang.

We turned into the car park of the great Memorial Cemetery, the same one Charlie had shown me back in March. A driver standing near a Mercedes Benz seemed relieved to see us as we pulled in. Lim jumped out, grabbed my case from the trunk and proceeded to have an earnest conversation with the other man. I began to open my door. Lim broke away from the conversation and strode over to let me out and see me into the Mercedes, into the back seat. He told me he would take me out for another tour tomorrow, so I thanked him for the lovely day. The government driver climbed in behind the wheel and off we cruised. As sweet music filled the car via an elaborate stereo system, and fragrance wafted through the cool air, I told myself not to get too used to being treated like a princess. I asked the driver his name, but after saying "Ernesto ma'am," he seemed unwilling to speak. Sensing that his English was not good, and that he was probably in his early twenties, I decided to speak only when necessary.

I became uneasy when we did not seem to be heading out of Millionaires' Row, and alarm bells clanged when we turned towards a towering iron gate in front of one of the mansions in the avenue. From inside the car Ernesto pressed a button and the gate slid sideways, a marvel I had never seen before, and as we drove slowly up a gravel driveway the gates slid shut behind us like magic. Now I felt like a nervous animal, trapped. Lawned and terraced slopes flanked the driveway, and soon we came to a halt in front of a porch where stood a young woman in maid's uniform. She wore a genuine smile.

I sat there like a block of wood as Ernesto fetched my case from the trunk and placed it carefully on the porch. He opened the door for me. My heart sank and my face flushed hot. "Ernesto, where am I?"

The puzzled chauffeur said, "Forbes Park ma'am. You would like to come out?"

"No thank you," I replied, "I would like to be taken to Malacañang Palace."

Ernesto flinched, turning to exchange a few words in Tagalog with the maid. The young woman stepped forward. "My name is Vee," she said. "Please ma'am, come, you can see your room."

My mind was racing as fast as my heartbeat. Perhaps this was During Araneta's house. If not, there must be a phone inside and I could ring

During or Susie Reith who (I realized with a sickening jolt) were the only two people I knew who resided in Manila. Slowly I alighted from the Mercedes, and with a sigh of relief Ernesto snatched up my case and strode inside to a passageway. All this time Vee was making welcoming noises while searching my face for signs of delight.

To the right of the passageway was a small parlour, then a tiny gym with an exercise bike. Vee proudly opened the door of the third room while Ernesto, who I later learned was Vee's brother, entered and put my case inside the door. This was a vast bedroom, featuring a giant four-poster bed with a snow-white coverlet and dark, intricately carved wood. On the right side of the bed was a small table on which gleamed a bottle of scotch and two crystal glasses. Nearby was another slightly larger table adorned with a bowl of fruit and a tin of biscuits. Against one wall stood an elaborately carved dressing table with a mirror, and a few steps away a door led to what I assumed was an ensuite bathroom.

It was luxury beyond anything I had ever seen, and as I gazed at this magnificent room my heart sank further. "Vee," I asked. "Who owns this house?" Flustered, she glanced at Ernesto, who squirmed as if he were on hot coals and slipped quietly from the room. "Why ma'am, this is private house of president."

It was what I had suspected from the moment we had driven through those self-operating gates, but now the fact was confirmed I felt a sharp stab of terror. The conversation I had overheard back in March between Hans and Johnny about their president harboring mistresses in Forbes Park returned with a rush, and my brain was spinning in a jumble of thoughts. *Have I been naïve, even stupid? Then again, how can Marcos not know my age? Perhaps he has no idea what a Rotary Exchange student is . . . maybe he thinks I am studying in Zamboanga for some private reason. I look much older than seventeen compared with Filipinas, but then again, didn't he assure me he was old enough to be my father?*

I tried to slow my brain down. *Remain calm. At least on the outside. Think this through. What else did I hear in that conversation at the Reiths?* "There is one thing in this catholic country that the president can't do— get caught!" *So . . . what will happen if I tell my friends the truth? They will try to protect me, in which case Marcos may silence them to avoid a damaging international scandal. And if he silences them, he will have to silence me.*

Vee's voice intruded on my thoughts. "Ma'am, you like to see round?"

Without enthusiasm I agreed. It would give me more time to think. She led me from the bedroom into a large space featuring an antique dining table and a modern stereo player. My eye darted to the phone table, but Vee was eager to point out other impressive features of this palatial mansion. Walking through the great glass sliding doors leading to the rear of the property I scanned the manicured lawns and palms which stretched as far as the eye could see, noting the twenty-five metre sparkling clear swimming pool almost backing on to the house. Perhaps Marcos was a better swimmer than he had implied at our meeting over dinner.

Vee was beaming from ear to ear. "Now, the kitchen ma'am," and we retreated inside, strolling past the dining table through a swing door to a vast galley kitchen with shining marble benches and floors. Fitted out with no less than two full-sized fridges, a massive freezer, three state-of-the-art ovens, the kitchen boasted every mod con you could imagine. And this was the unsettling part—the whole house and contents looked untouched, as if it had been constructed and fitted out just for me.

With great pride Vee opened the first fridge stacked with every fruit and vegetable imaginable. In the side of the door was an array of fruit juices, Cokes and soft drinks. The second fridge contained various meats—whole chickens, slabs of beef, cut steaks, pork chops and fresh fish fillets. "You like ice cream, I know!" exclaimed Vee, opening the freezer with great flourish. And there, on rack after rack, were tubs of every flavoured ice confection you could imagine. I flinched. Marcos had remembered our conversation about our mutual love of ice cream. I tried to smile, but my stomach was churning. Staring at food was making me nauseous. "What can I get for you ma'am?" Vee asked eagerly. "For your dinner?"

"Vee, I need to use the phone." This was clearly not the right answer. The young Filipina looked distressed as I left the kitchen and approached the phone table in the dining room. There was no directory, so I asked her to bring me one. She looked quite tragic, stammering, "I . . . we . . . there is no book . . . I can cook you anything ma'am, anything you want." I didn't think my heart could sink any further, but it did. Quickly I thought of a meal which needed at least an hour to cook.

"Roast chicken and vegetables please," I said. Vee was thrilled, exclaiming "And ice cream after, I know. I make for you. Now you rest."

I thanked her and hurried to the bedroom, opened my case and fumbled around until I found my address book. Naturally I knew the address of Susie Reith, but I had failed to bring her phone number! Luckily, however, I managed to find During Araneta's number, because he had specifically asked me to contact him while I was here in Manila. Vee was busy in the nearby kitchen. Walking quietly to the phone table, I picked up the receiver and dialed. *What will I say?* Quickly I hatched something plausible. I would tell During that there had been a mix-up. I would say that I had been very naïve in assuming that the president meant for me to stay at the palace. I would say that while I had been offered accommodation in the Manila Hotel I would prefer to stay at his place.

I became aware the phone was not ringing. I hung up, dialed again. No dial tone. It was dead. Now I could feel myself shaking from deep inside. I peeped into the kitchen. "Vee, could Ernesto please take me to the address of a dear friend I have in Manila?" Vee paled. "Ma'am, maybe yes, but after president is coming." She looked wretched. "I cannot say, only the president can say."

Okay, so now there was no misunderstanding—I was trapped here until I had the go ahead from Himself.

"When is he expected to arrive?"

Vee didn't know exactly—sometime this evening. I made a small decision. "I'll be in my room, so could you serve me my meal there please?" Instantly I regretted saying "my room."

Sitting on the rich brocade bedspread within the four-poster I felt flushed and hot. My thoughts whirled. A clock in a carved ebony frame told me it was 5.30 P.M.—almost sunset. Once more I dived into my case, pulled out another dress and my bathroom bag, entered the ensuite and turned to lock the door behind me. There was no lock. Nor was there a lock on the door to a small space on the other side of the ensuite. This room held a single bed with an exit leading to a sunroom overlooking that pristine swimming pool.

With no time to waste I undressed, glancing at the necklet holding the cross which Rob had lent me, my brain telling me it would not save me, my heart hoping it would. Desperate not to be caught naked, especially by Himself, I stood under the cool shower for only two minutes, unable to enjoy the scented soaps and shampoo in my feverish haste to get myself dry and covered before anyone barged through either door.

The bedroom was all-silent. I donned my pink draped dress, carefully tucking the cross out of sight in my cleavage. Then I noticed for the first time a compact antique writing desk—all it lacked was an inkwell and a quilled pen. *That's what I need to do!* I snatched a biro and writing paper from my case. In this way my brain might unscramble, my heart might calm down, and coping strategies might magically emerge onto the page. For obvious reasons it was vital this letter be kept secret until it could be safely revealed even to the most trusted of friends and family.

As my pen scribbled, I kept one nervous ear out for any sounds outside. I began with "Dear Rob," because it seemed silly to write to yourself. But this was one letter which was never going to hit the mailbox. "I feel like a prisoner in a gilded cage, I must be weak because I'm scared, really scared, the same scared feeling I experienced a few nights before I left Zambo." Then I began to describe everything that had happened from the start of that morning.

I had filled two sides of a page when I heard the unmistakable sound of tyres crunching gravel. I shoved pen and pad into the case, clicked it closed, grabbed up my handbag and flew out the door—almost colliding with the same rugged Colonel Ver who had jumped to obey his president's bidding at the dinner in Zamboanga. Although he seemed a little surprised to see me at the ready with handbag, he greeted me pleasantly enough and we shook hands. There was no sign of Vee or her brother.

Keeping my voice calm I launched into an urgent explanation of why it was necessary for me to relocate as soon as possible. I told him about Zambo's Rotary president Tony Mas, who was in Manila right now and was arranging a female companion for me. However, thinking that I was a guest at Malacañang, Tony would be waiting to hear from Mr Araneta that I had arrived and needed to meet my chaperone. "I should ring as soon as possible."

I stopped to draw breath.

A troubled Colonel Ver led me to a seat at the dining table while he thought the matter over. Finally he spoke. "Stephanie, you see, this is a *very* private house of the president." His eyes drilled disturbingly into mine. He was warning me, choosing his words with great care. "This is where his private guests stay and he doesn't want anyone to know about it."

I nodded, my heart beating loud, my voice low. "I understand Colonel Ver. But if I'm to stay here for six days or so, someone, especially from the Rotary Club, will have to know where I am." I watched his reaction intently. I remained wary of this man not because he had proved himself aggressive or even unkind, but because his very presence had an aura of absolute control, a quiet but formidable power. Taking his time, he finally concluded that he would try to have the president here by 7.30 P.M., when I could have a chat and get the matter straightened out.

We both stood up and shook hands. The colonel walked down the passage and disappeared out through the front door. I stood there, lost, listening to the fading crunch of gravel as he cruised back to the real world. Retrieving my pen and a new piece of paper, I wrote, "This is eerie, and I wish I were back in that little hut in Lisukan where I felt so much peace." A knock at the door, and Vee made a grand entry, cradling a huge oval plate which she set down on the round table. I tried not to look astonished. On the delicate porcelain was arranged a whole roast chicken cooked to crispy skin perfection, chips, vegetables of all kinds, toasts with the crusts removed, and two varieties of cheese next to pieces of fresh fruit. It reminded me of those pictorial advertisements in the *Women's Weekly*.

I tried to eat something so I wouldn't offend, picking like a nervous bird at this obscene feast, haunted all the while by the poor beggars I knew were starving less than an hour away. After thirty minutes Vee reappeared with creamy mango ice cream and glorious coffee. She told me if

I wanted anything at all I was to ring the buzzer, then pointed to a red button on the wall. I wrote minutes later, "What she doesn't know is that all I want right now is to get out of here, never see any presidents, aides, any roast chickens, any rich 'private' houses ever again . . . it's just this scary, uneasy feeling which is no normal scary feeling—an instinct, a premonition?"

Then I listed why I had good reasons to be scared, including being kept in the dark for so long about my destination; Lim being told I was a VIP and to ask no questions, implying a sense of hush-hush; President Marcos being known to keep mistresses somewhere in Forbes Park; the phone being dead plus no phone directory; the switching of cars at Memorial Park so that Lim and, well, no one else knew where I was; the absence of Mr Mas at the airport; my memory of During Araneta saying, "In Malacañang you will be safe, with the First Lady. If it was somewhere else, then that would be the time to worry!" and last but not least, the confiscation of most of the snapshots taken that night I met the president.

In the week before my departure from Zamboanga, two photos of that public meeting had been given to me, my face half-hidden by another diner in both but Marcos clearly visible facing me, laughing, and with his back to Mayor Enriquez who had every right to look stony. I guessed that Colonel Ver himself had vetted the films taken by each photographer in the mayor's house, permitting development of only those where the object of Marcos's attention is hard to identify. By 6.30 P.M. my strategy had firmed, outlined in two pages of my secret letter.

I started with fright at a timid knock at the door. "They are on their way ma'am," said Vee. For five minutes I paced up and down the room, mindlessly reciting Spanish verbs, my ears pricked for the faintest sound, on high alert. Then I forced myself to sit down and write more of the letter again.

Distant car engine; scrunch of tyres on gravel; hurried footsteps in the passage; door opening. The last thing I wrote was "It's happened. They're here! I'm going . . ."

My second meeting with President Ferdinand Marcos
Location: Somewhere in Forbes Park, Manila

It was almost 8 P.M. I left the bedroom, hovering for a few seconds outside in the passage. The front door opened and the president bounded towards me, with a practiced, youthful spring in his step.

We greeted each other warmly, me hoping I looked as pleased to see him as he did to see me. Inwardly I was a volcano. He clasped my hands and asked me how I had been, Colonel Ver standing behind him with his disturbed "ever ready" expression. Although Vee was nowhere in sight, President Marcos yelled towards the kitchen. "Hotdogs please Vee!" This indicated he hadn't eaten yet. Vee's head appeared for a second as she acknowledged his request, and then he and I sat on the sofa. Colonel Ver had vanished.

I'm not sure what we first talked about, but I do remember him looking concerned when I dropped into the conversation how many people knew of my trip to Manila at his invitation. I was calculating every word I said, my voice unnaturally monotone—way too calm to be the real me. When Vee briefly appeared and set the hot dogs on the dining table, I felt relieved to be off the sofa and chatting in a separate hard-backed chair. During the conversation I stupidly mentioned I liked dancing, whereupon he said he liked to dance too, and that he would dance with me after dinner. My unease grew, especially as Vee and Col Ver were nowhere to be seen. After dinner Marcos strode to the stereo and put on a record of slow sweet music. He took me in his arms and was holding me too close. As he began to nuzzle my neck it became horribly clear that my worst fears were playing out. From now on I would have to deal with the situation as best I could, from moment to moment.

I pulled away and asked if he'd like to see my poetry. Without enthusiasm he nodded, but I remembered with a sickening twist that my poetry book was in my case, in the bedroom! And that I hadn't hidden my secret letter! Naturally he followed me into the room, but when he headed for the ensuite I hastily shoved my secret letter into my handbag, and by the time he emerged I was delving into my case for my notebook. My nerves fraying as he stood behind me, I grabbed the battered exercise book and handed it over.

Sitting on the bed, he glanced politely at a few pages. But then he motioned for me to sit beside him, which I anticipated. Gingerly I sat, reading a three-versed poem called "Caged" about an imaginary king locked in a tower. I lowered the book as he uttered a few words of praise, but then he leaned sideways and kissed me, just gently, near my lips.

I jumped up and asked him if he'd like to see some photographs of my family, and before he could reply I was rummaging through my case for the photo album. This time I didn't sit down, and he made no more advances until he rose from the bed and we walked outside together into the hallway. By this time I had memorized the mantra I needed to extract myself from this house, for tonight at least.

"So I hope you can understand, Mr President, that for your reputation as well as mine, there must be not one night unaccounted for, or awkward questions will be asked."

He nodded in agreement. "What do you suggest would be the best way to proceed?"

At last I had the green light to explain my plan. "If someone could drive me to the Reiths' place tonight," I told him, "I will tell my hosts that I was taken on tour all day followed by nightclubbing, and that I got it wrong about the invitation to Malacañang. So rather than stay at the impersonal Manila Hotel, I asked to be driven to their home. I will tell no one about this place." This seemed to satisfy Marcos, for now anyway, and he turned his attention to taking me for a stroll outside on those fairy-lit lawns in the moonlight.

In different circumstances I may have been enchanted, but by now I felt sick with a mix of fear, the constant wariness of watching what I said, and tactfully avoiding his advances. We lingered by the pool, and he put his arm around my shoulder. Later I wrote in my secret letter, "I knew he was waiting for an opportunity to kiss me again, but I was extremely wary . . . and then I made a mistake, and he managed to kiss me—still very gently and then, thank God, Col Ver appeared and happened to mention it was 10.20 P.M."

Evidently and luckily for me, the president was supposed to have been somewhere at 10 P.M. The colonel left with orders to summon the presidential car, but this left at least ten minutes where Marcos and I were alone together in the dining room. He put on another record, and it was clear that slow dancing remained firmly on his agenda. He was not a good dancer and I was so nervous I guess we didn't exactly look like Fred Astaire and Ginger Rogers. And then, once again, he was nuzzling my neck, his mouth moving ever closer to mine while I turned my face away as far as I could without being overtly offensive.

This is what I wrote in my secret letter the next day, theoretically for Rob, but in fact for me as I desperately attempted to justify my lack of assertive action. "If you think I should have resisted more violently and less tactfully than I did, perhaps you're right. Perhaps I'm a coward. But I do know that if I had to go through the same thing again, I would act just the same. If he had been another man, or if he had not been going to go, or looked as if he had intentions of staying the night, then I would have had to act positively. As it was, I acted negatively, but I still think it was the best course."

Before he left with Colonel Ver, he said he would see me in Baguio, and that any time we met privately it would be here. *Next time.* Both he and the colonel explained that Baguio was a beautiful place up in the mountains of Luzon, but now I dreaded going there or to this house again or anywhere else where He might be. I tried to explain in my secret letter why it would be a bad mistake to confide in anyone. "Questions would be asked and I'd probably be shot secretly under government orders so I wouldn't let the cat out of the bag. That sounds melodramatic I know, but after that night I would not look at anything again optimistically."

After Marcos disappeared I rushed into the bedroom and zipped up my case. Vee appeared as if by magic to carry it to the front door. We hardly spoke. Silently I walked out onto the porch. Ernesto was nowhere to be seen, but two male officials were waiting to usher me into the back seat of the waiting Mercedes. I gave them the Reiths' address, and in my letter I described feeling like "a regal fugitive" as we set off out through the great gates and out of Forbes Park, through the vast deserted no-man's-land, then into the dirty streets of the slums before heading towards San Lorenzo Village. I felt a small feeling of relief to be physically gone from the house, but I knew the ordeal was far from over. *With no forewarning, will the Reiths be welcoming? Surely Susie will be, but how will I explain the late hour and the fact that I had not rung?* Somewhere inside me a small firm voice told me that if I didn't want to collapse with a nervous breakdown, I needed to deal with every situation one step at a time. *Just one step at a time . . .*

Location: Reith house, San Lorenzo Village, Manila

It was past 11 P.M. when we arrived at the Reith house which was shrouded in darkness. I asked the officials to wait. If the worst came to the worst and I couldn't get in, they would have to take me to the Manila Hotel, so with my heart hammering I knocked timidly at the front door. No response. I knocked louder, glancing back at the two dark figures seated in the Mercedes. After what seemed like a lifetime Augustine's voice sounded on the other side of the door. "Who eez eet?"

"Stephanie," I answered in a low voice.

"Who?"

"Augustine, it's Stephanie. Please let me in."

Rubbing his eyes, Augustine opened the door. I signaled to the figures in the car. One hopped out and with head lowered brought my case to the Reiths' front porch, dumped it without a word, and retreated to the car, which purred away.

I tipped my chin to my clasped hands in the gesture of sleep. "Can I sleep here tonight?" Looking at my suitcase, Augustine put two and two together and led me to George's room which had two single beds. Sadly George awoke, besieging me with eager questions while Augustine set about making up the second bed. Tired and scared, I mumbled some vague explanation. "Where's Charlie?" I asked. George replied that his typical night-owl brother was out, at the movies.

Exhausted though I was, I braced myself to wait until Charlie returned, when I would be forced to tell him all the lies I had prepared. It made me realize what an essentially truthful person I was. Bald-faced lying would present me with a real challenge. I was about to change in the bathroom when sounds beyond indicated Charlie had returned. *Next step*, I told myself as I fronted up to Charlie in the lounge room.

I told him that I had got it all wrong; that I had assumed I was staying at the palace, but that actually the president had arranged for all the tours to be undertaken from the Manila Hotel; that I had decided the hotel was too impersonal and so asked if I could come and stay with the Reiths instead. Everything sounded plausible, so plausible in fact that when Charlie sensed that I was depressed he jumped to the conclusion I was disappointed not to be staying at Malacañang anymore. Because I couldn't bear him thinking I was that shallow, my resolve broke and I looked him straight in the eye. "Charlie, not everything I've told you tonight has been the truth, but please believe me, I'm doing what I think is the only thing I can do right now."

I felt enormous gratitude to Charlie for simply staring at me for a few thoughtful seconds, then nodding his head in total acceptance. It proved to me that while he no longer believed my story, he believed in me as an individual, and that meant a lot.

Augustine brought me a cup of hot Ovaltine which I drank and then went to bed. Having just endured a real nightmare, it was impossible to sleep. Restless and hot, I replayed the events of the day over and over in my head while George slumbered soundly in the next bed. I tried to find comfort in the fact that Lim was taking me on a tour to the wondrous Pagsanjan Falls next morning, and so for one whole day I'd have a reprieve. But what would I do if the next evening Colonel Ver rang saying the president wanted to see me at the house? And what about the flight to Baguio? This was supposed to happen on Monday, only two days away. Burdened by my newfound cynicism I suspected this would be no ordinary tourist trip, and that the president would be less concerned about me being thrilled by the famous woodcarvings of Baguio than in meeting me privately, this time in his country hideaway.

* * *

I didn't see Mrs Reith or George the next morning because at 7.30 A.M. I needed to be up and dressed, ready for the tour to Pagsanjan Falls. I packed a small carry bag with swim gear.

Because from now on it was obvious that information would only be supplied to me on a need-to-know basis, I had no idea who'd be picking me up. An anonymous driver appeared at the door and said he would drive me to Manila Tours based at the Grand Hotel. In the white Mercedes we cruised grandly downtown, the driver asking me casually if I had a camera. "No," I replied, and he assured me that he would speak to the president's chief aide (Colonel Ver) and that one would be procured for me as soon as possible. My secret letter explains what I felt about this generous gesture: "For every gift that's given to me, and the more VIP I am treated, the more uneasy I become . . . I need so desperately to tell someone, but I cannot."

At the hotel a Danish lady and an Italian man in their thirties were waiting to join the tour, so off we drove in Lim's Toyota to the south, the man sitting next to Lim in the front and us two females in the back. It was a treat to be able to converse with two interesting people who were neither Filipino nor American, and I learnt interesting details about Denmark and Italy along that 270 km ride. We began a gradual climb upwards, after a while passing a town with hot volcanic springs, aptly called Los Baños. The name rang bells, and I suddenly realized that somewhere nearby stood the agricultural college where Chito was studying. My heart missed a beat. I begged Lim to take a detour and asked my fellow companions to humour me. It had seemed eons since I had farewelled Chito on that rainy night in his parents' jeep.

My heart sank as we drove into the college grounds. They were so vast. Eyes darting about, willing Chito to appear, I entered two of the main buildings and asked if anyone might know his whereabouts. But my quest was futile. Acutely aware that the foreign tourists were waiting and paying good money for this day tour, I abandoned the search and returned to the car. Perhaps it was just as well Chito and I didn't meet that day, because my need to tell someone what was happening may well have overwhelmed my common sense.

We drove through acres of sugarcane and rice paddies, at one stage crossing a narrow railway track carrying primitive carts on bearings, each small "truck" crammed with passengers and pushed along by young men. The whole system was ingenious, and quaint.

Eventually we were steeply winding our way upwards, and after passing through a town of ancient buildings unchanged since the Spanish conquest, we arrived at a lodge perched on the bank of a wide meandering river. It was time for lunch, and once again my meal was spectacular enough for me to make special mention of it to the folks at home—"a whole chicken roasted and falling from the bone, with all the trimmings." Afterwards we changed into our swimwear before grouping on the bank near a small quay.

We were helped down into two long, slim canoes, the Europeans seated on the floor in one and Lim and me in another. Two boatmen perched fore and aft, armed with long paddles. It was instantly clear that these canoes were designed for maximum speed and minimum resistance, but the downside was their lack of stability. As the boatmen toiled to take us upstream, the river gradually narrowed and quickened. The scenery on both sides was dense and lush green, and the sun above was sweet and warm and sparkled on the water. No one spoke, and the rhythm of the paddles dipping through the river's surface became an entrancing dream. For the first time for what seemed like eternity, all fears of presidents, secret houses and escape strategies vanished under the overwhelming beauty and serenity all about me.

The banks either side transformed into smooth black rock walls that somehow supported a vertical tropical jungle and towered over us, revealing a blue ribbon of sky far, far above. A myriad of thin waterfalls splashed down from unseen crevices of those shining black walls, bouncing over fluorescent green palms and ferns that somehow clung to the sides. For a girl from dry South Australia, the experience was quite marvellous.

Serenity shattered, replaced by excitement as we rounded a bend and faced the first series of rapids. Over the sound of rushing water the boatmen began shouting to each other in Tagalog, their native tongue, and from time to time they would leap out and haul the canoes away from the rocks, manhandling the craft against the fast moving current and somehow managing not to slip on the rocks. Their skills were equal to those amazing Moro vinta boatmen of Zamboanga. Reaching the crest of the rapids, we pushed upriver through a spectacular canyon. I felt tiny, like an ant on the floor of a cathedral. On one side gushed a waterfall, so powerful that when you turned towards it your face was blasted by the jetting spray. After that we began to hear a deep rumbling sound, and around every corner the thunderous sounds became louder. We braced ourselves for the sight of the main falls.

Suddenly we were floating in the churned-up water of a glorious aqua pool just beyond the main impact of the waterfall. Spray and droplets and noise filled the air, and although the curtain of water was too dense to see through, the rock walls on either side indicated a large cave hidden beyond. The tourists and I were permitted to flop out of the canoes and swim, and while that may have appeared dangerous, the boatmen knew that even the strongest swimmer would have no chance of getting anywhere near that wall of water thundering down. On the way back the excitement of being swept down the rapids at furious speed was breathtaking. Three times we nearly capsized, saved at the last second by the teamwork and agility of those boatmen.

During the drive back to Manila my fears came flooding back again. *Will I be summoned to the House tonight? Will I have one day's reprieve before I fly to Baguio, where "he" will be waiting?*

At the Reiths' that evening I rang During Araneta and spun the same lie that I had told Charlie the night before. "So, there is no need for a female chaperone now," I reassured During. "Could you please pass this information on to Mr Mas?"

"Of course," said During immediately, in a tone that sounded oddly sympathetic.

*   *   *

The following morning the big white Merc arrived with the anonymous driver, and once again I was dropped at the Manila Hotel where Lim scooped me up in the Toyota. As he drove we were chatting about our experiences at Pagsanjan when ahead of us loomed the wide gated entrance into Forbes Park. My heart started to thump, especially when we turned into the same car park of the Memorial Cemetery where the president's white Mercedes had been waiting for me only three days ago!

"I never got to show you this place," Lim said. With a rush of relief I realized this was simply part of the sightseeing he had organised for the day. Instead of standing at the edge of the carpark gazing at the scene, as Charlie and I had done eight months before, Lim and I wound our way up a long slope to the cemetery's hub, a white marble circular monolith from which we could take in a 360 degree view of twenty-seven thousand dazzling white marble crosses (imported from Italy). They were all set at exactly the same distance apart on a carpet of bright green grass sloping gently down and away from where we stood. In silence we absorbed the sadness and the beauty of that scene.

We headed out past the great walled mansions of Forbes Park, back through no-man's land then into the city, passing through the poorest districts where squatters sheltered in hovels cobbled together with wood and bits of tin from the rubbish dumps. The obscene contrast between Millionaires' Row and the slums never failed to shock me. We drew up outside Intramuros, the earliest walled city of "Maynila" constructed of palm logs and earth in the mid-1500s, under the control of an Islamic dynasty. By 1571, however, it had been replaced by the conquering Catholic Spaniards with their trademark blocks of stone, in some places towering six metres high, and the whole surrounded by a once deep moat fed by the River Pasig. For me, whose home state had been founded by the British in 1836, it was mind-blowing to see buildings and fortresses built more than 400 years ago.

Lim drove through the impressive ruins of the outer wall and parked at Fort Santiago. This citadel had been erected within Intramuros in 1593, under the supervision of conquistador Miguel Legaspi, on top of a vast stone chamber constructed the year before to store cannons and gunpowder. Over the years this underground chamber was converted to stone prison cells, a dreadful dungeon imprisoning any who dared to challenge Spanish authority.

The dungeon was not yet open to the public, but on the ground floor was a rudimentary information area which sold, amongst other souvenirs, prints of paintings relevant to the history of the place. One of these fascinated me. It depicts the melancholic afternoon before freedom fighter Dr Jose Rizal was taken from the fort and executed by firing squad in 1896. In the fort's chapel a priest in the background is lighting candles on a shrouded altar, and two uniformed and arrogant officers smoke as they casually watch Rizal's mother sobbing while her daughter embraces her brother in their last goodbye. It is said that during this embrace Rizal whispered to his sister that he had hidden something in the alcohol stove in his cell. The "treasure" turned out to be a poem now known as "Mi Ultima Adios." Rizal was not only a clever writer who had used his pen to rouse his people to oust the Spaniards, but I was intrigued to discover that he had specialised in ophthalmology, like my father. Two lines of "My Last Goodbye" I found particularly powerful:

> I'll go where there are no slaves, tyrants or hangmen
> Where faith does not kill and where God alone does reign.

President Marcos would not show himself to be a tyrant until the early 1970s. With hindsight I can only imagine how mortified Rizal would have been to witness a tyranny imposed, not by a foreign dictator from a far-flung Empire, but by one of his own countrymen.

From Intramuros we drove to the university of Santo Tomas, built in 1611, twenty-five years older than Harvard in the US. It was a vast stone building complex, somewhat like a Spanish town, and I remembered that Artu had been its top student only the year before. We ate lunch at some fine restaurant, but as we emerged into the full heat of midday I suddenly realized how much I was missing swimming. When I mentioned this to Lim he immediately turned the Toyota for the Manila Hotel. There, in a palatial private room, I changed into my bikini bottoms and midriff shirt before being led outside into the tropical gardens. These provided a spectacular backdrop for one of the most beautiful pools I had ever seen, fifty metres in length with diving boards of various heights and sparkling clear water. Practicing my trademark handstand dive I then swam six laps, washing away my cares for one refreshing hour.

As soon as I clambered from that cool water and toweled myself off, the dread of what would happen the next day—flying north to Baguio—settled heavily upon my mind. Probably because I now looked like a drowned rat, Lim asked if I would like to go to the beauty parlour. "I'm not sure I can afford that," I said, but Lim hastened to reassure me I shouldn't concern myself with such trivialities. He took me to a beauty parlour within the hotel itself. If I thought that Mrs Ebby in Zamboanga had treated me like a princess, then this parlour provided services fit for a queen. There were only two other female clients, and from their attire and plumpness I guessed they weren't exactly from the poor side of town. In between having a gentle head massage my hair was styled, my hands anointed with expensive oils, nails manicured, and delicious snacks were constantly on offer. Perhaps Lim thought I wasn't being spoiled enough, because he suddenly appeared with a carton of mango ice cream!

Shortly after he dropped me off in San Lorenzo Village, I looked around for Mrs Reith. So far I had managed to avoid any face-to-face conversation with this lovely lady since my unexpected arrival at her door. By now Charlie must have shared with her what I had said that first night, but I dreaded having to face Susie Reith almost as much as my next inevitable meeting with Marcos. Also, the fact that she had not yet appeared was quite unsettling.

George came out of his bedroom, eyeing me in a strange way as he informed me that someone had rung and cancelled my trip to Baguio. My heart leapt. *Maybe, just maybe, unexpected circumstances have trapped the president with his wife somewhere. All I need is one week more, and then I could flee back to Zambo without awkward questions being asked.*

"Who rang?"

George shrugged. "A man, someone from the government, he didn't say."

I tried to look disappointed. "Well, well," I said, "that's what happens when you get all beautified up for a trip—it gets cancelled."

"Actually," said George, "Postponed. He said postponed, not cancelled."

I was on a roller coaster, one moment up, the next down. But for now at least it seemed that another day's reprieve had been gifted to me. I rang During Araneta and told him that the Baguio trip had been postponed, and would it be all right if I came and spent the day with them? To my astonishment, he told me that he and his wife were about to head off for Baguio, and would I like to join them? My heart sank. I had no choice but to decline. I was a government guest controlled by Manila Tours—officially anyway. Fortunately During came to the rescue, asking if I'd like to visit his house the next day and swim with his son Nonito and his cousins, an offer I keenly accepted.

* * *

On Tuesday morning Nonito picked me up and we drove to a gated suburb. I liked Nonito. We chatted easily together about many topics, except of course my secret ongoing dilemma which I so badly needed to share with a friend. After a simple but delicious lunch, we changed and sauntered out to a pool. Two of Nonito's male cousins arrived, and we laughed a lot and generally had a good time. At 2 P.M. Nonito took me to pick up his sister in an area on the outskirts of Manila where all the prestigious schools and universities were clustered. We drove through Ateneo de Manila, an immense area containing impressive stone or brick buildings, lawns winding their way forever around the observatory, trees, gardens, sheltered basketball courts, science labs, a theatre, dormitories, and junior and senior schools. Ateneo also contained a vast library named after the college's alumni, Jose Rizal, that brave national hero who dared to seek independence for his beloved Philippines.

We picked up Nonito's sister from a girls' high school within the complex before cruising through the University of the Philippines. There the buildings were even older than at Ateneo. The entire property, which included a golf course, was so vast that students needed some sort of transport to get from one side of the grounds to the other.

Back at the Reiths' by 4 P.M., I showered, washed my hair, relaxed before the TV, then wrote a little more in my two letters (one destined for my family back in Australia, the other my secret letter). So far so good. No scary phone calls. And I still hadn't come face-to-face with Susie Reith. George returned from medical college, and after a while I sauntered into the palm garden where I spied him bent over a table. He was absorbed in something he was dissecting with a scalpel. "Homework?" I asked. He leant back to allow me to view his handiwork—a green frog, its arms and legs splayed out, pinned on a wooden board. Its chest had been split open. Then I saw with horror that its heart was beating. "He's alive!"

"Yes," George said with pride, "this way I can study how his heart beats and note what happens to the rest of his body." With that he promptly cut further to expose the stomach.

My hand went over my mouth, and the would-be doctor smiled a smug smile. "So many people feel sick at the sight of blood."

"No!" I yelled at him. "I feel sick because he's alive!"

George stared at me as if I'd lost my wits. "It's only a frog."

It was then I saw a brown bottle of liquid nearby, and a small piece of dry muslin. "Is that ether?" I demanded. George nodded. "Did you anaesthetise him?"

"Well no, because if I give it too much, it will die." George was defending himself. He had never seen me so heated.

"Okay, you've seen how his heart beats, so put the poor thing out of his misery!"

George wet a rag from a bottle of ether and held it over the frog's face until the muscles of the frog's arms and legs relaxed and it was obvious the creature was dead. As I turned to walk away, George muttered, "How else will I save human lives?"

I was too upset to stay and argue, but his words left me with the same kind of conundrum that Werner had presented to me when he announced that he would publicly torture human beings to ensure they never hurt any member of his family again. *So when does the end justify the means? What if someday the likes of George saves me or someone beloved on the operating table because he had the guts to be cruel to a frog?* After wrestling with myself for some time, I concluded that where cruelty is involved, the end can rarely justify the means.

I had dinner with George who was less talkative than usual, but then so was I. After the meal I headed for the piano, abandoning George to experiment on whatever animal he felt might help to save mankind. Creating tunes always calmed me. At 11 P.M. I was just thinking of going to bed when the phone rang. I tensed. People didn't usually ring as late as this. Augustine answered, put down the receiver, and turned to me. "Telephone ma'am."

I froze. Then I got to my feet and walked to the phone. "Hello."

"Good evening Stephanie," replied the colonel.

"Oh, Colonel Ver, good—"

The phone went dead. Bewildered, I waited, unsure of what to do, assuming the line had gone down. Augustine was hovering somewhere nearby. The phone rang again. I picked up. "Hello?"

Colonel Ver said, "You will never again say my name on the phone. Do you understand?"

I was as shocked as if he had slapped me in the face. "Yes."

"Good," said Colonel Ver. "You will be ready to fly to Baguio at seven on Thursday morning. You will be picked up at six a.m. Do you understand?"

I nodded miserably. "Yes."

"Please have a good evening," said the colonel, and hung up.

After that I clearly was *not* about to have a good evening. Augustine left the room, throwing me a strange look. Perhaps I read him wrongly, but I believed he understood that something distressing was happening to me and was sympathetic. I managed to get some sleep in the wee hours, knowing for now there'd be at least one more day's reprieve.

Early on Wednesday morning I rang During Araneta, telling him that Baguio had once more been postponed and asking if I could have a repeat of yesterday. The dear man agreed readily, and so again I spent a lovely day swimming and lounging around in the Araneta's pool and was not dropped back at San Lorenzo Village until 11 P.M. I set my alarm clock to get up super early, but no sooner than I had fallen asleep than the phone clanged. I woke with a jolt, heart racing.

Augustine made it to the phone seconds before I did. He picked up, listened, and silently handed me the receiver, giving me that same sympathetic look before diplomatically retreating to the next room. The colonel told me that "they" had decided to postpone Baguio once more, and that I was to await further instructions. After hanging up I staggered back to bed, feeling more dead than alive, remembering to switch off my alarm. Assuming I would be able to sleep in as long as I needed the following morning, I nodded off.

After what seemed like a few minutes Augustine knocked urgently on my door. It was 6 A.M.! "Ma'am, Manila Tour man!" The emotional roller coaster was in full swing again. I threw some clothes on and went out to find Lim standing alongside his Toyota. No one had thought to inform him that the Baguio trip was off the menu for today, and he had come to take me to the airport.

As he drove away I headed back to bed, eventually fell asleep, and was blissfully unconscious at 7.30 when Augustine knocked on the door. Mrs Enriquez, head of Manila Tours, had rung to say that Lim was on his way for a tour to Los Baños. I couldn't understand why he wanted to revisit this little town which we had passed through only days before. Perhaps Lim simply thought I'd like the novelty of swimming in the hot springs or (and this is when my hopes soared) he had seen how disappointed I was when my visit to the Agricultural College of the Philippines had drawn a blank with my friends. Just the thought of being with Raymond and Chito, even for a few minutes, was enough to forget my tiredness, grab up my swim gear, and fly out the front door just as the Toyota once again cruised up to the house.

Lim presented me with a Kodak camera, telling me there were thirty-six frames on the roll. Delighted, I asked him to stop many times along the way so I could take photos. I remember clicking away by a rice paddy where a farmer in a sombrero manhandled a primitive wooden plough behind his big horned carabao up to its knees in water; and another where two women were using a measuring stick to space the rice seedlings they were planting; and a man riding a carabao in front of a group of nipa huts. While we were driving along I took a pic of a young man standing on the back of a jeepney guarding its one and only passenger—a cow!

After 100 km from Manila we arrived at the outskirts of Los Baños where lay the vast grounds of the agricultural college housing my friends. Lim had indeed understood the disappointment I had felt last time, but on this morning, although I managed to find Raymond Bader, Chito remained elusive. After reluctantly taking my leave Lim drove me to a five-star resort for an exotic lunch and a swim in the clear blue pool before a relaxing lounge around in the green mineral waters of the hot spas. Again I was taken by Lim to the beauty parlour within the Manila Hotel, and as before I was treated like royalty. But despite all the pampering and luxury, my longing to be free of the dread of what might happen that night, or over the next seven days, clouded any pleasure I might otherwise have felt. I was delivered back to the Reiths' at 7 P.M., Lim telling me he would call by at 8.30 P.M. to take me to watch a game of Jai-Alai. Already I was tired, and as soon as I walked through the door Augustine, with pity in his eyes, informed me that the "man" had rung and would call back at 7.30 P.M. By this time my nerves were in tatters, but at 8 P.M. when Colonel Ver still hadn't rung, I began to harbor hopes that I could escape. *Just another half hour, that's all I need!* Then George, unaware that he was doing me a massive favour, began using the phone to make a number of calls. As long as he remained on the phone, the colonel would be unable to get through, and so at 8.30 I was dressed up and bolting out the front door.

Jai-Alai was great to watch. Fast and furious, it is similar to squash, its origins in the Basque country of Spain. Instead of a racquet with strings, a long scoop is wielded and the ball, bigger than a golf ball and just as hard, is flung against one of three walls to ricochet off the others. Lim asked if I wanted to bet, and because for the last eight days I hadn't had to spend one centavo, I happily handed over ten pesos with the stipulation that if I won, we would split the win between us. I bet my ten P on two players I thought would win overall, and Lim bet on another couple, and at the end of the round I found my players had won! The crowd craned forwards to see for themselves the dividends for the scoop of the evening, and suddenly the sign board flashed up the amount—185P! Even after splitting that sum with Lim, and going on to lose another twenty P, I as a poor student felt rich as Rockefeller.

A more mature girl would at that point have asked Lim to take her home, but my dread of the immediate future made me seek distraction for as long as possible. And so Lim drove me to the ritzy Bayside Nightclub which had no less than two big bands. When the first finished their round, the stage floor rose. They disappeared, while over the next minute the floor descended from above with the second band on board. Both bands were highly skilled, and Lim and I danced our socks off.

* * *

By the time I got home in the wee hours, I felt terribly nauseous and somehow knew that the multi-coloured ice cream I had ingested at the Jai-Alai had not agreed with me. I tossed and turned in bed until noon the next day when I dragged myself up, "showered" with buckets of cool water in the bathroom, dressed, and wandered out into the lounge room just in time to see a middle-aged woman being shown out by Augustine.

It was a shock when Mrs Reith suddenly appeared, obviously hot and bothered. "Stephanie," she began, and my heart sank. Normally she called me "Stephie," so I knew this was serious. "My friend is a spiritualist, we had a session this morning, and she said that you are in very deep trouble of some sort."

"Oh?" I tried desperately to look surprised, but Mrs Reith kept staring into my eyes with such intensity that further evasive tactics were useless. Her next questions rattled me with their accuracy. "Have you been taken to any private houses? Have you seen the president since you've been here in Manila?" I couldn't breathe for a long moment. *Can I lie to this woman I dearly love, while looking directly into her eyes?*

In the hardest decision of my life I decided I loved her too much to tell her the truth, justifying to myself that if I did, Susie would be desperately fearful for me the next time I "disappeared" from her house. Sensing that she loved me almost like the daughter she never had, I knew she would do anything to protect me, even if by doing so she put herself in danger. My face felt unbearably hot and my voice sounded high and false as I spun the lie, ending with, "But I didn't want to stay by myself at the hotel. I wanted to stay here, to be with you. So . . . so you don't have to worry." Her beautiful brown eyes hardened. She knew I was lying. Nothing would ever be the same again, and at that moment I hated secret houses, Colonel Ver, and most of all President Marcos. A few tears ran down my cheeks, and it was then she turned away. I could see she was mulling over in her mind what to do. Without looking at me she asked, "Would you like to come with us to the movies tonight?"

Overwhelmed with gratitude I told her I would love nothing better. Just to escape with people I knew and to feel safe for another night was my prime aim, and I dared to hope it was Mrs Reith's aim too. From all the strange late phone calls and comings and goings, she must have guessed from the very first night I landed on her front doorstep that all was not right.

At 6 P.M. the colonel rang with the blunt message "He wants to see you tonight." Although I had been expecting this for days, I nearly dropped the phone. Mrs Reith wasn't far away, and I braced myself to sound as casual as if I were talking to Lim. "I can't I'm afraid," I told him. "I have an important engagement tonight with my host family."

Colonel Ver seemed at a loss for words. After a few stunned seconds he asked, "What engagement?"

"We're going to see a movie." It sounded lame.

Then he asked what I thought was an irrelevant question. "A movie? What movie?"

"Wait a minute please." I turned, in a louder voice asking Mrs Reith the title of the movie we'd be watching that night.

"*Far from the Madding Crowd*," she called.

It was perfect. The colonel now knew for certain I was telling the truth, but he was reluctant to give up so easily. "He will not be pleased."

I lowered my voice. "I'm sorry. But he must understand if I cancel going out with my hosts, they will become suspicious. They will ask awkward questions."

"I will do what I can," said the colonel, "but I can tell you, he will not be pleased."

"I'm sorry," I repeated.

He hung up.

I stood there feeling a flutter of triumph. It had been a small battle, but I had won.

* * *

The weekend was uneventful, and for that I was grateful. On Saturday morning I mucked around on the piano with George, who seemed to have forgiven me for ordering him to kill his frog. Then we were driven to the Makati shopping centre where I bought a very silly card to send to my beloved SJ. In it I emphasized what a lovely time I'd been having, and how the government had been treating me like royalty, and how I had enjoyed fabulous adventures such as riding the rapids at Pagsanjan Falls.

On Sunday afternoon I had a lovely surprise. Augustine tapped at my door to tell me I had a visitor. And there in the lounge room stood Jun with his shy buck-toothed smile, the last person I expected to see. *How on earth did he know where I was?* He told me that he had flown up to Manila with Dr Alvarez and Litong. It was sobering to realize just how fast word had spread around Zamboanga that the Australian girl had got it wrong about being invited to the president's home and instead was staying at Charlie Reith's mother's home. It seemed all the townsfolk knew. After Jun had taken his leave the phone rang, but to my delight the person ringing was not Colonel Ver, but Chito! We talked for only a short time, Chito full of anguish at the fact he had missed seeing me not once, but twice. It was a difficult conversation. I could tell him nothing of my predicament, and he was tortured with the fact he was physically unable to travel from Los Baños to visit me. After I had hung up I was filled with such deep longing to be with those people I loved again, to feel safe, to be in the arms of SJ or bouncing along in the jeep with The Serenaders.

My reverie was rudely broken when once again the phone clanged through the house. This time, my heart pounding, I knew it was the colonel. My hand trembled above the receiver, then I picked up. "The Reiths' residence, Stephanie speaking."

"He *will* see you tonight."

This small but emphatic statement told me I could no longer duck out of this second private meeting with the president. If he forced himself on me, I would have no chance of escaping with my virginity intact, and my mental state would not be good for a long time. *I need to stay calm on the outside, and strong on the inside. That way I might live to see my family again.* "Right," was all I could think of to say.

"You will be picked up at five thirty P.M."

I looked around. Nobody was in sight, so I didn't need to play the acting game.

"I will be ready," I said, and hung up.

* * *

Later that afternoon, in my white figure-hugging cotton dress, and carrying a small bag filled with bikini bottoms, a blue shirt, and a few essentials, I was picked up by Colonel Ver in a white Merc. He was not the kind of person you chatted to, so I said little as we cruised along, fragrance in the air and some sort of classical music playing softly from the speakers. It gave me that same uneasy feeling you get when musak softly pervades the aircraft cabin minutes before a plane negotiates a difficult landing.

Driving out of San Lorenzo Village we soon reached that vast empty land between the harsh reality of the slums and the luxurious cocoon of Forbes Park. I gave a sideways glance at Colonel Ver. His rugged face was grimmer and more intense than usual. Without warning, he swung the car up and over the kerb and headed across the dried grass and bumpy ground towards the middle of a paddock. He braked abruptly. My heart jumped into my mouth.

Colonel Ver leant across me, opened the glovebox, and pulled out a pistol. *This is how I disappear*, I told myself. *He will order me out of the car, murder me, and no one will ever know what happened.*

The colonel got out and headed for the back of the car. I could scarcely breathe. The door of the glovebox remained open. Seconds passed. *Why is he not coming around to my door and asking me to get out?* In a rare moment of superstition I reached to touch Rob's crucifix around my neck. It wasn't there! It was back on the Reiths' dressing table. I dared to look around. The big man was leaning against the trunk, facing outwards, waiting. I assumed he was holding the gun.

After a long five minutes he came around to my side of the car and opened the passenger door. This was it. *What will a bullet feel like as it explodes in my back? Surely even Marcos's strongman can't look me in the face and shoot. Can he?*

Carefully he leaned in, returned the gun to the glovebox, closed it, and retreated, pushing my door shut with a muted click. The whole time he had not said one word.

Fifteen years later, when Marcos's chief opposition Ninoy Aquino dared to return from exile, he had just set foot on the tarmac when he was surrounded by soldiers and shot in the head. Fabian Ver, now promoted to General by Marcos, was not only present at the airport but was in command of that vast military contingent ostensibly sent to the airport to escort Aquino "safely" to prison.

As we approached the grand entrance to Forbes Park, my heart had slowed enough to allow me to ask, "Why did you stop back there?"

"We were being followed," was all he said.

I felt I should pinch myself to wake up from this all too realistic nightmare. Instead, I did something to try to make events seem normal. Fumbling in my bag, I found my camera and snapped a picture through the windscreen. It didn't portray the opulence of the district at all—just the wide street ahead and some palms cresting the high walls of a property to the side.

"May I have your camera please?" asked the colonel, still driving, staring straight ahead. I handed it across. Without glancing at me he took it and placed it in the soft side pocket of his door. "I will return it to you when I drive you home." It didn't take a genius to work out why the president's right-hand man didn't want any pictures taken near a private house of the president, but it was just another sinister reminder that secrecy was essential—or else.

Vee was standing on the porch to welcome me when we cruised up the gravel drive. She seemed genuinely excited to see me again. I was shown into the bedroom, and Colonel Ver seemed to vanish into thin air.

"Would you like anything for dinner ma'am?" Although the very thought of food nauseated me I asked her for a fruit and cheese platter. This should occupy her while I figured out my next strategy.

After the shock of literally "dodging a bullet" in no-man's-land, I felt calmer in this house than on that first night. This was strange, because the threat of sexual assault and death on this second private meeting had actually ramped up a notch. Perhaps my mind had accepted that I needed to work out what to do one step at a time, just one step at a time.

Suddenly Colonel Ver reappeared and led me into the first room at the front, a small parlour. We stood face-to-face as he apologized. The president had been forced to cancel our meeting just minutes ago. As I struggled to come to terms with this new situation he added, "However, he intends to meet with you tomorrow night, here. Then on Tuesday morning you will be driven up to Baguio, and he will see you there too." It almost seemed as if the Marcos's chief aide was trying to cheer me up!

He handed over a white rectangular envelope, unsealed. "He wants you to have this, to spend in Baguio."

I took the envelope and one peek inside confirmed it was money, a lot of money. "I cannot accept this," I told Colonel Ver, who adopted his troubled look again, saying, "But you must, otherwise he will be very offended."

Slowly I lowered my arm. "Please tell the president I am grateful for his generosity."

During the drive back to the Reiths' I began agonizing over what I would say if anyone asked where I had been for such a short time in the evening. By the time the white Merc stopped at the front door, while I had my camera back again, I still hadn't thought up a plausible reason for an evening absence of less than two hours. And what if George or his mother had seen the white Merc rather than Lim's Toyota? But apart from Augustine I saw no one. It was my lucky night. Just one more meeting to survive at the secret house, and another in Baguio. As soon as was practical after that I could escape back to Zamboanga, having spent enough time in Manila to avoid awkward questions.

I made sure I was alone when I examined the contents of the envelope—five hundred pesos! A veritable fortune. I stared at it, aware of the horrible irony—accepting these riches made me feel wretched. Now I was well and truly beholden to the President of the Philippines.

Retiring to bed early, I tossed and turned and tore at my perfectly manicured nails, my brain doing somersaults as it tried to find a way to extricate myself from every possible scenario. By midnight I had come to the scary decision that if Marcos forced himself on me, I would have to submit. Screaming or physically trying to fight him would be stupid and dangerous. My only chance—and this seemed a very feeble one—was to make it clear that if he did overpower me any friendship between us would be forfeited. *But, will he choose sex over friendship?* I had no way of knowing, but one thing was certain—utmost secrecy would need to be maintained. My life was more important than my virginity. With that imperfect plan made by midnight, I fell into a troubled sleep.

My third meeting with President Marcos
Location: Forbes Park, Manila

As expected, late that afternoon Colonel Ver rang to state he would pick me up at 5 P.M. I dressed and packed like I had done the night before, but this time I wore Rob's gold crucifix. I knew that if George or Susie Reith later questioned Augustine about my whereabouts, all he could say was that I had gone out.

On the drive to Forbes Park I took more notice of the colonel. His eyes repeatedly darted to the rear-vision mirror, but this time it seemed we were not being shadowed as we cruised towards Millionaires' Row. As the high gates slid open and we slowly approached the porch, as usual Vee was standing there with her beaming smile. After she escorted me to the bedroom I placed my little bag on one of the chairs, but this time I didn't hole up there like a scared mouse. Instead, I wandered around the dining and lounge room, examining the beautiful furniture and the few exquisite ornaments. Outside the little lights were twinkling all over the vast acreage of lawns and high up in the foliage of the palms. I slid open the glass doors and gazed at this fairyland, but I was more interested in the pool, lit up and sparkling. *Just one of my strategies to distract the president.*

No sooner had I returned inside to the dining room than Vee rushed from the kitchen. "The president is coming ma'am!" she cried. As I turned towards the front door she called, "No! This way ma'am!" Becoming aware of a mechanical thudding sound towards the rear of the property, I swung round to see the lights of a helicopter landing fifty metres away on the lawn. I remember thinking, *Why does anything surprise me anymore?* Taking a deep breath, dreading the time to come, I slid open the glass doors and stepped out to greet the president. Ducking briefly to avoid the rotors he bounded towards me with a huge smile on his face. The chopper lifted sideways into the night sky over the high stone wall, then vanished.

Apart from the chopper, the initial part of this meeting was almost identical to my previous private meeting with President Marcos. He was ravenously hungry, ordering a hamburger from Vee who was hovering in the kitchen. We sat at the dining table while I described my wonderful experience shooting the rapids at Pagsanjan Falls, but apart from that it was light chit-chat until Vee appeared with a wondrous looking burger. What he drank I have no idea. All I could think about was how I was going to survive the rest of the night. When Marcos finished his burger he got up and put on the slow dance record, and once again we danced, he becoming ever more amorous, nuzzling into my neck and trying to kiss me. Gently I pulled away. "Why don't we go swimming in that beautiful pool," I suggested.

"I haven't got any swimmers," he said, with a hint of triumph.

My brain raced. "You can swim in your underpants." *Have I really said that?*

Before he could refuse, other words with a life of their own emerged from my mouth. "I'll change into my bathers in the bathroom and meet you outside at the pool." With that I walked into the bedroom and grabbed up my little bag.

As I entered the ensuite bathroom I glanced back to see him wandering into the bedroom, looking bemused. I closed the door and hoped for the best, twisting to unzip the back of my white cotton dress. I let it slide down around my waist so that I could slip into the little blue shirt before tying the knot at the midriff.

I had just let the dress fall to the tiles, removed my panties and pulled up my bikini bottoms when the door opened and he was standing there, a trim figure in close-fitting underpants. His chest was smooth and his body toned. "Can you bring some towels?" I asked before darting off through the tight single room and into the conservatory that led to the pool.

The swimming scene was farcical. Diving in the deep end I swam a fast lap, Marcos splashing somewhere behind me. Then I jumped out and ran around to the deep end, repeating this "game" multiple times.

My suspicions about him being a good swimmer were confirmed. Each lap he gained on me. Even I was puffing by the time he stopped, saying "I'm tired. Shall we go inside?"

And so, literally, the game was up. The next few hours would be crucial. We towelled ourselves off before retracing our steps to the ensuite bathroom. He asked if I'd like to shower. "Yes please," I said. "If you wait in the bedroom, I'll be out in a minute."

Obediently he walked into the master bedroom. Quietly I shut the door behind him. Like lightning I stripped, had a one-minute shower, dried myself with a lovely fluffy towel, jumped into my panties, and grabbed up my bras. They were sopping. Cursing myself for not bringing another pair, I fastened the wet ones on and slipped into my cotton dress. As I reached behind to pull up the zip, Marcos walked into the bathroom, still in his damp underpants.

"Would you like some help with that?" he asked, immediately beginning to close the long zip which went all the way up to the neck. His body was way too close, and one of his hands was caressing the side of my breast. The zip was halfway up when he stopped. "Your bras are wet." I looked down at my front to see the wet bras showing through the white cotton of the dress.

"It doesn't matter," I chirped. "I'll finish dressing in the bedroom." And looking straight ahead I scurried out through the doorway.

The door remained open throughout Marcos's shower, and while alone I almost wrenched my shoulder in efforts to reach over and draw up the zip to the nape of the neck. Eventually, fully dressed including my white sandals, I sat at the round wooden table, the one topped with the bottle of whisky and two crystal glasses.

When he entered the room my heart sank to see that he was still in underpants. He came towards me, tut-tutting about my bras. "Here, let me unzip your dress. Your bras are wet. You must let me take your dress off."

In tones low and firm, I said, "No."

"But you could get a cold or something. You should really take your dress off."

Shaking my head slowly, with kindness in my tone, I repeated, "No."

He turned and went to the bed, hopped up and lay on his back. He patted the space next to him. "Come on, lie down next to me."

I stood up from the table. "I'm sorry, but no."

The president was rattled. He sighed. "I tell you what, lie down next to me, and I promise I won't hurt you."

Gingerly I walked to the bed, positioning myself carefully so that I was positioned as far away from him as possible, still with my sandals on which made the point that I was not going to get naked of my own free will. He patted the snowy white coverlet. "We will talk. Come a little closer." Feeling that to refuse this small command would be childish, I edged an inch further towards him. And then he took my hand. At that point I was certain he was going to roll on top of me and that would be it.

But then the strangest, most unexpected thing happened. We began talking. With genuine admiration I praised his speech at the Zamboanga airport three weeks earlier, describing how he had held the crowd in the palm of his hand. "You said that you got shot during the battle against the Japanese on Bataan Peninsula," I said. "How badly were you injured?"

"Ah," said Marcos, obviously thrilled that I had asked. He rolled a little so that his bare back was facing me. "Can you see it? They would not operate. It was too close to the spine."

Immediately I saw—below the shoulders—the cylindrical shape of a bullet near his backbone. "Can you feel it?" When I didn't hasten to touch it, he lifted my hand and guided my fingers until they were caressing the bullet shape under the skin. It was creepy, but at the same time I was intrigued.

With the second topic it was Marcos who asked the question. "No Philippines president has ever won a second term of office. Do you think I will be returned in the next election?"

In that moment I forgot about Senator Salonga, the humble man who had visited Zambo many months before and who had proved himself an orator equally as charismatic as Marcos, a man of the people who had risen from poverty to become Marcos's main rival. "I hope you do," I said, and I meant it. The president turned his face towards me. "Why is that Stephanie?" I had remembered part of Marcos's speech where he seemed genuinely passionate to build a better Philippines, literally. "Because everywhere I go in your country I see bridges and roads under construction. You need another term so that you can complete these infrastructures."

"Quite right, quite right," exclaimed Marcos, his eyes shining.

I recalled my traumatic visit to the Manila hospital, where I had seen Werner's blinded cousin and other shockingly injured patients lying in the corridors. "And hospitals," I added. "It would be a great legacy to create hospitals which have beds for the poor as well as the rich."

My seventeen-year-old idealism was on a roll, although it became obvious that the president did not seem nearly as thrilled by the idea of new hospitals as he had been with images of spectacular highways and bridges. "Yes, good girl," was all he said.

The third and last topic of conversation astounds me to this day. I'm not sure what led to my question, but perhaps only a teenage upstart will go where more mature angels fear to tread.

"I heard that a long time ago you were accused of murdering your father's political opponent, while he was cleaning his teeth!"

Marcos looked directly at me with a half-smile. "Yes, that's right."

Most wise adults would have left it at that and moved on, but not me. "So, did you do it?"

His answer summed up his smoothness, charm, and his sharpness of mind. For me it also confirmed his guilt. "I proved I was somewhere else at the time."

A knock at the door, but of course it did not open. Releasing my hand, which he had held all the time, Marcos calmly rolled from the bed, threw on a satin gown, and went to the door. I took the opportunity to roll from the bed and sit at the table. Through the closed door I could hear muffled male voices, and then Marcos returned alone. He came to me, placed his hands gently on my shoulders, and tried to kiss me on the mouth. Once again, I turned my face so that his lips brushed my cheek. "Stephanie," he said, "I am so sorry, but we have had a visit from the Turkish ambassador and his wife. I must leave you now.'"

"Of course you must," I said, trying to hide my relief. It was strangely late in the evening for anyone to make a social call at the palace, but I felt immense gratitude to the Turkish ambassador and his wife.

On his way to the single room to get dressed the president glanced back. "So I will see you in Baguio on Wednesday night, yes?"

"Yes, evidently."

"You will have a wonderful time in Baguio. There is a lot to see."

"Thank you, Mr President."

During the drive home with the colonel I felt numb with disbelief at how once again it seemed I had dodged a bullet—and how at one stage I had ordered the President of the Philippines around as if he were one of my swimming pupils. The whole evening, loaded with fear and uncertainty, had taken its toll on me. Instead of looking forward to the next day I felt nothing but dread. The longer the secret meetings went on, the bolder Marcos would become, and I knew that in the holiday resort town of Baguio there would be few official duties to distract him.

* * *

It was now Tuesday. By 7.30 A.M. I was seated in a car with the Danish couple, the Simonsens, heading north towards Baguio. Our guide was not Lim, but a man called Poy. It was going to be a long trip, much of it over the hot dusty plains of several provinces. I found the Danes to be dignified and interesting, their stories of Greenland and Iceland with their extreme winter climates intriguing for a South Australian who had never even experienced snow.

One of the cities we passed through was sprawling Angeles, in real life as seedy and unlovely as its reputation. Teeming with brothels and nightclubs, it was a hotbed of American soldiers on leave from the nearby Clark Airbase. There were no beautiful white beaches or jungle-clad mountains to refresh the soul or gladden the eye. Instead, the miserable poverty of the surrounding slums was all-pervading, a fierce desperation hanging in the dirt-heavy atmosphere. Poy would not allow us to get out of the car to take a photo. As we left the city we could see Mt Pinatubo rising from the plains in the far west.

This volcano would erupt in 1991, one of the world's worst-ever eruptions in a densely populated area.

We continued north into territory dominated by the Huks, a communistic peasant guerilla movement which had continued to fight against the Philippine Government ever since they put aside their differences to join the Allies in the World War II struggle to oust the Japanese. When we arrived at towns more benign than Angeles, although Poy allowed us out of the car, he took great pains to explain to curious bystanders that we were *not* American. We skirted around Tarlac city, Poy explaining that less than a month ago the Huks had attacked it, and that another attack was expected in about a week's time. It seemed that in this desperately deprived part of the country the pro-active peasants had decided to continue their war against the American and Philippine governments whom they saw as complicit in aiding and abetting the ever-widening gap between the rich and the poor.

At about 2 P.M. we arrived at the town where Poy lived with his family, so he took a detour down a dusty side street and stopped outside one of the tiny huts. As we got out I grabbed my camera and my bag which contained the envelope with the 500P. We were welcomed into the hut and sat on the floor while Poy's wife served us a modest meal of bread, dried fish, and fried egg. Having been surprised to see some calesas in this part of the country, a few minutes before the others got up from lunch I took my camera and stood outside the front of the house to wait for a calesa to pass. Each horse seemed healthier than those in Zamboanga, and Poy told me the calesas were gradually being replaced by tricycles.

Soon my companions emerged and we climbed back into the car. Throughout the sightseeing I had been cooking up a plan, a plan that involved flying out of Baguio some time the following day. If all went smoothly I'd spend Wednesday night at the Reiths' home instead of the president's private residence in Baguio. Then—I would fly back to Zamboanga the very next day. To all my friends, family, and Rotarians it would seem as if I had simply decided to return a few days short of the two-weeks holiday in Luzon.

By 3 P.M. we began climbing steeply up from the plains on a narrow road spiraling around the mountainside. Occasionally we could glimpse great canyons and rivers and waterfalls, and one sight I will never forget was two barefooted men bearing a pole on their shoulders walking towards us down the mountain. In the centre of the pole was a dog trussed upside down and crudely muzzled. It wasn't hard to guess the fate of this poor canine, and as our family had always loved dogs it was almost impossible to disguise my anguish. When I glanced at the Simonsens they seemed equally upset, which helped me to bite my tongue. None of us said a word, but memories of the ill-treated calesa horses in Zamboanga came flooding back, and helplessness and anger almost overwhelmed me. It wasn't that I was precious about animals being killed and eaten throughout Asia, but rather the needless cruelty inflicted on animals before they were killed.

The air became magically cooler until we began to see pines growing, the first I had seen in the Philippines. We had almost reached Baguio when I realized with a sickening jolt that I had left my handbag behind in Poy's house. I apologized profusely, but without a second thought Poy offered to show us into our hotel, to help me buy some woodcarvings at the market with the money he would lend me, and while his clients were enjoying dinner, to return and collect the bag. I felt wretched putting him to all that inconvenience.

It was 4.30 P.M. when we reached the Milton Hotel, which was very grand indeed. Quickly the Simonsens and I checked in before returning to the car and heading to the city markets. Immense and humming with life, this place housed the famous Igorot woodcarvers of Baguio. For the first time since I had landed in the Philippines, I enjoyed the bargaining, although my tactics weren't exactly slick. When I saw the price for a bowl of wooden fruit or a glorious rearing stallion, I would exclaim "Oh, I can get a lot cheaper in Zamboanga down south." I'd turn away, and when the vendors invariably pounced on me with a new price, I'd accept it immediately. To have overplayed the wealthy Westerner against these gifted artisans would have been obscene. I also bought one giant passionfruit and a jar of homemade strawberry jam to give to Mrs Reith.

Police whistles pierced the air, sounding the curfew that signaled it was time for vendors to pack up and customers to leave.

Back at the hotel I showered and dressed for dinner, joining the Scandinavian tourists in the dining room. Having been advised by Poy that I could choose whatever I fancied for dinner, I ordered all kinds of delicacies so that my companions could share them with me. For dessert I chose plain vanilla ice cream, and to the amusement of the Simonsens I brought out the passionfruit and squeezed it over the top.

By early the next morning my escape plan needed to be activated. All showered and dressed I was about to head off to the dining room when Poy knocked at the door and handed over my bag. Immediately I found the envelope containing the president's gift and repaid Poy the one hundred pesos owed to him plus a thirty pesos tip.

My reward was a beaming smile from Poy. "What would you like to see today ma-am?" he asked.

"I'd like to buy some more woodcarvings at the market," I told him.

"Certainly ma'am."

"And then I'd like to fly back to Manila please."

Poy's smile vanished. "Today, ma'am?"

I nodded. "As soon as possible this morning, thank you."

My poor guide stammered out a description of the rice terraces of Baguio, carved out and irrigated ingeniously by the descendants of the Ifugao thousands of years ago. It was a given that this Eighth Wonder of the World would have been an unforgettable experience, but another night with the president looked like proving equally memorable for all the wrong reasons. "I'm sorry Poy," I said, "But I need to return to Manila, urgently."

Like a beaten dog Poy made his way back down the corridor, and I noticed he had to pick his way past a cluster of workers who were squatting mending a patch of flooring in the corridor.

Before leaving my room I decided to grab 100P from the envelope and put it into the purse in my bag. Although I took special care to lock the door, to have left that envelope containing 270P in full view was naïve to say the least, but Aussies in the 50s and 60s rarely gave a thought to locking our houses when we went out for a short while. Clutching my handbag, I nodded good morning to the workers before descending in the lift to the dining room. The Simonsens did not appear so I dined alone, and then Poy arrived to say that he had organised my ticket for a plane departing at 8 A.M. I hastened back to the lift, and as I reached the second level I stepped out to see the workmen still bent over the floor. Once again I greeted them, but this time they kept their heads down. Because Filipinos on the lowest rungs of society often found it difficult to engage directly with those on the higher rung, I didn't think much of it, until I reached my room. There, of course, I found the envelope to be empty.

Storming from my room I stopped near the workers. In a mix of Spanish and English I asked whether anyone had entered my room while I was away, but they just shrugged and looked blank as if they had no idea what was upsetting me. I was about to descend in the lift again to report the missing money, when a thought hit me. *This fortune has never really been mine in the first place. It belongs to the people of the Philippines. If that money can help those workmen in the smallest way, then I'm happy!*

By 6.30 A.M. Poy and I were standing in the markets which were coming to life again, and for an hour or so I browsed, buying two more woodcarvings which Poy promised to package up and send to Australia courtesy of the government. We got back in the car and Poy drove 6 km or so down through the mountains until we came to a small airstrip. He offloaded my case and we waited for the plane. There was the usual delay, so in the meantime I studied the other passengers. Six of them were Japanese who had evidently come to visit a famous faith-healer in Baguio, but it seemed not all of them had been thoroughly cured, several needing to be carried on board the DC3 when it finally touched down.

It was a short but turbulent trip over the mountains to Manila. Lim was there to meet me. Thankfully he made no comment about my lightning Baguio visit, so no awkward questions needed answering. He dropped me off at the Reiths', and thankfully the ever-inquisitive George didn't put me on the spot either. He and I spent the time "composing" duets on the piano and laughing at our efforts. Then he spotted the battered old case I had brought from Australia. "You need a new suitcase Stephie," he proclaimed. "And it will need to be much bigger."

George was right. In the early afternoon the Reiths' driver took us to the Makati shopping centre where I purchased a huge suitcase for a very reasonable price, even though there was no bargaining allowed in such an upmarket establishment. Back "home" I grew tense as the afternoon wore on, fearing that a call would come through from a very angry Colonel Ver. But the phone didn't ring, and with more hope than I'd dared to feel in days, I sensed that safety of a kind was less than twenty-four hours away.

* * *

By 11.30 A.M. I was at Manila airport with my new case filled with several precious woodcarvings wrapped in my clothes to protect them. In typical Filipino fashion word had got round that I would be catching this plane, so during the two-hour delay I had great fun chatting with not only George, but Artu Lopez and Jun, and even Raymond Bader who was booked on the same plane back to Zamboanga. I noticed a Westerner in the crowd who seemed vaguely familiar, and after climbing aboard I found myself seated next to him. Soon I remembered. Three weeks earlier he had been one of the foreign reporters at the Zambo airport when President Marcos gave his speech. We introduced ourselves. His name was Garth Alexander, a British press correspondent who covered most of the big news all over Asia. He asked what I had been doing in Manila, but I was adept at telling the same old lie by this time—that my idea of being a guest at Malacañang, or even seeing the president had been ridiculous, and that all my time had been filled with generous tours.

Garth told me that while in Luzon he had been compiling an article about the Huks, the communist peasants who were waging war against the rich in northern Philippines. This freelance journalist, based in Djakarta, wrote for no less than twelve different newspapers around the world, the biggest of which included the *Daily Express* and the *Economist*. Travelling over all corners of Asia, Garth had spent time in Papua New

Guinea a few months earlier, interviewing hundreds who feared the imminent takeover by Indonesia.

Garth Alexander went on to write a book about the growing Chinese influence in SE Asia. Silent Invasion *was published by Ateneo de Manila Press in 1973.*

Garth's visa had run out two weeks earlier, and so his only way out of the country was to board a smuggling boat heading for Sabah. He explained if he got caught there would be "a hell of a row," adding, "I'm used to that." I'm not sure whether he was referring to pirates or Philippine police, but it was obvious this was one intrepid journalist who would risk great danger to get a good story.

Late October 1968
Location: Tetuan, Zamboanga
Host family — Araneta

That evening, when unpacking my new case at the Araneta's, Garth rang to ask whether I'd like to see a movie that evening. By that time, although I was beginning to unwind from the unrelenting tension over the last twelve days, exhaustion had set in through to my bones. Reluctantly I declined the invitation, but during our chat on the phone he casually informed me that the reason he wanted to see this film was that his father was one of the main actors! Garth confided that he had found a vinta to take him to Sabah, and that it would be departing under cover of darkness in the wee hours the following morning.

During my twelve days in Luzon, *The Advertiser* had printed a small article with a photo of me in my white one-piece bathers, the news cutting arriving a few days after I returned to Zamboanga. Headlined "Stephanie in the Swim," the opening paragraph read, "Teaching Filipino children to swim has helped to earn a seventeen-year-old girl an invitation to visit the Manila palace of President Marcos of the Philippines and teach him to swim." This article confirmed to me that both in Australia and the Philippines it was understood that I had been invited, openly by the president, to his home at the palace.

Soon after I arrived "home" was All Souls' Day, a public holiday when most Filipinos headed for the cemetery to visit their deceased loved ones. The dead are honoured by a feast of food, flowers, and even candles, and while the children frolic the adults sit and chat by the gravesites as everyone enjoys a picnic lunch. Feeling too burdened with my recent experience to participate in any picnicking, I decided to show Rob my secret letter. After all, it was addressed to him, and the immediate danger seemed over. There was also one gold icon to return to him, and although I doubted that God had stepped in to save me, I had to admit just having that crucifix around my neck had comforted me over that critical twelve days in Manila.

The all-important letter safely secreted in my handbag, I took a tricycle across to Santa Maria. After visiting Ma Alvarez to give her a hug I wandered across the road to see Rob. The first thing Rob did was to look me direct in the eye and ask me what had happened. I simply handed him the letter and sat down in a chair. After about one page his face began to redden, and when he reached page eight he slammed down the sheaves of tissue-thin pages. "You let him kiss you!" It was more of an outraged statement than a question. Now it was my face turning red, shocked.

"Not exactly, not on the mouth, he was nuzzling into my neck."

Rob loomed over me, close to shouting. "You let him nuzzle your neck?"

I could feel my jaw dropping, and I felt sick to the pit of my stomach. Rob's verbal attack stunned me. I was expecting outrage, yes, but against President Marcos, not with me. My reply seemed lame, my voice trembling. "What else was I supposed to do?"

"You should have resisted more strongly!"

Suddenly I was angry. "Like how? Like break away and scream?"

"Yes!"

"Well, I might not be standing here in front of you if I'd done that!"

My instincts proved to be well-founded. In 2017 South Australian media personality Jane Riley revealed on radio 5AA that in 1975 she won a beauty competition trip to Asia which included the Philippines. Finding herself alone with Marcos on the presidential yacht, she told him she would scream if touched her, whereupon he replied that if she did that, his minders would promptly attend, and it wouldn't be him who was shot!

Silence followed, Rob and I glaring at each other. Abruptly he sat down and read to where I had abandoned my story a few days before my final and most complex encounter with Marcos. "Did you see him again after that?" Rob demanded. I nodded, but added I would walk away with my letter right now unless he tried to see things from my point of view.

Reluctantly he agreed, and I told him everything, about how I thought I would die in no-man's-land by a bullet from Colonel Ver's gun; about how I had tried to tire out Marcos in the pool; about how I had just kept saying "no" and refusing to take off my dress; about how the president and I had talked for almost an hour lying side by side on the bed, him in his underpants, me in my white dress with wet bras; about how I fled from Baguio after only one night in the city.

We briefly discussed whether we would tell Jun when he returned from Manila, and I decided that I would. Jun would have died rather than reveal any secret that might have potentially harmed me, and so he deserved to know the truth. "No one else will know, until I get back to Australia," I declared to Rob. From that meeting I knew nothing would be quite the same between Rob and me. His impossible standards of morality had made me feel ashamed and wretched, but my inner voice told me his judgement was unfair. Seated in a tricycle back to the Araneta's I resolved not to brood on Rob's reaction. Some immediate and important issues needed attention. One was my Spanish exam to be faced on Monday; another was writing multiple dutiful letters back home; and yet another involved moving to Tony and Lotti Mas's residence atop Pasonanca Park. For one whole month I would have less than a five-minute walk to that glorious mountain pool.

A few days after I arrived back in Zambo, dear Hilda Araneta wrote a lovely letter to my mother, telling her that I had come second in my class Spanish exam while kindly omitting the word *Beginners*. Plump and motherly, Hilda added that I had taught her an exercise to make the stomach flat "which my husband and I follow regularly in the morning. We are proud to have her around." After stating that she and Po would always welcome me at their home, she wrote, "There's nothing to worry about Stephie now, really. My husband and I were for a while worried about her going to Manila. There had been pro and con on the invitation of the president, but thank heavens, it all turned out for the better and for Stephie's advantage most of all."

Whew. It seemed that the local Rotarians had swallowed my story, except for Charlie Reith whom I could rely on to keep his thoughts to himself. As long as Marcos did not try to contact me, I could breathe easy for the time being. Jun arrived back at the Alvarez home the day after I confided in Rob, and so I took a deep breath and told him everything. My belief in him was justified. He responded with nothing but sympathy and total understanding about why it was necessary to keep the whole experience a secret until I returned safely to Australia.

The following day Jun and I accompanied Rob to the airport. He was headed for a two-week Peace Corps conference in Cebu, and because this sprawling city was dusty, hot and flat he didn't look happy. As the airplane took off and headed north Jun dropped me back to the Araneta's in time for Jo-Jo to scoop me up for a swim at beautiful Caragasan. To my surprise Father McNally, principal of Ateneo College, was there alone about to take a dip, and so for at least an hour Jo-Jo and I lounged around in the sparkling green water having an in-depth conversation with the big Jesuit. He asked me how I had enjoyed my recent trip to Manila, and by this time I had little difficulty in spinning the much-practiced half-lie, half-truth.

* * *

Even though most tertiary students were arriving home from Manila, my lessons at Ateneo increased. I ditched History in favour of Advanced Spanish, recommenced Beginners Spanish, and even hung on to English Shakespeare. Most Atenean lessons were held in the late afternoon and evening, while three mornings of each week were taken up teaching children to swim, and almost every Saturday morning there was the usual collegiate softball match.

Student friends often drove me home at night, but during the daytime my transport was usually aboard jeepneys, my least favourite method of getting around. These vehicles were always crammed with people (often in need of a wash) along with sacks of various produce and baskets of fish. One day there were two mentally disabled men on board, and for some unknown reason the driver took us all over the place picking up sacks of copra and rice before we finally headed for the correct destination. By this time, however, I had learned to accept whatever weird events were going on and make the best of things.

And then there were the parties. In one day I would teach swimming in the morning, then be taken out by friends for a picnic, followed by lessons at Ateneo then perhaps a party at someone's home where I would dance under the stars until I dropped. Sometimes the parties were simply eat-fests, and even the poorest of families on significant occasions would feature the lechon (pig on a spit) amongst the plainer food of rice and noodles. Upon my arrival at any festivity the hostess would rush towards me with a plateful of pork crackling, the prime delicacy, before showing me to the most comfortable seat. As the spoiling and festivities continued I was able to quell my recent trauma to some extent. However, there were still two months to go before I boarded that Qantas plane for my Australian home where I could relax. And feel safe.

By this time the *Beacon* had published my short and sharp article about the Sabah issue. Back in South Australia, a Mr Chinner from *The Advertiser* had somehow seen it and invited me to send him another longer one for Australian readers, which I promptly wrote. However, without my permission two other local newspapers, *Mindanao Life* and *Southern Tribune* published the shorter version. No sooner had it hit the press than a DJ radio delivered a five-minute verbal attack on me. DXJW was the station which employed Jun as a drama series writer and which had praised my performances in his radio series, so it goes without saying that he and others of my staunch friends were livid, leaping into a verbal brawl to defend me. Having not heard the rant I was more intrigued than upset. As every fact in the piece was verifiable, on what grounds had I been attacked? I wrote home with the flippant remark "there could be nothing to criticize except my standard of journalism!"

Vic Solis urged me to allow my longer article to be published in the next issue of the *Beacon*, but just to reassure myself that there was nothing there that could give offence to any reasonable person, I ran it past other student journalists, Father McNally, and Hilda and Po Araneta. All of them praised it, the consensus being that the DJ was a rat. Consequently I threw caution to the wind and offered it up, resolving not to be thin-skinned should the reaction be negative. Although the article was splashed across the front page, all remained uneventful after the publication. Perhaps the DJ had been shamed into silence. And what did I learn from this? Nothing really, except that no journalist who ventures into politics can please all her readers all the time.

* * *

A letter arrived from Australia that took my breath away. It was from my beloved SJ, who claimed he had experienced a realistic dream where I was obsessed with a secret letter. Waking with the overpowering feeling that something was wrong, he had spent the next day trying to secure a berth aboard a Russian freighter bound for the Philippines so that he could see for himself that I was okay. Failing in that, he began entertaining the whacky idea of setting out on a yacht heading for Mindanao. Deeply moved but very alarmed, I wrote back immediately. "Don't tell this to anyone darling, but something did happen in Manila which scared me more than anything has ever scared me before, and while it was occurring I wrote about it in a letter because I couldn't tell anyone or confide. It was imperative that no one find this letter, and I lived in fear and dread each day that someone would find it. I will tell you all about it when I come home . . ."

I poured water on his yacht idea with the blunt warning, "If you sail anywhere near here the bandits would get you before you could shout 'Land Ho!'" but ended with "You ask why I love you? I don't know . . . I just accept the fact that when you kiss me everything goes topsy turvy . . ."

Location: Pasonanca, Zamboanga
Host family — Mas

Early in November I moved into the home of Lottie and Tony Mas. Much like the Lopez-Vitos, the Mas family was large and employed multiple maids and manservants. The house was quite modern with a vast number of rooms, and from one aspect it offered a breathtaking view of the volcanic mountain Pulong Bato, rearing up out of dense jungle. I was introduced to each of the children, their ages ranging from early twenties to a three-year-old nicknamed Tiger, a devilish little fellow and the apple of everyone's eye. I had already become acquainted with the three teenage sisters who had been amongst my first swimming pupils, and they were as unassuming as Tiger was full-on. I had a bedroom to myself which I appreciated, and although it was small and modest it was private and kept spotlessly clean by the maids.

On the second day of my arrival I was gobbling down a glorious breakfast when Lotti (Mummy) appeared from the kitchen where she liked to cook, albeit with maids helping. She asked if I had a long "mumu" dress to wear to the Rotary gathering that night. Because I didn't own one Mrs Mas insisted on giving me ten pesos to buy some material for the dress, and I was thankful but bewildered. The party was that very night, and my swimming lessons were at 10.30 A.M. How was that going to work? As usual in the Philippines, the impossible somehow happened. One of my "brothers" drove me down to the dockside markets where I hastily bought the material before we sped to a seamstress who agreed to make my dress within the day. Although I managed to arrive at Pasonanca Pool with a quarter of an hour to spare, already a record number of pupils had gathered, including the three Mas teenagers who were progressing with incredible speed. They became faster than me at breaststroke, a swim stroke that had never been my forte.

At 1 P.M. I walked the one hundred yards over the hill to the Mas house atop Pasonanca Park, had lunch, and fell asleep. A friend called by to pick me up for a swim at Caragasan, but luckily Lotti decided not to wake me up and gifted me a much-needed siesta. Upon waking it was another rush downtown to collect my dress and visit Angie's House of Charm for a manicure and hair set, still free in exchange for teaching Mrs Ebby's girls to swim.

At the Rotary get-together my new dad was invited to sing. Tony Mas may have been a small man, but his voice was huge, and I can remember listening with awe as his glorious baritone voice reached the stars from the hotel rooftop.

Afterwards we drove in various cars to another lavish party set in the height of luxury amongst palms and flowers and waterfalls. Most of my Atenean friends were there, so I felt right at home. All we girls in our bright-coloured mumus danced non-stop under a wondrous full moon, and once again it wasn't until the wee hours that we returned home. Neither Hans or Rosie, Charlie or the Velosos, in fact not one Rotarian mentioned a word about my trip to Luzon. They behaved as if I had never been away at all. Charlie, of course, twigged my story was full of holes, but luckily for me he decided to keep his suspicions to himself. As for the others, they may have avoided the subject, assuming I would be embarrassed that I had neither stayed at Malacañang Palace nor clapped eyes on their president.

* * *

The following morning I played with Tiger. The object of our game was to see if we could get away from his nanny who kept following us around. Because she couldn't speak English, she could not understand that we wanted to play by ourselves.

Even if she had understood, with hindsight I now understand that if anything untoward had happened to the family's favourite child, life would not have been worth living for this poor young woman.

Tiger and I finally managed to hide from her, and from that moment a bond was formed between the two of us. However, two weeks later I was standing in the driveway when Tiger flew into a tantrum and started hitting his nanny, who meekly accepted his blows. I was furious and told him off, only vaguely conscious that some of his brothers and sisters stood by agog with disbelief. *Little Tiger being chastised, just because he hit his nanny?*

I told Tiger to say sorry to his victim. He refused. I said I was very disappointed in him, then strode off out of sight to the back garden where I stood, breathing heavily, looking out over Pulong Bato. Then something interesting happened. The young boy appeared round the corner of the house and capered around, trying to make me laugh. I kept my face stern, and after a few minutes he came up and said he was sorry, his big brown eyes brimming with tears. Immediately I bent down and hugged him (even though he had apologized to the wrong person) and made him promise to never hurt his nanny again.

* * *

I was to be the special guest of a group of Muslim students headed by Ali, the successful DJ with the wide smile who had rescued me from the mosque incident in his town of Rio Hondo.

Loyal Jun got up before dawn so he could pick me up and deliver me down to the docks in time to catch the large ferry to Basilan Island. Ali was waiting there along with fourteen young Muslims, specially selected students and teachers granted scholarships by the Commission of National Integration. The CNI had been formed a decade before to enable at least some young Muslims to attend advanced schools and tertiary colleges. There was a photographer too, whose job it was to take a snapshot of me interacting with the different Muslim communities at every opportunity.

After an uneventful voyage across the strait, we arrived at the wharf in Basilan where two Muslim leaders waited to greet us. The group of us trudged through the hot dusty town to the Isabella High School where, in the rear of the assembly hall, we were served a breakfast of super sweet coffee and noodles. After that we were ushered into a hall and a mass assembly where I was guided up to the stage by Ali and expected to deliver a speech. Ali's speech was polished and well-prepared, but by now I had learned that speaking off-the-cuff was always better received. I talked in simple terms about my homeland, even mimicking a kangaroo hopping at one stage for comic relief.

Out into the bright sunlight our group straggled to where a small bus waited to take us to the outskirts of the town. Over the potholes we bounced until we arrived at the modest home of a Muslim councillor. There we were offered more simple food, and it was obvious from the expectant eyes upon me that I needed to appear ravenous. The matriarch of the family then presented me with a home-sewn gift, a frilly nylon bonnet to cover my hair. This was embarrassing. I could see that she expected me to put it on right there and then, and after I had done so she tied the ribbons at the front. The bonnet looked quaint and silly, but I kept it on as I sipped another sweet coffee. However, my discretion deserted me as we all got up to leave, and I casually pulled off the bonnet to place in my handbag. It was then that the matriarch jumped to her feet. With a gentle but rebuking smile she took the headpiece and once more arranged it carefully upon my head, tying the ribbons once more. It didn't particularly worry me that Muslim Filipinas covered their hair. In fact, a head covering in the tropical sun seemed very practical. But having it forced upon me left me quite conflicted. After all, I reasoned, how would the lady feel if she were visiting me in my Australian home, and I removed her head scarf?

Crammed into the bus we bounced out through dry, unlovely countryside until we came to another high school mostly occupied by the offspring of plantation laborers. I was taken into one enormous classroom while an English lesson was in progress, and inwardly I winced. It was learning by rote at its boring worst, and I wouldn't have blamed the kids if they hated English and school forever. Next we visited a small building where once more we were offered food, this time an array of oranges, biscuits, sandwiches and fruit juice. We travelled west to Lamitan, the second biggest town boasting a modern agricultural high school run by a

Me with Ali and his wonderful smile, Basilan Island.

Me as a guest in Moslem home, Basilan Island.

Jesuit priest. This delightful man led us into the canteen, on the off chance we were hungry! Feeling bloated by now we were about to board the bus when three policemen dressed in camouflage and packing M16 rifles sauntered up and began conferring with Ali. We weren't frightened, but their presence was a serious reminder that Basilan was not always a peaceful place. The tension heightened when they motioned us into the bus before climbing up and taking seats. Ali explained that he had requested the police to accompany us all the way for our protection, but they had only just appeared because of a mission they'd been engaged in elsewhere.

While the group stopped to visit one of the group's family, I asked if I could go to the market to see if I could find a bolo, one of those curved knives Raymond had used for hacking our way through the jungle at the base of Pulong Bato. At Ali's insistence the three policemen escorted me through the ramshackle cluster of stalls, but as it wasn't market day proper, most were closed. It was just as well I couldn't find the ferocious knife to take home to my brother, given the immediate circumstances where I was accompanied by no less than three men dressed in camouflage and armed with serious guns.

After glimpsing the sea sparkling through a grove of coconut palms, I requested a walk to the beach. They happily agreed, and our strange little group ended up on the seashore fringed with palms, gazing at a cluster of huts along the foreshore. A man emerged from a grove and began conversing with the police. To my surprise this chief stepped towards me, indicating I should follow him. We reached his home, slightly larger than the other dwellings, but still modest. While my escorts lingered outside the open door I walked inside. It took a few seconds for my brain to compute that this main room of the house was totally empty. The floor, which may have been concrete, was spotlessly clean, but there were no chairs, no table, nothing except one shelf affixed to the wooden wall. And on that shelf was a conch shell, its spotted brown and cream surface gleaming and the flash of secret orange inside. The sound of giggling trickled from a lean-to at the rear of the room, drawing my gaze to the tops of heads as the women of the home craned to peep through the high flywire window. Once again I longed to speak with them, but it seemed futile to ask, especially as the policemen loitered in full view just out from the doorway. Desperately searching for something nice to say, I exclaimed "Que hermosa concha!" Then, to my dismay, the chief leapt forward, grabbed the shell and took it to the rear where he handed it with terse orders through the doorway to the unseen women.

I started saying, "No, no!" but it was too late. The mistake was made. The only recourse left to me was to thank the man profusely in Chavacano when he presented me with a newspaper parcel—encasing the only ornament adorning his house.

Over the years this beautiful conch shell has taken pride of place on the mantel wherever I have lived. It serves to remind me of generosity and hospitality I will never forget.

When I returned to the house, the members of the CNI were eating yet again, even though we still hadn't had formal lunch! So it was back in the bus again with the three policemen, all of us hurtling along over a rutted track, our heads almost hitting the ceiling every time we lurched into a pothole. We became hysterical with laughter, barely noticing our surroundings when we pulled up outside the poorest of the poor Muslim villages, built over stinking swampland. Picking our way between tiny stilted wooden huts, on boardwalks barely covering the foul-smelling sludge beneath, we waved and smiled at the host of ragged urchins scampering all about us. We entered one of the bigger wooden huts. On the table was laid out a simple but delicious feast of fish, curry and green-pepper salad. Someone had remembered to tell the cook that the Australiana couldn't cope with hot spicy foods, and so the curry was toned down especially for me. Then someone, probably Ali, requested a song, so I belted out "Waltzing Matilda" which seemed to delight what had now become quite a crowd.

The ferry wouldn't leave for another two hours, so Ali suggested to the driver that if we hurried we could visit the large Menzi Corporation plantation. As the man behind the wheel had already proved he had a need for speed, once more we hurtled along several kilometres of dirt road, bouncing and laughing all the way until we came to the grand gated plantation. The different processing procedures of rubber, oil palms, cacao, and coffee were underway in vast separate sheds, and as we moved to inspect each one I was intrigued to see how the materials were developed from the raw products.

By 5 P.M. I was home with the Mas family at Pasonanca, naturally seeking an early night after such a huge day. Besides, I had to teach swimming for the next two mornings starting at 10 A.M., with classes still swelling in numbers.

* * *

Within the week Ali had asked me to join him on DXLL ostensibly to help him hold his hourly show together, but both of us aware that the serious agenda would come later when I interviewed Ali about Muslim/Christian relations in the region. The first hour was great fun—we chatted and laughed about everything under the sun until Jingy the guitarist stepped up to accompany me with "Hurry Sundown." I sang with great happiness knowing that Chito was due back in town any day now.

Then came the interview. With his sunny smile and intelligent responses, Ali made things easy, so by the end of the discussion we felt we had highlighted humanity and goodness in people from both sides of the coin, focusing on the similarities rather than the differences.

Several years after I returned to Australia, when President Marcos was stirring the political pot between Muslims and Christians to justify imposing martial law, I would learn to my horror that my foster father Tony Mas disappeared after visiting his coconut plantation on Basilan, one month before martial law was imposed in 1972. It seems likely that Tony was murdered by a Muslim gang in Basilan which was fast becoming known as "The Wild Wild West." Corporate plantations on the island, like the Menzi plantation, continued to be guarded by gun-happy paramilitary, but the small farms had no hope while Basilan's economy limped along the road to ruin. And the most tragic thing of all? During the years leading up to 1969, before Marcos's diabolical scheming to stay in power, there had been real progress towards achieving harmony between Muslim and Christian, especially amongst youth groups such as the Commission of National Integration who had so recently hosted me as special guest.

* * *

The day after the broadcast on DXLL Tony Mas rang me from his office to ask if I would show a German Rotary Foundation scholar from Cebu around town. Gerd was twenty-five years old, intelligent and funny, and I felt privileged to show him "my" Zamboanga. Deciding to once again brave a visit to Rio Hondo, the Muslim "barangay" (village) south of Fort Pilar, we took a jeepney downtown and walked across the park to the fort. I felt reasonably safe. After all, I had ensured that Ali would be at home, and I now understood that the inside of the mosque was out of bounds to both of us, barefoot or not. I had another agenda too. I wanted to lure Gerd into the trap of buying a "mas grande" candle, so that we could laugh at the enormity of his sins. But while Gerd was clearly impressed with the historic Spanish Fort, this morning for some unknown reason the Muslim women were not manning their candle-laden trestles. Under the hot sun we traipsed along the dusty breakwater before stepping off onto the squelchy track leading through the labyrinth of huts towards the mosque. Ali's mum was hard at work making garments on her treadle sewing machine, so I introduced her to Gerd and then Ali escorted us further in a walk around the mosque.

Gerd and I arrived back at the Mas residence, changed into swimwear and hopped across the park to the pool. I showed off my handstand and back dive. Keen to copy me, Gerd showed so much perseverance that by the end of an hour his dives were better than mine. Warm rain pricked the surface of the pool, and then with little warning the wind gusted and rain pelted into us with great force. Evidently a typhoon had hit Leyte north of Mindanao.

In blasting wind we staggered through the park to my host's house, jumped back into our dry clothes and headed downtown. For three hours in the bowling alley we clowned around, betting against each other and bowling wildly, amusing ourselves as well as the crowd who had gathered to watch. Suddenly we were ravenous, so the next stop was Laura's where we gobbled a tasty meal, me describing to Gerd how in this very place I had won a bet by eating half a gallon of chocolate fudge ice cream!

Chito was home at last. Over the next few days, in between lessons at Ateneo, I met up with a few Serenaders to make a tape of the latest folksongs that had caught our fancy. The recorder decided to play up, and as it alternately got faster or slower our singing sounded quite mad. I put each boy on the spot, ordering them to "say something" to my family, and assuming I would erase their statements they both said ridiculous things. When I declared their comments were recorded for eternity, Chito looked stricken. "Your parents will think I should be locked away!"

Charlie Reith's birthday was celebrated that night at the wonderful house on the seafront. Zamboanga had never seen anything like it. Dear old Sy must have been preparing the feast for days. A whole cow was roasting on a spit, so in between dancing in the torch-lit garden we fronted up for more serves of tender beef slices and other mouthwatering delicacies.

The Reiths had been kind enough to invite those people they knew were special friends of mine, such as Chito, Jo-Jo, and of course the latest visitor from Germany. All the Rotarians and their wives attended, and everyone had a marvellous time merrymaking until 3 A.M. During the night I told Gerd about my various adventures to Pulong Bato, about the first hike where Linda Gonda and our two male escorts had become severely dehydrated, and how we had to walk all the way back through town with our feet blistered and bleeding. Then I described the second major attempt with The Serenaders when I had "frozen" on the tiny slippery ledge on that sheer wall of rock. Full of enthusiasm Chito decided that Gerd must join us in the third conquering of Pulong Bato, and as our guest was due to fly back to Cebu in two days it seemed obvious that the three of us should set off without delay.

At nine the next morning my two bleary-eyed "conquistadors" drew up in a jeep at the top of the park. I was bleary-eyed too, but soon we were frying some bananas in the Mas kitchen to take with us and ensuring we had plenty of water and a small medical kit. At last we strode off down the jungle track on a mission not only to tackle the rock on its sheer face, but to somehow find, dig up and bring back some rare yucca palms for my "mum" Lottie Mas. Because these palms only grew near Pulong Bato's summit, it was imperative we reach the top.

We had no sooner reached the base of the rock when drenching rain fell. Little waterfalls began to course from the clefts in the stone and spurt from the jungle foliage itself. My courage was weakening, but none of us voiced our fears and we began to climb. My foot dislodged a rock that crashed down through the palms and ferns, and suddenly a raucous shrieking broke out. We froze, then spotted a troupe of monkeys leaping through the trees, sounding the alarm at the presence of unwanted human beings. I immediately pictured their other major predator, the great monkey-eating eagle, either gliding silently and free in the heavens, or pinioned in some cruel cage for humans to gawk at.

The monkeys moved on. We continued to struggle upwards until at long last, step by shaky step, we reached the summit. Sitting triumphantly atop the rock in the rain, lords of all we surveyed, we nibbled our fried bananas and laughed with relief. Chito suddenly spotted the fronds of a yucca palm, so we made for a small clearing where about six yuccas of varying sizes conveniently grew. Selecting three of the smallest we began digging them out. As we tackled the descent, we realized the only way to carry each plant and watch our feet at the same time, was to sling it over one shoulder. Yet that meant each of us would lose the use of one hand during the climb down.

To descend by the sheer rockface would be foolhardy. We stopped, staring towards the rear of the mountain. While none of us could make out a pathway, the terrain was slightly less steep and there was more jungle growth to clasp with our one free hand should we fall. We slipped and slid, mostly on our backsides, mud smearing us from head to toe. We had no idea where we were, but at least we were descending.

It was rough going, taking more than an hour before we sensed the ground levelling out. But the jungle was so thick it seemed impossible to find an escape route. At one stage we stopped, looked each other up and down, then fell about laughing. We were sorry-looking human beings, and the palms looked sad and sorry too. Our merriment ceased when we began to realize each of us had lost something—Chito's water bottle, Gerd's headband, and the opal ring that my parents had given me and which I had worn constantly in the Philippines. There was no point bemoaning our losses, because we now urgently needed to find our way over the rivers and up through the lighter jungle to Pasonanca Park. The return trek proved a marathon, and when we finally collapsed on the Mas's lawn both we and the plants were total wrecks. Our hands and feet were bloodied with cuts from the sharp fronds, our shoulders bruised and tender. Somehow we found the energy to get cleaned up and go to a party, but as soon as we'd stayed for the required amount of time we roared around in Chito's ancient jeep with several Serenaders singing at top throat to the guitars—until midnight.

* * *

The next morning reality hit. Not only did I feel fatigued and battered, but Gerd was flying back to Cebu and I needed to be at the airport bright and early to say farewell. After that came swimming classes, and it was during these that a commotion broke out at the deep end of the pool. Over by the diving board a man and his family in Muslim dress were yelling frantically as they watched their seven-year-old son vainly struggling to stay afloat. I leapt out of the pool and rushed to the deep end. Seeing the child so close to drowning, I panicked, jumped in with a huge splash, and enveloped the boy with a wave of water. It was then I remembered the drill—duck-dive to surface behind him, turn him on his back, hook one arm around his chest, and use my other arm to propel me and my cargo to the side of the pool. Willing hands were waiting to haul him out onto the edge, and adrenalin helped me to heave myself out of the pool and lie the child on his side. To my relief he retched up what seemed like half of the pool and was soon able to sit up. His deeply distressed parents were trying to thank me in their language. I gathered they were taking a small holiday in Zamboanga from where they lived further south. After I had reassured them that their son was okay, I returned to my lessons, berating myself that the rescue had been so clumsy.

* * *

Student journalists in the *Beacon* office greeted me excitedly. "President Marcos is coming down to Zambo tomorrow for a press conference, so you will want to be there won't you?"

A bomb exploded in my stomach. "Oh, I'm not sure . . ."

Vic Solis spoke up. "He will be expecting you to be there Stephie, because everybody in town knows that he is a friend of yours, isn't he?"

"I guess so," I said.

"Of course he is!" exclaimed Vic, "you were his guest for a whole two weeks in Manila. What would he think if you stayed away?" He followed with details of place and time, and the other students smiled and nodded as if I hadn't quite appreciated what it meant to be favoured by their president. Vic added in typical chief editor fashion, "Oh, and see if you can find out details of the press conference for your next article."

Filled with dread I hurried alone across the college grounds to find a jeepney. *What if he invites me aboard his yacht? What if he invites me to lunch? How are we supposed to act together in front of a crowd?* On the way back to Pasonanca I hopped off the jeepney at Santa Maria and darted into the Alvarez home to grab Jun and take him across the road to discuss the situation with Rob. Both men immediately sized up my dilemma, agreeing that on the surface I had to appear to be keen to meet up once more with my illustrious "friend." However, they assured me that tomorrow morning they would stick to my side like glue, so that from the very first greeting Marcos would know that there were solid human obstacles in his way.

During the meal at the Mas house that night I feigned mild excitement at the prospect of seeing the president again, thus fulfilling the expectations of everyone at the table. Relatively early I excused myself and fell into bed, my head swirling with unanswered what ifs. The following morning I caught a jeepney to Santa Maria where Jun and Rob were dressed in their best and waiting on the verge. With the boys flanking me we walked, mostly in silence, up to the edge of the park to the hall where the press conference was due to take place. While journalists arrived on foot, jeepney, tricycle and car we seated ourselves together at the very back so that we could slip out and escape at a moment's notice, hopefully without drawing too much attention. The hall quickly filled with journalists clutching pens and notepads, and a provincial governor and the president's male secretary ascended to a raised dais at the front. Foreign Correspondent Garth Alexander was nowhere to be seen, which was not surprising given that he had illegally fled the country only a month before. I found myself disappointed on one level, yet relieved on another, aware that Garth's keen sense of observation would have noted any awkwardness between Marcos and me, and his questions may have caught me out. The seated journalists were murmuring to each other and glancing around to see if there was any sign of the president. I was tense, aware of the Marcos style of grand and very late appearances.

A quarter of an hour after start time the governor began speaking at the podium, but instead of announcing that the president would be late he began to drone on and on, about border disputes, smuggling, the situation up north with the communists, and a few incursions that had happened here in the deep dark South. Not one mention of Marcos. The atmosphere was humid and sweaty, and I scribbled frantically to keep my brain occupied. The journalists asked questions, and one enquired, "Why is the president unable to attend today?" The secretary stepped forward with an embarrassed smile. "You will have to ask the president that." The crowd shuffled and murmured.

"So he is coming then?" persisted the questioner, but the secretary, looking sheepish, simply shrugged. After that the press men focused on the relevant topics under scrutiny, and the politicians' replies were careful and mostly boring. After an hour it was certain Marcos would not be gracing our presence on this day.

I never discovered where Marcos was staying at the time of the conference, but I always suspected that Colonel Ver's common sense had ruled the day. He, like me, would have understood this to be a situation fraught with danger for both parties. Whatever Marcos's reason for staying away, once again I counted my lucky stars and could relax for now. The morning, though wasted for Rob and Jun, had at least provided me with enough interesting morsels for my final article in the *Beacon*.

There was only a month to go until I would leave Zamboanga via Manila on my way back to Australia. In Manila I would need to stay at the Reiths' for as long as it would take to get formalities sorted for the big flight, but I convinced myself that if I kept under the Marcos radar until I stepped onto Australian soil, the nightmare would surely be over.

* * *

Most of my foster parents were wonderful human beings. Hilda Araneta had already written to my parents reassuring them there was nothing to worry about any more now that I had returned from Manila. Following Hilda's letter, Leticia "Ma" Alvarez wrote to my mother declaring I had endeared myself "to many of us who came to know her. She is young of course, but she has been very sensible . . . although she found things not very convenient, she took it tactfully and with a smile. You can be assured that she has been a real ambassador of goodwill and a credit to her parents." And then there was Lotti (mummy) Mas, who fussed about in the kitchen preparing every dish she thought I might like, and constantly worried that I might not find her meals good enough.

One day I asked Tiger, the three-year-old lovable devil of the Mas family, whether he would like to escort Chito and me across to Pasonanca pool for a swim. Instantly rapturous he ran around the house yelling for the maids to fetch his trunks and his towel. After two minutes he appeared, clutching his swimwear and said, "Sigi na man!" ("Let's go!"). I replied with a negative because Chito had not yet arrived. "Don't like," he said. "Sigi na man."

"No. We wait for Chito," I said.

"Don't like to wait for Chito," said Tiger, and he kept repeating this until I lost my temper and shouted, "No!"

Dumbfounded, Tiger disappeared. After five minutes he peeped in, his face a mask of tragedy. "I no go to pool now," he said.

"Okay," I said, and resumed studying Spanish. From the corner of my eye I saw his face twist in puzzled shock.

Chito arrived at the house and was ushered into the lounge by a maid. Tony was home and conversed with him for a minute or two before I entered the lounge with my swim bag. As I joined in the conversation, I noticed Tony trying to suppress his laughter, glancing at the corner. And there was Tiger, sitting on a small stool, and if looks could kill . . .

* * *

At the end of November I played softball as catcher, and there were seven innings under the tropical sun which were strenuous to say the least. A persistent headache began, enough to make me feel lousy, so after the match I returned home and lay down for an hour in semi-darkness. The headache wouldn't budge, and so I cancelled a Thanksgiving dinner with the Peace Corps fraternity, the movies with Chito, and a big Jaycee dance before I settled down again to sleep, this time with no pressure. I slept for some hours, and when I awoke the headache was gone and I felt refreshed. It was getting dark by now, too late to change my mind without making a mess of things, so I began to write letters home. At 10 P.M. one of the Mas girls knocked on my door saying, "Don't you hear them? I think you have visitors." I switched off the fan, and the lovely sound of folksongs wafted through the window. When I wandered out under a clear night sky, the full moon cast its light upon Chito and eleven other Serenaders. The fifteen of us sat on the front lawn and sang our hearts out until midnight. As they crowded into the jeep and waved goodbye, I wandered back into the house in a dreamy state of fulfilment and joy.

The following Saturday morning, Chito and other Serenaders were amongst the crowd who came to watch the softball in the Ateneo grounds. My team was up against the pre-nursing fraternity, and we were fielding first, me in the important position of protecting first base. Luckily I never missed a catch, but when I stepped up to bat my coordination failed. I swung hard, the ball tipping the bat and dribbling from the end. Caught off-guard, the pitcher charged in to retrieve the ball, only to find I had already made it to first base. This happened again and again, ironically giving us the game, courtesy of my innovative new stroke, the Bat Dribble.

Chito then drove all Serenaders to Caragasan. We sang to guitar melodies under the coconut palms and ate fried bananas before attempting, with hilarious results, to balance on some logs rolling around in that sparkling clear water. I ended up with the usual sunburnt and supremely happy face when the boys delivered me to Angie's. There I was groomed for a very important ball that evening, marking the end of a national press conference. The invited guests included journalists from all over the country, and the local press from Zambo.

Wondering what dress I would wear to the ball, I made my way home by jeepney to find a package waiting for me. It contained handmade culottes of pale green silk, a diaphanous red silk top, and a letter written in stilted English from a Muslim boy whose young brother I had saved from drowning a week earlier. The victim's mother had determined to show her thanks by creating this beautiful outfit—perfect for the ball so long as I wore a sleeveless blouse under the see-through top. Evidently the young man had discovered where I was staying just in time to deliver the gift and board a boat heading south to his home in the Sulu Sea.

I scored dances with several VIP officials, but the man I remember was the foreign minister and secretary general of the Philippines, Carlo Romulo, because he was two inches shorter than my height of five feet, six inches.

As with Senator Salonga, I had no inkling of Romulo's sterling character. In the 40s he had been strongly involved in the United Nations as a champion of freedom, democracy and world peace. When a Russian UN member insulted him with, "You are just a little man in a little country" Romulo retorted: "It is the duty of the little Davids of this world to fling the pebbles of truth in the eyes of the blustering Goliaths and force them to behave!" Although he had become Foreign Secretary under Marcos in 1968, by 1983 he had resigned, sickened by the suspicious murder of his friend Ninoy Aquino.

* * *

I had heard that cockfighting in the Philippines was a favourite "sport." When a wealthy young man called Bebot offered to take me to a cockfight, I hesitated. It was a given that I would hate it, but curiosity overwhelmed me. One Sunday we drove to the very outskirts of town, and in a bare paddock stood a vast shabby tent in which a wooden framework of seats surrounded a sandy square—the "cockpit." No less than 4,000 men sat in that stifling tent, all shouting and brandishing paper money. When Bebot led me inside and up some wooden steps to a platform, there was a visible and audible stir amongst the audience. The platform overlooked the "ring," and now I was all too aware that I was the only female in the tent. Trying to ignore the terrible closeness and heat, I sat on my rickety seat and took note of the scene. The sandy square had bars around it, and inside the bars the top gamblers sat on low benches, their "callers" standing beside them to call out their bets. A pair of cocks were brought in by their owners, one a hatless man and the other wearing a sombrero. The audience stopped shouting, turning their attention to the "pecking" ritual. Hatless turned the neck of his bird from side to side while Sombrero's bird was urged to peck at his rival's neck, then vice versa. This served to arouse the anger of the cocks while also acting as a guide for punters to sense which bird had seemed the most aggressive.

A bell rang and the betting began in earnest, the hullaballoo of shouting making me wince. During the recording of the bets, both Hatless and Sombrero removed the covers from the steel knives attached to their birds' left legs. Bebot asked me for my preference, accepted my wild guess and informed his caller who registered the bet amongst the mayhem.

The birds were set down to face each other. The entire place fell deathly quiet. The cocks rushed at each other, and the feathers flew. They drew apart for a second, one obviously wounded. They both rushed again. When they drew apart it was easy to tell which bird was the loser, although both were bleeding. In one last valiant struggle they stumbled towards each other, but before either was killed they were lifted up by the referees to face each other, the loser bird's neck exposed for the victor to peck. The crowd roared as the vanquished was hauled off unceremoniously upside down, no doubt headed for the soup pot, while the hero was carried outside to be stitched up without anesthetic. Bebot explained that even if he was in no shape to fight again, at least he might breed a family of winners in the future. He also told me that every Sunday about 150 fighting cocks die in Zamboanga alone.

I wrote home "It's a bloody sport, interesting, but as far as I'm concerned, once is enough."

* * *

The fraternities at Ateneo had formed three groups, each to produce an hour-long play, the winner to be awarded one hundred pesos. One fraternity asked if I would play the lead in a medieval farce called *Pierre Patelin*. After reading the script, although I wasn't sure that comedy was my forte, I agreed. My character Guillemette, the only female in the cast of five, was even more feisty and independent than Kate had been in Shakespeare's *The Taming of the Shrew*, so it was hard to resist. Besides, the young director seemed sane as well as creative, characteristics which don't always go together in the world of theatre.

One fraternity chose a play which I dismissed as having little chance of winning, but the third chose *Antigone*, a Greek tragedy. Because I had previously experienced this play performed by a professional company in Adelaide, I knew it had the potential to be powerful and very moving, therefore proving a serious contender. The cast had begun rehearsing for the past six weeks and starred Babouchi, the extrovert mestiza with the striking personality—perfect for the part of Antigone. Not only that, but the director was a mature-age teacher whose directing skills were famous in Zamboanga.

There were several other factors working against us. First, we had been rehearsing for only two weeks despite committing to rehearsal every evening after lessons until midnight. Secondly, our director was a student and new to the game. Thirdly, our play was a farce, neither moving nor powerful, and I had observed that comedies are less likely than dramas to win competitions. And last but crucially, *Pierre Patelin* features interjections and eccentric remarks, demanding quick responses and perfect timing.

While a tubby student playing the whacky Judge rose to the occasion every time with an arresting portrayal, the actors playing Pierre and the Tailor consistently botched their lines. In the early stages of rehearsal the botching caused chuckles, but as performance night loomed ever closer I began to worry. The director was becoming uneasy too.

I recalled my preschool days in Port Lincoln when I was given the role of Head Angel in the nativity play. On the big night, in a white robe made from a sheet, a wire halo wobbling on my head and huge wings sagging from my shoulders, I pronounced my lines with passion before sweeping from the stage as regally as a Head Angel should. But to my disgust, the three Wise Men needed prodding with one of the shepherd's crooks to get them onstage, where they stood like a trio of dummies. There was nothing for it but for me to reappear in all my glory and speak their lines, word for word. Mum and Dad cringed, and the incident went down in family history, never to be forgotten.

* * *

On Thursday 6 December, two nights before the performance, the cast of *Pierre Patelin* practiced from 8 P.M. until midnight, but any enjoyment of the play was diminished by deep concerns shared by the director and me—Pierre and the Tailor were still woeful at remembering their lines.

On Friday, after teaching swimming all morning, I met Jun at the ice cream parlour to swap news and gobble down the usual sweet treat. Because my Spanish lesson was only half an hour away we both headed for Ateneo. As I stepped off the pavement my sandal twisted under my left foot, and I gasped with pain. The ankle area began to swell, so Jun insisted on hailing a jeepney and taking me to a very humble hut on the outskirts of town. Inside sat a wrinkled old man who in no way resembled a doctor, but having great faith in Jun (my translator) I perched on a stool in front of the healer and gingerly placed my bare foot on his lap. As my hands gripped each side of the stool he began massaging some type of liniment around the sprained joint. Yet while the treatment left me sweating and exhausted, the ankle itself seemed to calm down enough for me to make my six o'clock English lesson with only the slightest of limps. By the time dress rehearsal was due to start at eight, as long as I took care not to swivel, few would have guessed when I walked into the theatre that I had been writhing in pain only hours earlier.

Director, cast and crew had gathered onstage for the dress rehearsal—all of us, that is, except Pierre and the Tailor. By 9 P.M. they were still missing in action. Furious and nursing an aching ankle, I stormed from the theatre across the dimly lit grounds, intending to go home but unsure whether a jeepney would be operating at this time of night. Luckily Bebot was cruising past and insisted on driving me up to Pasonanca, but as soon as we reached the park I had cooled off and asked if he would return me to the theatre. We reached downtown and turned into a side street only to find ourselves in the middle of a street fight, rock-throwing youths against baton-wielding security guards. A stone hit the car just above the passenger door, missing my head by a whisker! Bebot had the good sense to speed up and keep going until we were safely inside the college grounds, but we were both shaken. I thanked my savior, hoping that his car was not too damaged. I was also aware that if it hadn't been for that offer of a lift I could easily have wandered into the brawl, a scenario that didn't bear thinking about.

Upon arriving at the theatre I was informed that the two miscreants, although they had finally turned up, had vanished—to look for me! I scolded myself for ever leaving in the first place, and now I was desperately concerned that Pierre and the Tailor were caught up in the fight. They might have been dragged off to jail!

I needn't have worried. Both wandered in, smirking inanely and not too steady on their feet. Master Pierre, though tipsy, dramatically fell to his knees and begged my forgiveness. However, after both boys tried to assure us that they had been learning lines all day, the Tailor swayed off into the adjoining gym and collapsed onto one of the foam mats.

We began the final rehearsal, and my wayward husband Pierre had never acted better. For the first time I really began to enjoy the play, realizing that although I could hardly do a repeat of Head Angel, I could, as the brash wife Guillemette, fill in any gaps with some spontaneous nagging when needed. However, when the Tailor was cued to appear, he staggered out from the gym and was in no state to remember anything, let alone his lines. At this point the director sensibly decided a prompt was needed for the big night, to be concealed behind the tablecloth of the kitchen table.

Master Patelin and the inebriated Tailor, probably as penance, saw me safely home around midnight in a pre-arranged taxi, a rare form of transport in Zamboanga. Exhausted, I fell into bed without eating and slept soundly.

* * *

The next morning, my ankle holding out well, I threw myself into yet another softball match. During the fielding I had caught every improbable ball, low or high, and began to feel quite the Olympian. Then came our turn to bat and I was last in line. By the time I stepped up to the plate we were losing by one run. The pitcher pitched and my bat resounded with a satisfying "whack!" The ball flew fast and low to the edge of the field. With the crowd cheering I began the sprint from base to base. Halfway home I was aware that the fielder had retrieved the ball and was now hurling it towards the catcher. As she caught the ball I put on a valiant spurt of speed, knowing it still wasn't enough, and that's when I tripped. My body arced through the air and landed over the home base a split second before she touched me with the ball. "Safe!" yelled the referee. The audience went wild. What a sacrifice the Aussie girl had made, diving selflessly at the plate, her one thought to save the team!

Half an hour later, the praise and glory wearing thin and my adrenalin waning, I began to feel the pain of being bruised from top to toe, including my right heel. Now lumbered with two sore feet and huge fatigue, I treated myself to a super-long siesta. Towards evening Lottie, Tony and their married daughter headed off for the show while I piled my hair up in curlers and affixed little tats of coloured rags in each curl, then climbed into my costume and painted a red dot on each cheek. To avoid being seen by any of the audience I waited until after dark when the first play had begun. Dear Jun picked me up, soon offloading an outrageous looking French housewife into the rear of the theatre. In the gloom I tip-toed up the wooden stairs from the stage wings to the upstairs dressing room. The cast of *Pierre Patelin* were donning costumes and applying makeup, and when one by one they turned to see dippy Guillemette with her multi-coloured hairdo and huge round eyes, long shabby skirt and canary yellow ballet slippers, they clapped their hands over their mouths to stifle laughter.

It was my turn to grin when I spied my "husband" decked out in a gaudy jacket with puffy red and yellow sleeves, tight pantaloons, and the real killer—a ridiculous Charlie Chaplin moustache. How on earth was I going to frown at him onstage? I observed that while the Tailor was pale with stage fright, at least he didn't seem drunk.

At last we heard mild clapping from the audience as the first play finished, and soon we were called to the wings and were on. In the first few minutes we were causing such hilarity that not only was I beginning to settle down for one of the funniest hours of my life, but many times I had to wait for audience merriment to die down before I could deliver each line. The director had failed to bribe a prompt for the courtroom scene where the judge went head-to-head with Pierre, and so I provided my husband with some whispered help from the wings. We lined up for curtain call and the audience seemed rapturous. With cast and director hyped and happy, we gathered back up in the dressing room.

At the end of a small interval *Antigone* began, and three of us decided to creep down the stairs and around the back of the auditorium so that we could witness the performance. I quickly removed the worst of the make-up, ripped out most of the hair rags, and as silently as possible I followed my ex-husband Pierre and the Tailor down the steep wooden stairs to the space level with the wings. Halfway down I could hear Antigone delivering her tragic lines, and it was then the unthinkable happened. I'll never know whether to blame the long skirt or the recent ankle sprains, but I pitched forwards while my feet stayed trapped between two steps before I ended up in a crumpled heap at the bottom of the steps. Looming over me Pierre whispered, "What's wrong?"

"My feet!" I gasped. Thinking that I had got a cramp, he began pressing and twisting my feet, escalating the agony. Magically Rob and Jun appeared, quickly sizing up the situation. While Jun went for a doctor, Rob somehow carried me up those steep dark stairs and lay me gently on the floor of the dressing room. I had suppressed any noise, but tears and sweat flooded my face. Everyone was trying to help, one cast member fanning me and Rob telling me funny stories. A doctor arrived, and after taking a quick look at my rapidly swelling ankles he disappeared, soon returning with liniment, bandages and painkillers. After each foot was tightly bound, Rob helped me to the vertical position, but there was no way I could stand unsupported. And so once again he carried me, this time down the stairs and all the way round to the back of the auditorium. Someone had found us seats, and so I sat amongst my steadfast friends and watched the rest of *Antigone*, trying to immerse myself in the drama so that I could, for a while at least, forget the pain.

Antigone and others in the cast, although delivering their lines valiantly, often elicited unwelcome laughs from the audience. It didn't help when the blackouts between scene changes weren't black enough, so that Creon the king could clearly be seen carrying his own throne onto the stage. Lights came on quickly at the end, and so did the judges—announcing that *Antigone* had been awarded second place, with *Pierre Patelin* the winner!

From there it was all happiness and congratulations, and after most of the audience had vanished Jun and Rob helped carry me to the jeep where I sat with my feet up on Butch Alvarez's lap. The Mas family headed for home, but we young ones were in party mood, eating barbeque on Cawa Cawa Boulevard before driving in pouring rain to a house filled with cast and crew, all celebrating in wild fashion. Even though I sat on the sidelines, no one left me alone for a second, the story of my dramatic fall rapidly becoming part of the excitement of one of the most memorable nights of my life.

* * *

Jun drove the jeep as close as possible to the Mas's front door. All the household was fast asleep, so we tried to keep the noise down as Rob carried me inside and into my bedroom while Jun and Butch followed behind cracking jokes. The painkillers were working, so I found the situation hilarious. We said our goodbyes, but as Rob turned to leave I realized I needed a pitcher of water and a toothbrush, and after brushing I would need all the lights turned off except the one by my bed. After that, I calculated, I would be able to undress myself and go to sleep. The boys rushed to do my bidding, then disappeared.

I was halfway through awkwardly extracting myself from my clothing when I received an urgent call of nature. There was nothing for it except to crawl on my hands and knees to the bathroom. I somehow managed to get myself "enthroned," and on the return trip I tested the standing position. Oddly enough my left foot, the one that had suffered the sprain on Thursday, could bear a small portion of weight, but the other was definitely no-go. Once again I needed to crawl back to bed. Before falling asleep I remember wishing my mum had been in the audience that night. An excellent actress, she was an honest critic too. In 1967, when Woodlands Girls and Pulteney Boys colleges had combined to produce Agatha Christie's *Witness for the Prosecution*, I was given the very challenging star role. While Mum had praised me, she had also confessed to being frustrated that I rarely turned towards the audience. Wise words, which I had taken to heart in *Pierre Patelin*.

At nine the next morning Lotti peeped her head around the door, realized I was going nowhere fast, and called Tony to discuss the matter. Because Doc Marasigan was away in Manila, they asked Dr Alvarez if he would pay me a visit. Because I could put just a little weight on one foot, I determined to ask "Pa" Alvarez if he might obtain some crutches so I could attend the Ateneo rooftop ball that night. The occasion was to mark the end of the school year, even though lessons would continue almost until Christmas.

Darling Pa showed up with crutches. So that night, in a new dress and with many of the males in the fraternity assisting, I managed to ascend three flights of stairs to the garden rooftop of Ateneo where the band filled the air with throbbing music under the stars. Most of the evening I sat beside the flurry of non-stop dancing, but never did my friends desert me. So many Filipino students came up to congratulate and chat that the time rushed by in a swirl of goodwill. I became overwhelmed with a contentment that was curious, given the dramas of the last twenty-four hours.

* * *

During the morning when my back began to give me stabs of pain, especially when I bent or turned, I wrote home that what with hobbling along on two swollen feet plus a twinging back, I was feeling "old as Moses." However, I was able to spend a distracting and pleasant few hours when someone brought in my mail. This included a hilarious tape, especially recorded for my pending birthday by an Aussie friend who had somehow managed to gather together my extended family and record messages and general silliness. The problem was, like most typewriters in the Philippines, the tape recorder in the Mas household was a dinosaur with a bad habit of slowing down so that a "Happy Birthday" singalong sounded as if the performers had been hit by a typhoon before being knocked sideways into deep snoring. It was, as usual, a mix of hilarity and frustration. I opened a birthday card from my SJ and another from brother Steve. Both had purchased their cards in Melbourne on their way to Tasmania—as first year Uni students needing a holiday job, they'd be dropped by a mining company helicopter into the forests of Tasmania to take soil samples over several weeks.

I saved SJ's big card until last. I unfolded it once, then twice, then many times until I was holding a placard-sized sheet of paper with every spare inch and both sides covered in pink hearts. All warm and fuzzy I gazed at this field of hearts, and for several moments my sore feet and back were overwhelmed by sweet dreams of reunion with the man I loved and intended to marry as soon as feasible.

* * *

The X-ray on my feet showed nothing was broken. As my entire family had never once broken a bone, despite falls from horses, fences, cliffs and trees, I was able to reassure my parents in a letter "the family history of sound bones remains intact."

However, my ankles were swollen up like two small balloons. Tony Mas wanted me to see an old lady who had been curing dislocations and sprains for as long as his family could remember. She had been doing this since she was ten years old, he told me, and people had even flown from Manila to be treated by her. However, the ancient one had recently suffered a mild stroke and was still weak. Coming from a traditional doctor's family I was dubious about going to a "quack," but I had to admit that the venerable healer whom Jun had taken me to see only a few days ago had made things better—certainly not worse. Tony was adamant. I must be treated by this lady as soon as possible.

Lottie and her very pregnant daughter Ally Lou drove me to a humble hut just down the hill from Pasonanca Park. Both women helped me up the steep wooden stairs, and the Old One was waiting for me. Wizened and frail, she looked far too weak to kill a fly, let alone apply pressure to my feet. When Lottie turned to me saying, "You'll cry. Be prepared," I replied with a scornful smile, "Don't be silly!" Since I was ten years old the only time I had ever sobbed in earnest was after last Saturday night's agonizing fall down the stairs. This afternoon I was braced for whatever was coming, and anyway, both my parents had taught me that bravery was to be admired, and I agreed wholeheartedly.

Gingerly I sat down in front of the lady. Taking my left foot onto her knee, she unwrapped the elastic bandage the doctor had applied, then looked up at Lottie who translated, "You should have come sooner." The old one gently felt the foot all over until she got to the ankle. I winced, but instead of backing off, her gnarled old fingers began with ever increasing pressure to circle like a shark towards the ankle joint itself.

It was only then I became aware that Lottie and Ally Lou were lending their entire body weights to my leg, clamping it still. I began to gasp, and then shriek, and then scream and groan. The fingers became like a vice around the joint as they kept probing into what she called the "dimple," the word translated by Lottie.

The modern-day treatment for injured ankles, where the ligaments have been over-extended, also uses the word "dimple." It will forever remain a mystery how such a person, obviously raised in dire poverty, gained her medical knowledge.

The healer kept on probing, and I kept on screaming, until at last she ceased, leaving me drenched in sweat and panting like a dog. The Old One muttered something in Chavacano to Lottie who turned to me and said, "Your ankle had come out of its socket. She has put it back." I nodded, trying to look grateful, unable to speak.

Before I could rally, Lottie and Ally Lou had gone round to my other side and were lifting my other even more swollen foot into the Old

One's lap. Now I braced myself for what I knew would be hell to come, Lottie and Ally Lou transferring their combined weight on the right leg. After the first careful physical examination I was already gasping when the old woman told Lottie that this foot was worse. Within seconds I was screaming blue murder, but the healer simply increased her pressure, pushing and probing into the puffy soft tissue of the foot until she felt bone. The torture went on and on, until eventually, mercifully, she released my foot. Again I collapsed into a sweating, panting wreck. Ally Lou gave me a drink of water from what looked like a jam jar. The old lady rose, collected some wide green leaves from the table and dropped these into a pan of boiling water on the stove. While they were "cooking" she told Lottie that the bones were in place now, but the pain would be bad until the day after tomorrow.

Tomorrow was my birthday, but nothing seemed to matter anymore except escaping from that agony. After the leaves had cooled slightly the old lady wrapped them gently round each foot, expertly binding them in place with the elastic bandages. She told me not to get them wet, and then she did something surprising, something sweet. As if she knew my back was sore, she sat behind me and softly massaged up and down either side of the vertebrae. Because my pain was deep inside the joints themselves, this caressing gave me great relief and had the effect of calming my tightly wound nerves.

When my two tough angels helped me into the back seat of the car I collapsed, wrung out and utterly exhausted. By the time we reached home I felt as if I were heavily drugged, and it took huge effort to heave myself out. Supported either side by Lottie and Ally Lou into my room, I fell onto the bed and slept like the dead.

When I woke Jun was sitting beside me, telling me he had brought medicine that never fails to cure. Smiling his buck-toothed smile, he held aloft a bucket of delicious, cool, soothing, creamy—mango ice cream!

* * *

Jun had just left the Mas residence when his sister Claro, she who had joined Rob and me in the Malaria survey, arrived bearing a parcel. The darling had sewed me a dress out of silk, a labor of love that must have taken her at least a day.

All that night I dreamed of pain. When I woke next morning I lay in bed, too scared to get up and test my feet. A muffled commotion started up outside my door. The entire Mas family had gathered to sing "Happy Birthday." Someone struck up the birthday tune loudly on the piano in the lounge. Then one by one they all filed in to kiss me, including Tiger who decided to put on his "hard to get" face.

After breakfast the wonders kept happening. No sooner had Tony and Lottie invited me to join their family for barbeque at Cawa Cawa Boulevard that night, a telegram arrived from Chito who was still in Manila. Adorned with a picture of bright red roses it simply said, "No way I know of can be as quick for sending my love and a birthday kiss," and on cue the doorbell rang and Chito's mother was at the door with her son's present to me, a shell bracelet and mother-of-pearl earrings.

After I had donned my new silk dress, I hobbled out to Tony's car just as a truck drew up in the driveway, the occupants alighting and offloading crates of Coca Cola. "Good grief!" I exclaimed. "Just how many bottles of coke do you plan to drink over the next two years!" Ally Lou, who was standing nearby, told me that her twin sisters were looking forward to their birthday party in two weeks and it was cheaper to buy now rather than around Christmas time. Accepting her story without question, I headed off with Tony to the Rotary meeting at the usual glorious venue atop the Zambo Hotel.

The Rotarians made a huge fuss of me, crowding around with best wishes, asking about my feet. Even the newest Rotarian, Father McNally, shook my hand asking, "How's the actress?" When the crowd thinned I spotted a gigantic pink castle of a birthday cake on the main table. Halfway through the meeting Charlie, as past president, was asked to formally present me with the cake. Rising to his feet with his trademark mischievous grin he went through theatrical motions of presenting me with the pink castle, all Rotarians cheering and whistling. Then he took the microphone. "Well, fellow Rotarians, we expect all of you and your wives to be present this evening at the house of Tony Mas." Tony jumped up to silence him, but it was too late. The secret was out. Charlie turned as pink as the cake, and his fellow Rotarians glared, but all I could do was smile, and I couldn't stop smiling. Maybe it was infectious, because laughter broke out and everyone filed up for a piece of cake which I cut and served. A guest began to sing to the accompaniment of the regular band of blind instrumentalists, and I felt dizzy with happiness.

When Tony drove me home, we had to admit to Lottie that the cat was out of the bag, and the poor lady almost burst into tears. Realizing the huge efforts made by all the Mas family to surprise me that night, I reassured her with a hug that I was thrilled to bits and that was what mattered.

A great bouquet of roses arrived from the Alvarez family, and the gifts kept coming—a generous piece of hand-embroidered material from the wives of the Rotarians, and from the Mas family several small golden purses especially designed for make-up, loose change, etc. Rob turned up with two holy books he assured me were valuable, and Jun arrived with a green jade necklace and a pink handbag. A book of German short stories arrived from Gerd, black coral earrings from a kind Rotarian who owned a shell shop, and all the while cards from Australian friends seemed to appear from nowhere.

Unwinding the bandages from my feet I threw away the remnants of the healing leaves. Without the bandages it was more painful to walk, but so long as I moved carefully and slowly I felt confident enough.

The Mas garden looked like fairyland when the party began, flaming torches lighting up ferns and the second giant birthday cake in one day taking pride of place on a pedestal. All Rotarians with wives and friends turned up, including Charlie looking sheepish and heading for a stiff drink at the bar, and Jo-Jo bearing his gift of an exquisite fan. Just as I was thinking, *How perfect it would be if just a couple of Ateneo friends turned up*, the sound of singing wafted from around the front of the house. And there they were in the driveway, more than fifty students singing "Happy Birthday," totally unexpected by the Mas family, who were forced to run all over the place finding plates and glasses for so many extra serves. I hobbled round greeting each person, bursting with joy, lavished with even more gifts and trying to commit to memory who had given what so that I could thank them during the following days.

During the evening Nina and Tony Veloso, the beautiful young couple who had taken me for so many spectacular rides and beach picnics in their speed boat, said that while they understood that time was running out for me in Zambo, they would love to have me stay over Christmas. I had already grown to love this couple, so I agreed to move to their house the following week for what I knew would be a short but fun-filled stay.

It was three in the morning when Charlie and I were the only ones remaining, sipping coffee and feeling very mellow indeed. I think Charlie was trying to sober up a little before he departed, not because the police cared two hoots about drunk driving, but because he needed to find his way home! Suddenly one of the Mas girls appeared, calling urgently for her mother. It seemed that Ally Lou's baby was demanding to be born!

I felt sympathy for Lottie and Tony Mas. After such a huge day they now needed to drive their daughter to hospital and stay there for the birth of her son, who appeared at 5 A.M. By late the next morning news came through that all had gone well, excitement flaring throughout the Mas household. I spent the morning writing a detailed letter to my family, describing the last incredible twenty-four hours in which not one but two birthdays had been celebrated. I signed off, "Steph, 18 yrs old!"

* * *

Two days later Lottie Mas tapped on my bedroom door and told me I had a visitor. "Who is it?" I asked. Lottie shook her head. She had never seen this man before.

And nor had I. In his mid-twenties, he was sitting on the lounge room sofa as I limped in. He stared up at me with moon-struck eyes. "Hello," I greeted him, "how can I help you?" With that he began to stammer and stutter, admitting he was too embarrassed to speak, and could he please write down his message. Intrigued, I ducked into my bedroom, brought out a writing pad and biro, and sat a respectable distance away on a single chair. The man busied himself for a short while and then handed me the pad upon which was printed "I have strong feelings for you. I would like my boat to sail into your harbour." This was accompanied by the sketch of a harbour with a boat sailing in through the entrance.

My face flushed hot as I leapt up and moved to the dining table where I wrote, "If your boat moves anywhere near my harbour it will be blasted out of the water." With that I drew two cannons, one each side of the entrance, aiming at the boat. Handing this to him I stepped back, thinking that he would cringe and take off through the front door. But he looked up, saying he didn't believe me. "Please leave," I requested, but he insisted he would stay until he had satisfaction. Lottie, hovering nearby, spoke up. "What is the trouble?"

"This gentleman will not leave," I told her. Lottie informed the man that if Stephanie wanted him to leave, he must leave. Stubbornly he shook his head.

Lottie used harsher tones. "I will contact my husband if you don't leave right now!" But the man stared ahead as if deaf and dumb. Lottie's eyes met mine, and she indicated with a slight flick of her head that I should go back to my room. I heard her voice on the phone as she rang Tony, and I kept thinking this crackpot would up and let himself out. However, he sat on that sofa for a good twenty minutes until Tony arrived home.

I could hear Tony talking, his tone rising with annoyance then outright anger as the man refused to obey his orders to leave. But at last I heard the front door open and voices receding as Tony saw the intruder off the premises and returned to join Lottie in the lounge. When I dared to reappear the three of us had a brief discussion about what had just happened. When I showed them my sketch and written reply Lottie giggled, and Tony's anger subsided. However, he warned me that if I should ever see this guy stalking me, to seek support immediately. And even though I had always welcomed new experiences, this whole episode had been creepy—not the kind of experience I wanted to repeat.

* * *

Most nights now I dreamed about returning home, but in my head was a sharp divide—on the one hand desperate to be with my beloveds back home, and on the other dreading parting from all my loyal Filipino friends, probably forever. The dream seemed more real as the dates and times were made for my departure. It was planned that I would leave Zamboanga at the end of December, travelling to Cebu for a New Year's Rotary party before continuing on to Manila on the first day of 1969 to stay for a short while with Mrs Reith. All being well I would board a Qantas plane at midnight on January 6. One slightly disturbing factor was that Mrs Enriquez, owner of Manila Tours and mother of my guide Lim, had been tasked by Zamboanga Rotary to organise my ticket home. As this business lady was related to President Marcos, I had a nagging feeling that word might reach him that I would once again be staying in Manila. If all went to plan I would be vulnerable for only a few days, but the oft-quoted observation from Robbie Burns refused to go away.

"The best laid plans of mice and men do often go awry."

Location: Zamboanga
Host family — Veloso

I moved to the Veloso's in time for Christmas. Nina and Tony were more like friends than foster Mum and Dad, and we had lots of funny conversations. There were three children, two girls aged seven and five, and noisy little Buddy Boy attending kindergarten. Their house was vast, with all the mod cons of the day, and my bedroom was luxurious. A manservant waited upon me every time I showed up for breakfast. Coffee strong and hot was always waiting for me, and within seconds I would be served half a papaya garnished with the tiny citrus fruit, calamansi. This would be followed by two fried eggs and as many pieces of toast as desired.

On Christmas Eve I accompanied Nina and Tony to a ball held atop the thick walls of the ruins of Fort Pilar. Torchlight guided us amongst the trees and through the great entrance. It was an awe-inspiring experience to find myself within those thick stone walls that I had only ever seen from the outside. Wooden steps led up to the parapets, where guitars strummed, people danced, tables groaned with delicacies, and frangipanni wafted its fragrance over that perfect evening.

It was a fitting and glorious end to my stay in Zamboanga, but as I gazed across at the shoreline of this ancient Spanish city which I had come to love, I felt as if a knife was twisting in my heart. Below us lay the swamp village of Rio Hondo where I had ventured recently with Gerd, and where in April I had been lured by the shining dome of the mosque before being "rescued" by my friend Ali. Out on the dark sea lights twinkled from every vinta and every big ship, and when my head turned towards the western shoreline I could see the tiny piece of sand where Rob and I had sat one night gazing out to sea after dining at the

Hotel Byot. The police had cruised up to warn us about venturing into this area, their vehicle sliding into a ditch. And the Hotel itself—clearly outlined by strings of tiny lights extending out onto the decking from where Jo-Jo and I had once purchased shells from the Moros. Further in the distance I could just make out the rooftop of the home which served as the Zamboangan base for the Reith family, and hardly discernible was the balcony atop the Bernado house from where I had given a wink of approval to the little thief up the tree stealing guavas.

* * *

It was the day before leaving the City of Flowers. The Serenaders and I frolicked up at the Pasonanca Pool. Although we clowned around, the atmosphere was bittersweet. At one point Chito swept me up in his arms and carried me down a slope to a garden bench. Fiercely he stared at me, as if he were etching my face into his memory, and he pulled from his finger a ring which I had never noticed before. "Stephie," he said. "I want you to have this. No matter what happens, I want you to wear it, so you will never forget me."

Me with some Serenaders in Pasonanca Park.

It was a wide band of rose gold set with a large rectangular stone. At some angles it gleamed red, at others tangerine. Overcome with emotions, I found it hard to speak as I slipped it on my right ring finger. "I don't need something so beautiful to remember. I will *always* remember you."

What I said was true. For as long as I live there will be a place in my heart for this special Filipino boy who lit up my soul from the very first time his eyes had met mine.

Location, Cebu

At the New Year's party in Cebu I danced mostly with my German friend Gerd, slowly and carefully so I did not twist my feet. Everyone went ballistic as 1969 arrived in a cloud of streamers and fun and "Auld Lang Syne," but most of that night all I could think of was going home, home to Australia. Now that it was just a matter of days, the longing to see my family and friends and SJ became fierce and all-consuming.

As the Cebu exchange students accompanied me to the airport where a Fokker Friendship would take me on to Manila, Gerd gave me a card featuring a photo of himself holding aloft a plastic Christmas tree while sitting astride a water buffalo. Once again I farewelled a loveable person I'd be unlikely to ever see again.

Gerd's version of a Filipino Xmas Card.

January 1969
Location: Reiths' house, San Lorenzo Village, Manila

The Reiths' needed to serve as a base from which I could organise my departure. My visa to stay in the Philippines had been extended to March, so an expired visa was not the chief obstacle. However, there was a sticking point, something mysterious to do with my passport. Every day after I arrived at the Reiths', either Hans or Charlie drove me to downtown Manila to the Bureau of Immigration to try to get clearance to leave on 6 January as planned. The BOI room was vast with hundreds of stony-faced workers behind their desks. It was almost impossible to deduce which one to approach and why none of them seemed at all interested in sorting out the problem.

Every evening I dreaded that Colonel Ver would ring, demanding I see the president at his private house in Forbes Park.

The underlying truth concerning the lack of cooperation from the bureau began to emerge. I had just enough pesos to pay for each official step of the process, but I had no extra money to pass under the table to secure one vital stamp on my passport. Even if I had possessed the extra money, handing over a bribe would have galled me.

The departure date came and went. I was frustrated beyond belief. Because it was not possible to ring Australia, I guessed my family and friends had gone to the Adelaide airport on the morning I was due home. How their imaginations must have run riot! On 7 January I fronted up at the bureau with Charlie by my side, and whether the dear man paid the bribe I will never know, but the passport was duly stamped and the departure time was set for midnight the following day.

I spent hours packing and repacking, attempting to protect gifts such as the wonderful wood carving from Baguio—a glorious rearing stallion which was destined for my mother. While I managed to stuff all articles in, I did wonder how I would pay for any excess luggage if that were required. As 8 January dawned clear and bright, the departure date being set, I felt safe from any more overtures from the president. I spent part of the afternoon with darling Mrs Reith, and said my goodbyes and heartfelt thanks to George, Charlie, and the devoted Augustine.

An hour before I was due to leave for the airport, when darkness had fallen, it happened. A white Mercedes Benz pulled up, and the driver came to the door asking if this was where Miss Wicks was staying. "Can we talk in private?" asked the stranger, eyeing Mrs Reith and George who were hovering in the lounge. I wandered with the man towards the car, as he began apologizing. "Ma'am, the president is so very sorry, but he only discovered this day you are in Manila, and that you will be leaving soon." I felt my face flush. *Who had told Marcos I was here, and the details of my departure?* I hastened to assure the man that he was correct—I would be gone by midnight.

The man glanced around to make sure we were not being watched, then pulled a card from his trouser pocket. "The president would like you to correspond with him, but you must under no circumstance use his real name. Just this name here." He pointed to the anagram of the first four letters of Ferdinand, "Fred," written above a post box address. Feeling as though I were a character inside one of Jun's farcical radio plays I nodded, took the card, and turned back to the house. "Oh, wait," he said, "I might need some help." With that he leaned into the back seat of the car, pulling out armfuls of orchids and boxes of chocolates in such quantities that both our arms were overflowing as we returned to the lounge room.

George and his mother exchanged strange looks. Now I was in a pickle. But as the Mercedes cruised away, I realized that on this occasion I didn't need to lie. "These are from President Marcos. Somehow he learned that I was heading home." I had already hidden the card from George's prying eyes, and although I knew that the family wondered why the president would lavish me with such gifts when I had only ever met him once, in Zamboanga, there seemed nothing else I could say that would be constructive. "How will you carry all these onto the plane Stephanie?" George demanded.

I told him that I had no intention of taking any of the gifts aboard the plane, and that it would be a good idea if he and his family enjoyed the chocolates and adorned the house with orchids to remind them of me for a few days after I had gone. When I went to my bedroom to lock my case, I tore the card into small bits and threw them in the wastepaper basket. Then, knowing full well that George was a born detective with fierce curiosity, I retrieved a handful of the bits and stuffed them into my handbag.

The big red Dodge cruised to the front of the house. It was time.

* * *

Charlie stayed with me at the airport until 11.30 P.M. when I headed off alone on the vast tarmac towards the Qantas plane. At first I thought I was dreaming when Chito came running up behind me. *Wasn't he supposed to be back in Zamboanga, and how on earth had he found out my new departure time?* Without wasting valuable moments discussing the hows and whys, he handed me an envelope with instructions to open it on the plane. Then he confessed he didn't know how he would endure life without me. We hugged for a long time, the marvellous ring gleaming from my right hand, and I promised him that although I was going home to marry SJ, I would never, never forget the sheer happiness in my soul every time we had shared each other's company.

The Qantas steward called out, and with a last glance at Chito's anguished face I turned quickly and almost ran to the steward waiting at the bottom of the aircraft steps. Tears streamed down my face as I returned his smile in a furious mix of emotions. "Gudday mate, welcome aboard," said the Australian steward, and as we both climbed the steps I began to feel as if I were already home.

Location: South Australia

Perhaps extreme tiredness prevented me from remembering much about the return to Australia, except that as the plane lifted into the skies above Manila I read Chito's poem, my heart churning. The first stanza read: "This poem is yours my Stephie, It's plain and honest as can be, It's not made for praises, But simply for the love of thee."

On a smaller plane from Sydney, I arrived at Adelaide's modest airport at about 8 A.M. on a January day fast heating up. As I crossed the tarmac towards the low building where family and friends had farewelled me ten months ago, I held the naïve hope they would all be there to welcome me home. But of course, none of them knew the actual date of my arrival.

The airport building was a sad and lonely place as I collected my luggage from the carousel and hauled it out into the dry, sweet sunlight of South Australia. Suddenly it dawned on me—I had no money for either a taxi or even a phone call. Approaching one of the few taxis I asked the driver if he would take me to my home where I would collect the fare from my mother. The dear man must have thought I had a trustworthy face, and I settled back to enjoy the familiar sights along the route from the plains to the foothills. He drove me around to the rear of the house, standing by my case as I opened the back door and walked inside.

No one was home!

In the kitchen I scurried to the drawer where Mum usually kept some money, thankful to find enough to pay the taxi driver who kindly hauled the case through into the lounge before driving off.

I surveyed the scene. It was as though I had gone away for a day, not ten months. Suddenly all adrenalin drained away and fatigue hit hard. I showered, got into a light dressing gown, and lay down on my parents' bed so that I could see through into the back verandah. I fell into a light sleep until a car door slammed shut somewhere.

Hugging a huge bag of shopping, Mum entered the back verandah and came through into the lounge. Not wanting to scare her, I appeared in the bedroom doorway with a smile. "Hello little mother." Mum took one look at me, her knees buckled, and she collapsed in a pile of runaway groceries on the lounge carpet. Both of us were hysterical, half laughing, half crying, hugging each other amongst the carnage of fallen fruit and veg.

* * *

That night Mum cooked for all the family, including SJ who had raced up as soon as he knew I was home. We had the traditional Aussie lamb chops, mashed potatoes, peas and carrots, and I relished every mouthful. We had just finished when my Rotary mentor (Mr X) arrived. All of us made ourselves comfortable in the loungeroom, and I told them in detail about my encounters with Marcos until our coffee cups had been empty for hours. I was surprised when my voice and hands trembled as I relived the trauma, and my small audience was shocked to the core. Mum and Dad kept repeating they would never have let me go had they known this would happen, and Mr X was speechless. SJ nodded fiercely. "I knew something was wrong, I knew it!"

We all agreed to keep the story a secret for now, because we couldn't see any constructive outcome by telling the world. Yes, Marcos had abused his power, but at the end of the day he had not knowingly harmed me or any of my Filipino friends. Nevertheless, suspecting that the tentacles of a president can spread far and wide, we decided that to publicize the event could be dangerous, even on a personal level.

The following morning a big bouquet of flowers arrived from Mr X, my mentor, who was not only grateful that I had shared my story with him, but hugely relieved that for now I had agreed to keep the episode from Rotary. I'm sure he hoped the whole sordid episode would stay under wraps forever, and at that moment I saw no point in revealing my ordeal to anyone but close family and friends.

Soon after arriving home an *Advertiser* photographer arrived to take my photo above an article titled, "VIP Tour for SA Student." I am smiling as I hold aloft the rearing horse from Baguio, and while the item mentions that my Manila tour was "sponsored by the government" after being lucky enough to meet President Marcos over dinner, I had ensured there'd be no suspicion of private houses or secret meetings. It described how I roughed it during the malaria survey with Rob and Claro, how I had taught Filipino children how to swim, and how I hoped to return to the Philippines once I had finished my drama studies at Flinders University.

I had arrived home, but unfortunately that was not the end of the story. The repercussions kept coming, snowballing one on top of the other, impacting on my Filipino friends and me in ways I could never have dreamed of, changing my relatively benign feelings towards Marcos into those of hatred, fury and the desire for revenge.

Epilogue

1969

Letters and postcards from the Philippines followed thick and fast after my return, from close friends but also a few which caught me off-guard. Vee, housemaid in the president's private house, sent me no fewer than four postcards, each addressing me as "Dearest friend" or "Dearest One" and declaring how much she missed me. It was a challenge to reply kindly yet appropriately, myself uncomfortably aware that our few moments together had occurred in a top-secret situation.

Then there was a postcard from Poy at Manila Tours, the guide who had driven me to Baguio and accompanied me to the markets there. It had disturbed him deeply that I had fled so quickly from the beautiful mountain city before he had a chance to show me the ancient rice terraces. His postcard depicted Filipino peasants cultivating the terraces by hand in full national costume, with Poy urging me to return to his country so that he could show me these wonders for myself.

A letter from Jun addressed to SJ arrived late January, reassuring Steve that I had unerringly remained faithful to him, which had made him admire me even more. Adding that while he had always thought Western girls "don't take love seriously . . . Stephanie proved that was only a myth."

Throughout January and February Chito's cards and letters had sounded reasonably upbeat, mentioning his studies as a mechanical engineer and his newfound interest in scuba diving. He had even sent me my article about the White Australia Policy freshly printed in the *Beacon* along with the comment, "I think you'll be having many Filipino immigrants this coming year, and they will all be saying 'thanks to Miss Stephie Wicks,' and who knows, I might be one of them."

But in March, his letter took a more disturbing tone. "I really do miss you Steph . . . Whenever I sing a folk song your image bursts into my mind and sadness clouds within me, and for this reason I dare not sing again." It hurt to think my dearest Chito had stopped singing—to sing was as necessary to him as water is to life. But I was busy enrolling in the drama course at Flinders University, spending time with other students, even learning to scuba dive myself, and of course enjoying a full-on courtship from SJ. All I could do was to fervently hope that my special friend would suddenly discover a lovely girl who would restore some joy to his soul.

I wrote several return letters, as tactfully and as truthfully as was possible, but there was no response until a letter arrived dated 5 May. This one floored me. Chito said he had been sick, and when his friends suspected I was the cause, he had tried to convince them this was not the case. But he confessed he was lying. "They think I'm getting worse Steph. I thought I could forget you by going home to Zamboanga, but when that failed I tried drinking but all was useless . . . Remember the day I told you that I was ready to accept any hardship when you left? I said it with boldness in me but look at what's happening to me now. I'm not a man . . . I cannot handle the situation . . . I'm ruined since that dreadful day you left for Australia." Chito then suggested we quit writing to each other so that he might forget me. He apologized repeatedly, professed he would always love me, and finished with a small but powerful poem ending with: "If you knew I loved you and more, If you knew just how much I do, then you would come back to me . . ."

Feeling wretched, my only reasonable course of action was to write and assure him that I would cease communication if that might help. Early in November a more positive letter arrived from Manila—Chito obviously deciding that to quit writing altogether was counterproductive. Due to return to Zambo by boat, with a cabin all to himself, he wrote, "Won't it be just wonderful, looking at the endless ocean?" He was also keen to tell me of The Serenaders' new clubhouse, masterminded by Teddy and Raymond Bader and built almost entirely of signboards stolen over several nights from Marcos's election campaign. Chito wrote, "I'm just glad they are not caught. I wonder what President Marcos would do if he finds out? I think we should send him a 'thank you' card . . . wouldn't he be surprised?" At this point Chito had no animosity towards Marcos because I had not yet breathed a word to him about my secret encounters.

However, he did note that politics was getting very dirty, very personal, and that already many people had died in the lead up to the election. The last paragraphs were full of sadness that I couldn't be with him, and that he would wait patiently for me to return. However, the tone was not as despairing as in his previous letter, and he finished by sending his regards to my parents and brother, hoping to meet them one day so he could tell them "how their daughter had captured my heart."

Marcos won his second term of office on 11 November 1969. Jun's following observations about the election campaign, while similar, were more detailed than Chito's—"It has been the most expensive and dirtiest election in the history of the PI with the Election Commissioner Perez a crony of Marcos." These two Filipinos, one from the middle class and the other from the working class, confirmed my instincts that Marcos had stopped at nothing to win his second term of office. Warning bells rang loud when soon after winning the election Marcos set about suspending Habeas Corpus, the right of people to challenge the legality of their imprisonment. The reason he gave was that the Moro National Liberation Front (MNLF) had been formed in Mindanao and were engaged in active insurgencies, but at this stage I simply assumed that in four years from now someone would replace him, perhaps Senator Salonga or Benigno (Ninoy) Aquino, and that Filipinos would easily rebuild and enjoy their precious democracy as before.

The end of 1969 was ironic. When details of the sickening Mai Lai massacre in Vietnam were made public, Marcos had his excuse to withdraw his forces, no doubt with the idea he could use extra manpower for his own agendas. My brother Steve won the "Birthday Ballot"—a free mandatory ticket to join the conflict. The Wicks family held its breath, until we received the wondrous yet irrational news that because Steve was serving in the Navy Reserve, he would be exempt.

As for my SJ, his twentieth birthday would not occur until April 1970. A strong individual who never followed the flock, he braced himself for the worst, vowing that if his number came up he would suffer the horrible consequences of being a conscientious objector rather than bear arms in this conflict. He and I had attended several powerful lectures by an eminent professor who made no bones about the immorality and wrongfulness of the Vietnam War. As a result, both of us often found ourselves engaged in heated discussion of the issue over the dinner table with our parents.

1970

In January something extraordinary happened in the Philippines which remained unknown to most of the world. Dovie Beams, an American starlet in her late thirties, proclaimed to the Philippine press that after she had been recruited at the end of 1968 to play the love interest in the film *Maharlika*, she had become Marcos's mistress. Keen to support the movie which was designed to mirror his brave exploits during World War II, Marcos had begun a torrid affair with Dovie that proved highly dangerous for his career and for her life.

In a "safe" house in Forbes Park, perhaps the very "gilded cage" where I had been taken three times in October 1968, Dovie hid a tape recorder under their bed with the motive of shoring up insurance in case Marcos turned against her. Sure enough, eventually Dovie claimed that her life had been threatened, and proceeded to play the erotic tapes to a delighted press.

With Malacañang reeling from the scandal, Dovie returned to America while Marcos and his ministry denied and covered up the story as best they could. But a few months later the actress returned to Manila, this time demanding 150,000 US dollars which she claimed was owed to her from her lover. But because she now had no bargaining tool, a furious Imelda demanded she be sent packing with not one dollar, and promptly engaged in her own blackmail, promising her husband she would present a united front as man and wife so long as he allowed her ambitions free rein. One of those was to become governor of Manila.

A quote from dispatches between the governor's office in Hong Kong and the British Embassy in Manila states Dovie, "was seen on to the plane by a staff member of the US embassy but, as soon as he left the plane, the seat next to her was taken by Delfin V Cueto, one of Marcos's hatchet men. Although he made no approach to her during the flight, she was thoroughly frightened and on arrival in Hong Kong moved hotels frequently to avoid him."

Because of this scandal, the film *Maharlika* remained effectively quashed and unseen throughout all the years of Marcos's dictatorship.

In August, at the same time the fearful Dovie fled the country, I wedded SJ who in April had been lucky enough to escape conscription and was studying arts with me at Flinders University. We took out a loan and bought a cottage for $6000, and so from now on we'd be, as the saying goes, "living on the smell of an oily rag." Our time was spent studying, making friends, restoring the cottage and occasionally joining the protest rallies against the Vietnam War. Both of us were dismayed by those of our student colleagues who waved red flags and dubbed our soldiers "baby-killers." Knowing that the war was counterproductive, we simply wanted it to stop.

The ring that Chito had given to me gleamed constantly from my right hand, even though every evening I laboured, sanding and painting and generally restoring the cottage. SJ knew why this ring was important to me, and to his credit he never expressed any jealousy.

Meanwhile, back in Manila, it became clear from Jun's letters that the Marcos tentacles were reaching into every corner of society—armed forces, grand hotels, significant corporations, all major newspapers, all TV channels, and perhaps most alarming, the Supreme Court Justices, the last hope of democracy.

But I was pregnant, preoccupied with setting up our home and future family, and had no energy to spare being too concerned about the Philippines. After all, it was against the constitution for Marcos to stay in the presidency for a third term, wasn't it? Naively I believed that in three more years he would be gone, and I would have little cause to think about him again.

1971

In February I received a letter from a Filipina who observed, "The future is bleak and dreary in our Philippines... bloody demonstrations occurring now in Manila and suburbs." She quoted a minor newspaper's headline "Threat of Martial Law." However, distracted with my life, I barely gave a thought of what the ramifications of martial law might be for the democracy-loving Filipinos.

At this stage Zamboanga itself had not been particularly affected by protests or unrest, but nearby in Basilan and remote parts of Mindanao things were starting to get ugly. Instead of working to unite and strengthen his country as his last term of office drew closer, the president devised a way of creating enormous chaos, enough to warrant martial law which would override the constitution. He turned his attention to the two areas of the Philippines which were inherently unstable—the north where the ideals of communism were increasingly gaining traction, and the south where Muslim resentment had been simmering for centuries. According to Jun, whose extended family helped him put together the pieces of the jigsaw, Marcos had been responsible for setting free many of the most hardened Christian criminals from Muntinlupa Penal farm on the outskirts of Manila. (The penitentiary boss happened to be a second cousin to Marcos.) The prisoners' freedom came with the proviso they would be shipped down south to Mindanao with secret orders to attack as many Muslim communities as possible. Forming a strike force called the Llagas (Rats), they went to work with a will, plundering, looting, raping, and killing. The Muslims were quick to form retaliatory paramilitary groups called the Barracudas and the Blackshirts, and all too soon the cycle of reprisals was out of control. Jun was disgusted at the hypocrisy of Marcos, who ordered his "peacekeeping" forces to the affected areas "to maintain the unity between Christian and Muslim brothers," a move calculated to pour fuel onto the fires.

From this time on, any Filipino owning property further south than Zamboanga would be forced to either fight to retain their properties or surrender them, and any foreign missionaries and loggers living in remote areas felt extremely vulnerable. I thought about the Hall family living in the Litukan valley; I thought about Werner Garmsen's family defending their island properties; I thought about my typing friend Bing and my Rotarian father Tony Mas, both needing to tend their small coconut farms in Basilan. I even thought about my Muslim friend Ali in the swamp village of Rio Hondo, wondering whether he would be forced to take sides and thereby lose his precious job at radio DXLL.

By July leaders from all Filipino Muslim communities had published a manifesto demanding that the government take action to quell the attacks. The fact that Marcos immediately dubbed this manifesto a "threat" confirmed his grand plan to fuel the unrest, his response leading to the formation of the Moro National Liberation Front (MNLF), based in Basilan and supplied from Sabah. Those more politically savvy than me, people like Jun, knew that once martial law was in place Marcos would stay entrenched for as many years as he could maintain control.

Meanwhile I was busy juggling baby Skye with my studies. SJ and I would take her in a wash basket to university campus and smuggle her into lectures where she won over professors and students alike with her gurgles and smiles.

On 21 August Senator Salonga, the charismatic Rotarian guest who had sat beside me in Tony Mas's limo and made such a riveting speech that night, ran for re-election. During his party's proclamation rally at Plaza Miranda in Manila a bomb exploded, leaving nine dead and several, including Salonga, critically injured. Marcos blamed the communists for the attack, adding that the New People's Army (NPA) had framed him for the outrage. But whether the perpetrators were Marcos's military or the NPA, the president must have been rattled to hear that not only had Jovito Salonga survived his multiple injuries, but that he would go on to top the senatorial race with a host of fellow liberals. Quickly Filipinos made their own judgement as to who had been responsible for the Plaza Miranda atrocity.

In a November letter Jun described his recent journey by bus through a southern province when he witnessed many Muslim houses burnt to the ground. Asking one of his fellow passengers whether this was the work of the Llagas he was told that Filipino soldiers had torched those homes. "And right there," wrote Jun, "I felt something fishy."

1972

During the previous year I had ploughed on with my studies while my mother took over primary day care of my daughter. But in January Mum offered a snippet of advice that was nothing short of life-changing, warning that while she would love nothing better than to raise Skye, "one day when she is troubled about something, it'll be me she comes to, not you."

It took me a second to make up my mind to defer my arts degree and become a stay-at-home Mum, but creative writing continued to flow from my typewriter at home. Jun and Chito kept me informed about themselves personally, but it was Jun the political "beastie" who included summaries from the underground newspapers to provide me with the detailed truth about what Marcos was up to.

In May a shocking episode unfolded when American police shot and killed several Kent State University students protesting the Vietnam War. The iconic photograph of the Napalm Girl, the picture that shook decent people to their foundations, provided the flashpoint. From now on Richard Nixon would have his work cut out to justify the continuation of the war, and an even tougher time justifying taxpayers' millions to persuade Marcos to keep hosting the US military bases.

There was a full-on Muslim insurgency on Basilan Island when, on the first day of August, my dear host father Tony Mas took the ferry and crossed the Strait to visit his hobby plantation. Failing to return home, and because his body was never recovered, it seems likely he was murdered.

By September the situation was so volatile Marcos judged the time was right to impose martial law, but not before he had rounded up all his critics, including Senator Salonga and Ninoy Aquino, imprisoning them on trumped-up charges. And who was the president's chief enforcer of the round-up? General Fabian Ver who had climbed the promotional ladder, the same man who had ferried me back and forth to the president's secret "safe house" in Forbes Park during October 1968.

Another chief enforcer was Juan Ponce Enrile, who would stage an attack on his own white Mercedes Benz literally hours before Marcos announced martial law. This fake attack, although not admitted by Enrile until Marcos was ousted, was to further his boss's justification of the implementation of martial law which was officially declared on 22 September, the acts of tyranny escalating even as Marcos shut down Congress. Consequently, even though Salonga was released after a brief time at Fort Bonifacio, he lost his job as senator. Refusing to take warning from his summary arrest, he and his law partners turned their attention to providing free legal assistance to all those political prisoners crammed into the regime's jails. Salonga's friend Ninoy Aquino languished in solitary confinement in a three-square metre cell, unbearably hot and crawling with insects. From this time on Aquino, Salonga and the eccentric long-haired Cesar Climaco knowingly put themselves at great risk by taking every opportunity to expose Marcos. From this point on it was horribly clear that my steadfast friend Jun was also in danger each time he posted a letter to Australia, our communications becoming increasingly cryptic to avoid detection.

1973

My son Jim was born in March, and the next three months were as hectic as is the norm with a newborn and a toddler in the family. During this phase I was blissfully unaware of the full horrors going on in the country I had inhabited only five years earlier. Just one example is what happened to Liliosa Hileo, twenty-three years young, the same age as me. During her tertiary studies she wrote several essays criticizing the Marcos government. Soldiers came to her home without a warrant, beat her up in front of her family, dragged her off to Camp Crame, and within days had tortured and killed her. She was the first of many to die during the martial law imprisonments.

In July, I became ill with Stills Disease, a virulent form of juvenile arthritis which I had suffered in early adolescence at boarding school.

As with the first onset at the age of twelve, I spent a month in hospital, and a month at home to recuperate. In both cases I was given a fifty-fifty chance—either I would get better or end up in a wheelchair. Thankfully I recovered as before, superficially at least. When at last I could hold a pen I wrote to Chito in late August, telling him all that had happened. A month later his return letter arrived, expressing worry and sadness for me and my little family. "I like the four of you to be happy because it makes me happy too." This was true love—one that transcends sexual attraction and wishes only happiness for the beloved.

When Chito mentioned he had scored a job as Mechanical Engineer and Assistant Operations Manager in a logging camp in the Zamboanga del Sur mountains, I was surprised to see that this logging concession belonged to none other than the Veloso's, my last Rotarian host family in Zamboanga. Tony was the fine man who had treated family and friends to wild rides on his cruise boat out to Santa Cruz Island. Perhaps it was this coincidence that distracted me from any concern about the location of Chito's work, or the increasing danger that any remote community was likely to attract.

Towards the end of 1973 both Chito and Jun sent news that their dreams of leaving the Philippines and migrating to Australia or America had been dashed: Marcos's Philippine New Society Program was actively discouraging technicians, engineers, doctors and any intellectuals from emigrating to other countries. While superficially it might have seemed laudable that Marcos wished to halt the brain-drain from his country, the irony was clear. The very reason so many educated Filipinos were now looking to live elsewhere was because their president seemed hell-bent on trashing their much-prized democracy at every turn. The Marasigans, my first Zamboanga Rotary host family, were amongst those who fled to America.

1974

In September there was a massacre of Muslims at a coastal town at Palimbang in Southern Mindanao. The perpetrators were alleged to be the Philippine Constabulary.

I now know that not far from Palimbang Chito lived and worked in the logging camp. But in 1974 I had no knowledge of the massacre or of Chito's exact location.

On one of his days off in November, Chito came down from the camp, purchased an expensive Christmas card at Palimbang and posted it to "Stephie, Steve and the children." It arrived, as he had hoped, just before Christmas. I placed the card in pride of place on the kitchen mantelpiece and set about preparing for the big day.

Four days after Christmas I was standing in the kitchen chopping up carrots when there was a loud "clang!" as something flew from my hand and hit the tin pedal bin. I doubled over, as if I'd been shot in the stomach, noticing that the stone from Chito's ring lay on the floor. Clutching my belly, trying to catch my breath, I picked up the stone and almost staggered to the back door where I called out to SJ who was gardening. "Something bad has happened to Chito," I called, before attempting to describe the strange happening and what I had felt. Once again, to his great credit, rather than mocking me he pondered for a few seconds before deciding, "He must be okay, because he sent you that card. It came only a week ago."

Returning to the kitchen I retrieved the card from the mantelpiece, trying to feel comforted as I reread it. By the time I came to the last paragraph I reasoned my imagination must have run away with me. After all, he had signed off with "I'm doing fine, in spite of the loneliness in the mountains and being single, I still manage to go along just fine. Always, Chito."

1975

Early in January I visited one of South Australia's top jewelers who told me to return in a quarter of an hour, by which time he would have secured the stone into Chito's ring. When I fronted up he seemed annoyed. "Are you sure this stone belongs to this ring?" Astonished, I assured him I had been wearing both stone and ring for many years now. "Come back in half an hour," he said, and so pushing the pram containing baby Jim, little Skye tottering along by my side, we spent half an hour window shopping.

This time the jeweler was super stressed. The stone would still not fit into the ring, and when he insinuated that I was deliberately deceiving him all I could do was to repeat the facts. He asked me to come back in a week, which I did, and there was the ring back to normal and gleaming. The poor man was fuming. What he had deduced would take him a quarter of an hour had swallowed up half a day, but he could only charge me for fifteen minutes' work.

Soon after this I wrote to Chito, careful not to mention the strange happening with the ring, thanking him for his card before describing our Christmas and New Year activities.

March came and went, and still Chito had not replied. But the Philippine Post being reliably unreliable, especially from the more remote regions, I assumed that Chito's latest letter had gone astray. I wrote towards the end of April, asking him to write soon. May came and went, and still no word. In June I wrote again, this time chastising him gently for not staying in contact, and enclosing two photos of my family.

Another month went by without any contact, and so when one afternoon in July I wandered out to the mailbox and discovered a letter from the Philippines bearing Chito's tell-tale handwriting, I yelled with joy. Jim and Skye raced up to share the excitement, and as we walked together down the passage I exclaimed, "At last! A letter from Chito!" All three of us sat on the sofa, all three of us smiling expectantly as I tore open the envelope.

Within a few seconds my joy had turned to horror. The letter dated 23 June began, in writing so like Chito's, "My Dear Stefanie, the doctor and myself would like to apologize for our failure to inform you earlier of what actually happened to our son Chito. We have desired so much to write you much earlier of the incident, but we never found the courage to do so. However, after receiving your letter dated June 6 we deemed it no longer right to keep you from knowing."

Tears welled up so that the following was almost impossible to read as I pictured Chito's Mum—instead of that sweet smile all I could envisage was heart-wrenching anguish. The children sensed something terrible had happened. "What Mummy? What is it?" but I couldn't reply as I struggled to read on. "We know that the tidings we bring is painful because we ourselves cannot accept the fact that he is gone."

The following is a summary of Mrs Limcangco's news. In 1974 on 28 December Muslim rebels attacked Tony Veloso's logging camp in the mountains and set about killing the men they found—except Chito and twelve other office personnel whom they kidnapped, probably in a rush of indecision as to whether these men would be more useful held as hostages for ransom money. However, a few days later, the decomposing bodies of all these young men were found strewn together some way from the camp in no-man's-land, an area still seen as too dangerous for the bereaved parents to collect the bodies of their sons.

"You see Stefie, we wanted you to be spared from this painful news, but we also believe that you have the right to know. We received your three letters together with the pictures of your family—but then Chito never had the chance to see or read them . . . please forgive us if we have to cut this letter short—before we might get sentimental again . . . do write to us . . . we will be very happy to hear from you because we are pretty sure that it is what Chito will want . . . do receive our best wishes and regards to you and Steve and the children—Lovingly, Horacio and Tillie." These are the very names I later found engraved on the inside of the ring.

I cried for days. When I wasn't crying openly, I was crying inside. Eventually I posted a letter to Drs Horacio and Otilia Limcangco, but I have no memory of what I wrote. At this time, although ignorant of the Palimbang massacre, I already knew enough to suspect that the key architect of the recent wars between the different cultures and religions was Marcos himself. One day, I vowed, I would put all the main pieces of the jigsaw together and alert the world to the big picture. For now, and for my husband's sake, I needed to store Chito away in a corner of my heart and get on with life in Australia.

Less than five years after the Dovie Beams scandal, the Jane Reilly incident occurred but, like mine, remained a necessary secret at the time.

One of her beauty competition prizes was a free trip throughout Asia in 1975, and while in the Philippines she caught the eye of President Marcos.

Jane went on to become a much-loved TV and radio personality, and in 2017 she decided to make public the details of what turned out to be a very traumatic time. One reason she had kept the secret for so many years was that it was upsetting to relive her experience, a feeling to which I can relate strongly. The following is some of her story as transcribed from radio 5AA in Adelaide . . .

"It just so happened that President Marcos took a shine to me and he requested that I be in his company for a couple of formal events . . . we ended up on his boat and somehow I end up in his private dining room on my own with him. He's sitting very, very close to me and he starts to touch me on the leg. I said, 'If you touch me again I'm going to scream and I'm going to run out of this room.' He said, 'Miss, if you do that the guard at the door with the gun will shoot you.' This is a true story."

Some time in 1985, a baby was born, presumably in Australia, and she was called Analisa Josefa, her second name attributable to Dona Josefa, Marcos's grandmother. The baby's mother was a Playboy model, and her father was Ferdinand Marcos. It would be 2025 before the fifty-one-year-old Analisa Josefa came to my attention, when mainstream news reported that Marcos's love child had been arrested for drunken and disorderly behaviour on a Jetstar flight. Perhaps it was this dalliance in the mid-1970s that was the final straw for Imelda, who in November 1975 struck a deal with her husband—in exchange for her turning a blind eye to his womanising, he appointed her Governor of Manila.

1977

This was the year when a young Australian man called Keith Dalton arrived in Manila with "a backpack, a typewriter, and a burning ambition to be a foreign correspondent."[2] He would stay until Marcos and family were ousted, occasionally visiting the eighth-floor office of the United

---

2. Dalton, Keith, *Reinventing Marcos*, (Dalton Books, 2024), 8.

Press International office, overlooking Malacañang palace. He may have passed Jun in the street, or lived in the same block, but of course neither Jun nor I were aware of Keith's existence in 1977, or the tumultuous decade to come.

Keith's personal experiences, shrewd observations and dangerous encounters are vividly described in Reinventing Marcos, *a book he felt compelled to write when Marcos's son Bongbong was elected president of the (Philippines) in 2022. I had no knowledge of Keith until early in 2025 when I read his book and realized we shared mutual feelings of horror and outrage that a tyrant's dynasty had craftily managed to "reinvent" history to suit its political agenda.*

In May, Jun's uncle was aboard a Philippines Airlines plane when six young male Muslims hijacked the aircraft and forced it to land at Zamboanga. Their aim was to negotiate their safe passage to the Middle East. When the plane landed the hijackers allowed most of the women and children to leave the plane. But then, according to Jun's uncle, the Philippine Constabulary surrounded the aircraft and opened fire with every size gun imaginable, spraying everyone with bullets regardless of whether they were passengers or terrorists. The fact that only seventeen passengers died was remarkable, and the survivors, including some of the hijackers, were equally horrified at the ferocity of the indiscriminate attack. Jun wrote, "One of the passengers happened to be an Australian journalist, and when the troopers stormed inside the plane this Aussie kicked the first trooper that approached him shouting, 'You SOB . . . you don't have any respect for innocent lives!' He was quickly overpowered . . . and deported immediately." Military man Lieutenant Colonel Estocapio stated that it was only when the hijackers had begun throwing grenades that the military had opened fire. However, Jun's uncle, a civilian, makes no mention of grenades, claiming that the young terrorists were relatively "considerate, even friendly."

In November Ma Alvarez wrote to me describing the lawless state of Zamboanga. "The situation is tense because the rebels turned bandits are plundering villages. When Government forces fight back, more civilians, especially women and children, get hurt." She added that the bandits were trying to take the city "because the air base and the armed forces HQ are here . . . all we can do is be prepared and fight back. Civilians are being armed now . . ."

Shortly after Ma wrote that letter, a military tribunal sentenced Ninoy Aquino to death by firing squad. But Marcos shrewdly calculated that if the sentence were carried out, Aquino's death would create a martyr who might well spearhead a mass uprising against his government. So, for now at least, although Aquino continued to languish in jail, he would have a stay of execution.

1978

I'm not sure why, but almost a year flew by without Jun and me corresponding. When at last a letter arrived from me a "deliriously happy" Jun responded, swearing that neither of us would lose contact again. That is when he wrote the prophetic words, "On my word of honour Steph, only death will stop me writing to you, now that I've found you again." Over the years I had learned that Jun was a man of huge integrity—he did not use those words lightly.

It was now one decade since my year in the Philippines, and all naïve hope of Marcos as a benign dictator had vanished. No longer did the ordinary people believe his accusations of communist or terrorist bombings. Putting two and two together they had discovered that not one corporate interest linked with the president had been bombed. Jun pointed out that the attacks were occurring everywhere except (strangely enough) the Marcos-controlled army installations, TV and radio stations, and corporations.

By March, desperate to help all those Filipinos who had been so kind to me and were struggling financially and socially under the oppressive regime, I decided to write to Marcos himself. It could not be sent to "Fred" at a secret box number because a decade earlier, within moments of receiving his coded name and post box number, I had destroyed the piece of paper it was written on. My typed letter was therefore addressed to Malacañang Palace, a handwritten copy made for safekeeping.

Without mentioning secret houses or rendezvous, I simply reminded him of our brief friendship, appealing to his "kindness, honour and reason" to stop the tyranny. I inserted just enough details to make him aware of how much I knew, without of course giving away my main source. I also mentioned his legacy, asking him to imagine people years from now recalling that F. Marcos was "the only leader recorded in the annals of history who backed from his own repressive policies with dignity and transformed his country once more into the Show-Window of Democracy in the Pacific."

I indirectly warned Marcos that if there were no changes for the better in Philippine politics, I would make sure the truth seeped "like oil under the Iron Curtain for the rest of the world... to judge accordingly." Inwardly I vowed to leak not just my story to the Australian press, but all the information which my insider informant was supplying.

Within the next two months Jun sent several pieces of news which were political dynamite. After five years of martial law, with criticisms echoing around the world, Marcos had publicly announced he would hold an election on 7 April, bragging that even the detainees could run for office. I could only imagine his shock when Aquino decided to take him up on the offer, running as candidate from where he sat in prison. This immediately gave a real boost of hope to the ordinary Filipino, who knew that in any honest election Aquino would win in a landslide. But herein was the catch—in any *honest* election.

Aquino requested that Marcos allow him to leave prison sporadically to hit the campaign trail, even if this meant guards escorting him to and from his cell. The request was denied, the justification being that Aquino was too dangerous! Jun wrote: "Marcos is afraid to set Aquino free even for a minute since he knows very well the appeal of this young genius of a senator."

Aquino proceeded to form his own party, nicknamed Laban. While the Laban night rallies often suffered blackouts, all those held by Imelda Marcos's New Society Party, the KBL, ran smoothly with no disruptions. "Right now, here in Manila," wrote Jun, "you can feel the intense opposition to Imelda and her cohorts. People from shoeshine boys, taxi drivers, college/high-school students and professionals are shouting 'Laban!' on the streets." But Jun predicted that Marcos and his cronies would rig the ballots to prevent the Laban Party from winning. And there are no prizes for guessing he was correct, with few if any impartial newspapers surviving to report the facts.

One day a letter arrived from Jun that had obviously been tampered with and re-sealed. Instantly I felt alarm. While one of my safeguards was to always use my married name, none of us could be sure of the extent of Marcos's spy network. I worried what might happen to Jun if he were identified leaking damning information to the Australian press. Living in Australia I would be less of a target, but nevertheless we resolved to stay alert.

Renting a humble abode on the outskirts of Manila proper, Jun wrote in April that it must have been "Australian Customs who opened my letter—because if it was otherwise then I wouldn't be writing to you at this moment." He advised that while he would need to register his outgoing mail, my letters should remain unregistered to avoid arousing suspicion in the Philippines. The situation in Manila sounded intolerable. He did not even dare take a walk downtown because of the "fires and bombings."

And the situation was no better in Zamboanga. A grenade had been thrown inside the Plaza Theatre, two people having been killed and one badly injured. Jun naturally worried because his family so often frequented the movies. Shocked, I remembered the number of times I had sat in this cinema during 1968 where the only scary incident had been a rat running over my foot. The thought of my Zambo friends now being afraid for their lives every day and night was truly sad. Jun added, "I don't think I have to tell you who is behind this evil deed."

During June the Interim National Assembly, rubber-stamped by Marcos, met for the first time, only to find the meeting hall infested with flies—the delegates' fly-swatting all caught on television and becoming the joke of the week. Jun declared it was hardly surprising. "All those SOBs inside are rotten, so naturally they will attract the flies!"

From now on Marcos was running scared. Increasingly aware that his people now saw through his schemes, his paranoia reached terrifying heights, and the brutality of the regime ramped up accordingly. Aquino still languished in jail, his only comfort knowing that he was adored by the great majority of his countrymen.

In July 1978 the Philippines Charge d'Affairs in Canberra, Joselito Azurin, unsuccessfully sought asylum in Australia after learning that upon his return to his homeland he would be charged with treason because he had joined the Movement for a Free Philippines. Perhaps the White Australia Policy was still alive and well, but whatever the reasoning had been, Azurin fled to safety in the US instead.

At this point Jun expressed ever deeper despair, railing against the passivity of Filipinos. "Most are illiterates and easy prey for a vulture like Marcos. I feel like a coward, but if I raise a storm right now I'll be dead." He repeated, "Only death will stop me writing to you."

That did it. I determined to interest the foreign editor of *The Advertiser* about what was really going on in the Philippines. If Jun couldn't protest publicly without ending up dead, then at least his passion for democracy would be rewarded. I contacted foreign correspondent Bill Guy, and after hearing my reasons for giving him political information he came to interview me for several hours. At this point we agreed that Jun's name be withheld, and mine too, for obvious reasons.

In mid-November Bill's substantial article, "The Marcos Dictatorship" appeared in Saturday's *Advertiser*, explaining that this information was via an intermediary and that the source itself could "only be named at his peril . . . a young city worker, well-educated despite an unprivileged childhood with no ideological hang-ups. He is passionate in his patriotism but fearful for his country's future."[3]

Thus, Bill Guy was able to describe with confidence Marcos's agenda and his manipulation of his people through control of the four major media outlets—either owned by himself, a crony, or someone related to the family. (Jun could name them all.) For the first time Australians were hearing an ordinary Filipino's opinions based on fact, and the punchline, a direct quote from Jun, summed up the situation perfectly. "The only thing we believe in our newspapers now are the death notices."

Bill's article had gone beyond my expectations, satisfying me that Jun's hard work, Tony Mas's disappearance, and Chito's murder had not

---

3. Bill Guy, "The Marcos Dictatorship," *The Advertiser*, 18 November 1978.

been entirely in vain. One day, I vowed, I would write my own book telling the whole story. But that would be some time in the future. When destiny determined that the time was right.

1979

In between my obsession with the Marcos's tyranny and family life in Adelaide, I was in my element writing screenplay. One of the stories, which only ever reached what was called treatment stage, was based on my visit to the Philippines General Hospital in 1968. Werner's beautiful cousin who had been raped and blinded by a gang, morphed for my film into an educated Moro princess character who is attacked and left for dead. Her brother repeats the endless cycle of revenge by tracking down the perpetrators and slowly torturing them to death, just as Werner had vowed to do.

I asked Jun for more details to give authenticity to my fictional story, and my loyal friend scrambled to help me, searching far and wide to find the answers to my questions despite working in his office until midnight six days a week for a coconut oil company. In one letter he announced that he had been subjected to so many lies from the Marcos machine for so long he feared for his mental health. "It's only . . . friends like you . . . that keeps me going . . . and normal. In fact, I'm not sure if I still am."

1980

Jun was visiting Zamboanga where now there was a curfew. This meant no public transport after 6 P.M. and risking life and limb to wander downtown after dark. But he sent good news too, excitedly telling me that he had met the love of his life and would marry in April. His chosen one, Bel, was a teacher who was "humble and very sweet." I felt great relief for my friend, who had been so stressed and would now have someone with whom to share the fast-unfolding horrors. However, it was not lost on either of us that from now on he would have to be even more cautious in speaking out against the regime.

Three days before the wedding a big fire broke out in downtown Zambo, razing a whole block of shops except for one small building which contained Bel's bridal dress. Naturally everyone connected with the couple considered this to be a wonderful omen which would bestow great happiness on the marriage. The wedding was a simple affair because the couple needed every peso to start a new life and family, but according to Jun the occasion was exceptionally beautiful because so many close friends and relatives worked hard to make it so. He counted himself the luckiest man in the world.

Jun and Bel immediately moved to Manila, renting a relative's small flat for 350P a month, a third of the normal price, Jun slaving away in his company's office. Only one newspaper Jun vowed was telling the "real truth," the eight-page *WE FORUM* founded in 1977 and compiled by a courageous bunch of young men and women working from an old bungalow. "The reason why Marcos won't touch them," he wrote, "is because this newspaper is very popular with the University of the Philippines, New York Times, Washington Post . . . and other free press." Despite its support from such illustrious sources, the staff of this gutsy little newspaper were constantly harassed by the constabulary, just to keep them fearful of every word they wrote.

Only 3 km away from where Jun and Bel lived, Ninoy Aquino suffered a heart attack after seven years of solitary confinement at Fort Bonifacio. Marcos and his ambitious wife were suddenly faced with a conundrum. If the adored Aquino were to die, even from natural causes rather than firing squad, he would instantly become the martyred figurehead of a mass uprising. Imelda announced that she would allow Aquino to leave the country, a clever move which made her seem compassionate but at the same time ridding her dynasty of its most potent enemy. By May, Aquino, and his wife Cory were winging their way to America where Aquino would undergo life-saving surgery.

Marcos announced that on 23 September (the date he had imposed martial law eight years ago) his country would celebrate Thanksgiving. A journalist from *WE FORUM* called this a "sick joke on the nation."

In October the Philippines Convention Center was bombed, the president narrowly escaping the blast. The incident provided Marcos with the excuse to again arrest Jovito Salonga, this time on suspicion of masterminding the bombing and attempting to assassinate him. This was a grave mistake. Despite mainstream news blatantly attempting to garner sympathy for Marcos, public outrage was now so great that by November the government, forced to back off, released Salonga, who calmly continued to legally represent other political prisoners in their bid for freedom.

It is quite likely that Rafael Climaco, close relative of my former hosts, the Alvarez family, and brother of that wonderful character Cesar who had recently staged a comeback as Mayor of Zamboanga, was one of the few surviving incorruptible judges in the Manila Supreme Court who may have allowed some of the prisoners to walk free. As for Cesar, a close friend of Aquino and the one who had refused to cut his long hair until martial law was lifted, he maintained ongoing and loud criticism of the Marcos government despite the danger. I remembered him with great fondness, vividly recalling St John's Day 1968 when he had scooped me up from the Alvarez home and driven me downtown to allow me to enjoy the tradition of water-flinging.

Late in 1980 Cesar Climaco wrote an article for *WE FORUM* newspaper which produced twenty thousand copies, claimed by Jun to be "gobbled up in a blink." The mayor lamented that his "City of Flowers, of beauty and of love" had become under martial law "a dirty and deadly city . . . of tears and of fears." He even went so far as to criticize the military as being some of the worst perpetrators of violent crimes. The loveable Climaco, writing articles like these, must have known he was on borrowed time.

1981

In January martial law came to an end, officially that is. While Marcos refused to relinquish his decree-making powers, Climaco refused to cut his hair, claiming that "Marcos did not lift Martial law. He just tilted it." On 13 February, in the heart of Manila, nuns and priests bearing a giant cross led one thousand people in the largest anti-Marcos demonstration since the imposition of martial law. It was no accident they had chosen to protest shortly before Pope John Paul XI's visit to the Philippines. A mass arrest of clergy would have made discourse between the Pope and Marcos awkward to say the least, especially as Cardinal Sin had signalled his intention to focus the Pontiff's attention on the social injustices and poverty all over the country. Foreign correspondent Keith Dalton observed that "Sin was wily and he knew he wielded influence ... as the spiritual head of more than forty million Filipinos."[4] The Cardinal had also quipped that the three quickest forms of communication had become "telephone, telegram, and tell-a-nun."[5]

A million people gathered to hear Pope John Paul's speech shortly after he landed. His rebuke to Marcos and Imelda, though carefully considered and couched in general terms, must have hit home to Marcos and those who supported him. "Legitimate concern for the security of a nation ... could lead to the temptation of subjugating the human being and his or her dignity and rights to the state."

In that same February an Italian priest was ambushed in Siocon, the village near the estuary where Rob, Jun's sister and I had disembarked from the overladen cargo boat to conduct a malaria survey in the jungle-clad mountains. Father D'Ambra had lived a simple life in this area since 1977, attempting to bring peace between Muslim, Christian and the indigenous Subanon in much the same way as our hosts the Halls had operated, by attending to their medical needs, learning their languages, and getting to know them as individuals.

D'Ambra made the decision to meet with the leader of the Moro National Liberation Front despite being aware of Marcos's divide and conquer scheme. The military was sent to silence the priest because, as he himself put it, his "plan of peace disturbed their strategy of war." D'Ambra himself escaped (most likely aided by the MNLF), but a staff-member was murdered.

In March former Senator Salonga and wife were exiled to Hawaii, and at the same instant Salonga was hit with a subversion charge, by now a familiar tactic used by Marcos to discourage his enemies from returning.

---

4. Dalton, *Reinventing Marcos*, 140.
5. Dalton, *Reinventing Marcos*, 125.

Around this time Jun's son was born, and the new father was besotted. "I spend endless hours with him just gazing and watching his every move . . . at night I'm rocking him to sleep with the radio music on . . . but we are not going to spoil him so he'll remain loveable." However, my friend still made time for political commentary. "The presidential election on 16 June is a farce . . . after sixteen years those gullible ones will be wiser now Stephie . . . Marcos will be repudiated at the poll, but the Marcos machine will proclaim him President again and again." Jun's prediction came to pass. The First Couple, their paranoia rising steeply as they sensed their people were now eager to oust them, indulged in atrocity after atrocity.

On September 15 one of the worst outrages occurred in a central Philippines village, Sag-od, where at least half the population were murdered, not by the communists, but by the Civilian Home Defense Force (CHDF), a paramilitary force comprising the worst of the worst characters working for the San Jose Timber Corporation bordering the village. The owner of the corporation was none other than one of the Philippines Military's topmost ruthless enforcer—Juan Ponce Enrile.

One small eight-year-old girl survived to tell the horrific tale of what she experienced, described in detail by foreign correspondent Keith Dalton, who interviewed the traumatised child in the care of nuns. Keith was so incensed by what he heard, he organised another interview—this time with Enrile himself. This did not go well, the arrogant Enrile with a stoney face refusing to answer any of Keith's questions before finally giving the nod to his bodyguard goons who abducted this brave reporter. In their jeep they drove to a deserted industrial property. Keith feared for his life as they held a gun to his head and threatened that if he reported anything, he would suffer the consequences. Then they pushed him from the vehicle, leaving him to find his own way home.

When I read Dalton's account my own memories came flooding back—memories of October 1968 when Marcos's hatchet man Fabian Ver drove me to no-man's-land outside Millionaires' Row and lounged casually at the back of car, brandishing his pistol. Like Keith, I feared for my life, and the aftermath of what Dalton experienced had familiar overtones. "For several weeks after this incident my phone was bugged, a military vehicle was stationed outside my home, and I was followed on several occasions."[6]

1982

In April, acclaimed Australian filmmaker Peter Weir was directing *The Year of Living Dangerously* in a Muslim area of Manila when threats from Filipino Muslims caused him and crew to flee from the Philippines and finish off the last six weeks of filming in Australia. The story of the film, set in tumultuous Indonesia during 1965 when Sukarno was deposed by a coup, is ironic given that the horrors suffered by the lead characters at the hands of the military were horribly akin to the everyday outrages occurring in the Philippines.

In August the BBC released a documentary *The Third Eye*, which angered Marcos because it featured comments from several former political prisoners as well as Cardinal Sin, the archbishop of Manila, who claimed that Mr Marcos identified national security with his own security. When the Cardinal was subpoenaed to testify in the Supreme Court he refused to accept the summons, and from this pivotal moment the Catholic Church was openly at war with Marcos and Imelda. The couple would now need fine judgement. How far could they suppress the clergy in this fervently Catholic country before the metaphoric powder keg exploded in their faces?

In September 1982 Ferdinand and Imelda embarked on an extravagant trip to the US to meet President Reagan, who harboured an agenda to discuss how the couple might transition to stable non-authoritarian rule. No doubt the Marcoses in turn were keen to sense from the US president how far they could continue to abuse human rights before the US withdrew financial support. Imelda must have turned on the charm, because from that moment Reagan seemed to turn a blind eye to the ongoing atrocities in her country. This was partly as insurance for continuing use of those US defence forces based in the Philippines, but also to ward off a communist takeover. Imelda visited Ninoy Aquino in New York, but

---

6. Dalton, *Reinventing Marcos*, 205.

although she begged him to recant, he flatly refused. Having been to hell and back, he was not about to forsake his moral principles now.

Despite the New People's Army confessing to the March 1982 vigilante-style murder of a mayor and four aides in the sugar-producing province of Negros Occidental, in October trumped-up charges for the killings were laid against three priests and six Filipino laymen. The Negros Nine were arrested, but Marcos had overreached. One of the priests was Father O'Brien from Ireland, and the other was Father Gore from Australia, both countries important to his regime. To avoid bad press abroad, Marcos allowed the three priests to stay under house arrest until their day in court, while the six Filipinos were flung into jail.

At the end of the year Jun wrote with more depressing news, informing me that the communist New People's Army had been nicknamed Nice People Around, many of the Christian populace having now become sympathetic to their cause. Jun gave an example whereby the daughter of a poor farmer had been raped by the son of a government official, but when the father tried to prosecute the offender the Marcos-skewed judge proclaimed that it was the victim who was to blame. And so "the next day the rapist was found dead, with a bullet wound. The case is closed . . . results? Another supporter of the NPA." This crushing of democracy and human rights, declared Jun, was the reason why many Filipino priests and nuns who had not already been detained were fleeing to the mountains. "They cannot stomach any more the abusive officials and soldiers of the Marcos regime." The NPA was now fast winning the hearts and minds of the people, whatever their religion.

Jun added that the military, no longer able to attract any right-thinking young Filipinos, were now recruiting misfits, ex-cons, killers, and anybody willing to get paid to carry guns and shoot the subversives. He summed up with "Instead of being the protectors, they are the perpetrators." On 7 December *WE FORUM* was raided, with editor/owner Joe Burgos and several other colleagues arrested on charges of a plot to overthrow the government. They were imprisoned. In fact, Marcos had shut down the paper because of an article containing evidence that he had faked his war medals.

Jun described how the trial became farcical. Notable characters in this farce were the Marcos-selected judge Jose Castro, often booed by the court spectators, and the young defence lawyer bold enough to exclaim, "Your Honour, what we are after is a speedy trial, not a speedy conviction!" One of the two witnesses "bought" by the military couldn't continue with his false story and broke down crying, Jun declaring, "It is very hard to defend lies Stephie . . ."

When fifty US Congressmen wrote to Marcos protesting the closure of *WE FORUM*, Joe Burgos, under house arrest, felt emboldened enough to continue publishing. People flocked to buy the few copies. Jun told me he would have sent me many more cuttings, except that a thick packet addressed to me would have aroused suspicion. Already we had devised a way of disguising names and addresses on my postage to Jun, and as I had not yet divulged my married name to the Australian press, I felt safe enough for Jun to use my married name. Safe enough for now, anyway.

1983

This was a year choc-a-bloc with political, social, and personal bombshells. In an extreme irony, on 14 February, Valentine's Day, my divorce came through. Steve and I had suffered a tumultuous break-up, and for the first time in my life I doubted myself, my judgement, and my instincts. I felt lost.

Two days later, Australia suffered one its worst bushfires ever recorded. On that first morning I stared over the cottage fence towards the north, uneasy at the red brown colour of the sky and a weird kind of silence over the city. As the morning progressed radio reports trickled through. Parts of the Adelaide Hills were in flames, and soon the breaking news became a tsunami of unfolding disasters. The fire raged through forests and properties from South Australia into Victoria, where survivors had fled their homes and gathered on the beaches.

The Ash Wednesday fire was sensational enough to make Philippine news, and in March a letter arrived from Jun who needed reassurance that we were okay. As for Jun's safety, given that the lifting of martial law had been a farce, and free speech was still not tolerated in his beloved country, I worried that he was taking a grave risk every time he wrote to me.

On 21 August the fifty-year-old Ninoy Aquino boarded a China Airlines plane to take him home. While believing that by returning to his country he might persuade Marcos to restore democracy, he was nevertheless cynical enough to wear a bullet-proof vest.

The military, headed by General Ver, were thick on the ground at Manila airport, "combat ready armed soldiers"[7] corralling Australian foreign correspondent Keith Dalton and other reporters several hundred metres from the plane, so that none of them saw anything.

However, a fellow passenger Rebecca Quijana did witness the assassination. Just as Aquino stepped onto the tarmac, a gunman disguised as a mechanic shot him point-blank in the head. Hysterical with grief and shock, Rebecca screamed to anyone within earshot, "They have killed him already!"

Keith Dalton explains that "everyone knew, instinctively, that 'they' meant the military."[8] Rebecca was immediately led away and three days later arrested on fraud charges, a desperate ploy to prevent her from testifying.

However, one brave photographer managed not only to snap some pictures of the immediate aftermath of the killing, but also to save both himself and copies of the precious film. His name was Recto Mercene. Somehow he had avoided being barricaded with the other journalists in the airport building and was on a nearby airbridge when the murder took place. After a couple of snaps, he saw a man amongst the military escort aim his gun directly at him, so Recto ducked below the window but still held his camera aloft and kept snapping. As soon as possible he managed to escape the chaos, returning to the headquarters of his newspaper with the urgent request to make as many copies as possible before the Marcos military broke down the door. This they did, and Recto Mercene's photographs, in today's language, "went viral," appearing in news items all over the world.

---

7. Dalton, *Reinventing Marcos*, 129.
8. Dalton, *Reinventing Marcos*, 129.

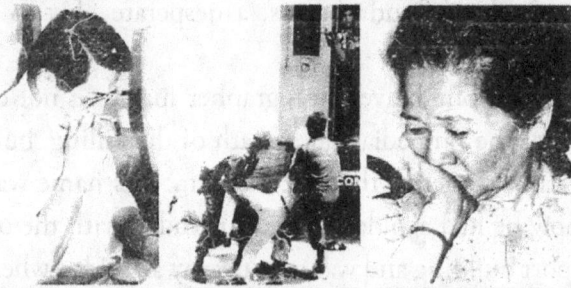

Front page article by Garth Alexander of Benigno Aquino's assassination, Aug 1983, News Ltd, Newspix.

Although Armed Forces Commander-in-Chief General Fabian Ver had not actually pulled the trigger, that same rugged individual who had in 1968 been entrusted by Marcos to arrange those dangerous encounters with a seventeen-year-old girl in Millionaires' Row, instantly became the chief suspect.

So momentous was the assassination of Aquino that the story became front page news in Australia. The lead article in my local paper, *The Advertiser*, was written by none other than Garth Alexander, the very journalist who had sat next to me during my flight back to Zamboanga after my ten-day ordeal with President Marcos.

During the following days Cory Aquino and her mother-in-law wanted the thousands of people who filed past Ninoy's coffin to see his bruised and shattered face just as it looked after the murder. Australian reporter Keith Dalton attended, describing what he observed along with the emotional reactions from the crowd which "flittered from stunned disbelief to furious anger, to stifled vows of revenge."[9]

Aquino's funeral procession was the biggest mass event in Philippine history, the two million onlookers chanting "Ninoy!" and "Marcos killer!" and "Who killed Ninoy?" That night, according to Dalton, the news from the mainstream Marcos-controlled media began with a story about bus fares before a "cursory ten second"[10] mention of the funeral.

Soon after this pivotal event Jun wrote that Marcos had just made "the *greatest* mistake of his life." Like many other Filipinos Jun now realized that he could no longer play a passive role in the fight for freedom and some sort of future for his children. The Philippines was now in foreign debt to the tune of twenty-six billion US dollars, 300,000 people in Manila alone no longer had jobs, and a significant proportion of the population, having little to lose, braced themselves to go on the attack. Jun quoted from his famous countryman, Jose Rizal, who maintained, "There can be no tyrants if there are no slaves." Riots now became the norm throughout downtown Manila, the people emboldened as Marcos's health began to go downhill. They believed now, perhaps for the first time, that with sheer numbers they might actually manage to oust the dictator from office.

Mayor of Zamboanga, Cesar Climaco, boldly continued to criticize the Marcos government at every opportunity, even naming one of his city's main squares "Aquino Plaza" in honour of his recently murdered friend.

---

9. Dalton, *Reinventing Marcos*, 130.
10. Dalton, *Reinventing Marcos*, 132.

By doing so, this wonderful character was recklessly, perhaps deliberately, tempting fate.

1984

On 5 Jan the three foreign priests under house arrest, Father Gore, O'Brien, and Dangan, were enjoying a hearty breakfast at their base when they became overwhelmed with guilt—their imprisoned colleagues were starving. So the trio, accompanied by guards, visited their friends in jail, but when it came time to leave, they refused. The story of the Negros Nine contains astonishing irony. Most prisoners seek to break out of jail, but true to their Christian principles this trio sacrificed their freedom to be with their colleagues. The Nine continued to make news abroad, grabbing attention by going on hunger strikes and being given full moral support from Cardinal Sin.

Jun's work took him to Hong Kong for a few days in March. Fired with enthusiasm for this prime example of democracy in Asia, he declared his fervent hope that he would live to see a free and balanced Philippines with "*real* democracy." His hope was that the Philippines would "become a great nation in the very near future . . . where Marcos will no longer be on the scene . . . a new generation will take over . . . and everybody will live happily ever after." Two months later *Time* magazine's feature story highlighted the pre-election state of the Philippines, quoting Cardinal Sin's blunt statement "If we cannot decide important matters through the ballot, then they will be settled through the gun."[11] Quite spectacular stuff from a leading cleric. On 14 May the elections took place, riddled with corruption and gross fraud until, unsurprisingly, results declared Marcos the winner.

Jun felt overwhelmed with despair. "The only thing that will stop this country going to the dogs is that Marcos should resign gracefully. It's this, or violence." In July Marcos played the beneficent ruler by freeing the Negros Nine, including the two foreign priests, Fathers Gore and O'Brien, with the proviso that they leave the country. Jun passionately assured me and "the whole Australian nation that nobody . . . but *nobody*, believes that these priests are guilty."

---

11. *Time Magazine*, 14 May 1984.

General Fabian Ver wasn't the only one facing the five-member Agrava Commission over Aquino's murder. Two other generals, three colonels, and more than a dozen soldiers of lesser rank, were also under suspicion. As Bill Guy claimed in *The Advertiser*, "whatever the outcome of the proceedings, and we can be sure they will be enveloped in smokescreens designed to obscure the truth, relations between Mr Marcos and the military elite will never be the same."[12] It was July. The five-man commission had taken six months to reach a finding, and the local joke was that "only five people in the country still don't know who killed Ninoy." At the enquiry held in a packed hall, Aquino's brother Agapito refused to testify on the grounds that he no longer trusted the judiciary, the military, or the government to protect any of those witnesses who had approached him with the truth. The courtroom crowd cheered. Under pressure, the commission finally found that Ver was complicit in Aquino's murder, leaving Marcos with little choice but to send him on long leave. It was a shallow gesture, Ver managing to remain conveniently active in absentia. And at that point Marcos made his second big mistake—sacking Chief of Defense Juan Ponce Enrile and promoting General Ver in his place. From that moment on Enrile was a slippery, opportunistic enemy lurking in the wings, waiting his chance.

On 21 of September, the anniversary of the day Marcos imposed martial law, 50,000 Filipinos demonstrated peacefully in Manila. Jun was one of them.

In November, the inevitable happened to that fearless champion of freedom, Cesar Climaco, Mayor of Zamboanga. Astride his motorbike he raced to the scene of a fire downtown, and after supervising the fire brigade to quell the flames, he turned to mount his bike for the return home. He pointed to a display of caskets in a nearby funeral home and quipped, "Save one of those for me." It was then that a man stepped from the crowd and shot Climaco point-blank in the nape of his neck.

The police immediately blamed a Muslim gang for the murder, but Climaco had always warned his wife that should he come to harm, the police would try to pin the blame on this same group. His widow stated publicly she believed it was the military who had carried out the

---

12. Bill Guy, *The Advertiser*, 24 November 1984.

assassination, her statement all the more credible because no one was ever caught and charged. Many thousands of people, including the Italian priest D'Ambra who himself had narrowly escaped being murdered by the military at Siocon, attended the wake. My former host family Alvarez would also have been present, their grief deep, not just for their Climaco relatives, but for Zamboanga which had indeed, as claimed by Cesar, turned forever from the City of Flowers to the City of Tears.

Climaco's death and Jun's hopelessness spurred me to a critical decision. I needed to help Jun in a more practical way than merely leaking information from him to foreign editor Bill Guy. After all, for me it was disgraceful and embarrassing that both Australia and the US were still propping up the Marcos regime with economic and military aid. It was time that my country, better still the world, were given some insights into the natures and ambitions of both Ferdinand Marcos and Fabian Ver.

I gave Guy the go-ahead to describe my private experience with the proviso that he gave equal emphasis to my personal reasons for "going public," which were the loss of my beloved Chito, my foster father Tony Mas, Cesar Climaco, and my grave fears for the future of all those other Filipinos who had been so good to me. And how their deaths were inextricably linked with Marcos. My heart was racing when on 24 November I opened *The Advertiser* to find a massive spreadsheet heading up the Saturday Review. There was a picture of thirty-four-year-old me holding my Philippines photo album; an equally large photo of Marcos; a smaller pic of me diving into Pasonanca pool; and tucked in amongst the text was a face-shot of General Ver. The preface summarised the "Arabian Nights-style interlude" in which Stephanie was "treated like a princess but for which, it gradually became apparent to her, she was expected to pay a price . . . Stephanie remained silent about that experience for fear of compromising her friends in the Philippines and of embarrassing the Rotary student exchange scheme. The sixteen-year time lapse has neutralised those fears but it has not made her story less relevant. It offers unexpected insights into the nature of President Marcos, now struggling to retain power, and points up his relationship with General Fabian Ver,

Feature article by Bill Guy, Nov 1984, News Ltd, Newspix.

now facing charges of being implicated in the assassination of Senator Benigno Aquino."

And then came the detail, starting from that day in October '68 when, as seventeen-year-old journalist, I first met the Philippine President at the dinner in Zamboanga; my expectation of staying as a formal guest in Malacañang Palace; finding myself a virtual prisoner in one of Marcos's private houses; and my secret letter written to myself to help me deploy the strategy needed for my physical and mental survival throughout the two-week ordeal.

Four days later a response from the Philippine embassy screamed the headline "Woman's story a fairytale!" The segment was cunningly crafted, taking my words out of context, indicating I had concocted an intricate lie slandering the president to save my friends. And like most of those in the recent Me Too movement, my story was discredited because of the time that had passed between events and the public accusation.

This hurt, but there was worse to come. Within two days the *Sydney Morning Herald* had rung me for an interview. I was wary, replying in the negative. But then the reporter warned that if I didn't give my side of the story he would run his own version of events anyway. I was cornered. In the following phone interview, although I attempted to emphasize my political reasons for going public, it was to no avail. The sensational horse had bolted, and all too soon the front page of the *Herald* shrieked the tacky headline "Marcos met me in his underpants, woman claims." Stunned, I was only slightly mollified to see the paper had included some of my reasons for going public, quoting me as saying "I wanted to throw some light on the cloak and dagger stuff that was going on in the Philippine, even at that time when Marcos was legally in power."

In no time at all a Canberra paper printed an article similar to the first reaction from the Philippines, its embassy claiming that my story was nothing less than a "hallucination," and my motives were part of an Australian movement to "vilify and insult the President of the Philippines." Never again would I be so naïve. I never dreamed that reporters would seek comments from the Philippine embassy which would, of course, refute the story by attacking my credibility. And it didn't help my cause that in 1984 neither the public nor I was aware of what had happened in 1975 between Marcos and Australia's much-loved media personality Jane Reilly, or Marcos's love child born that same year. Also, thanks to the Marcos-controlled media, the general public had never heard of the 1969/70 Dovie Beams affair.

I sent a letter to Jun, describing the article and the Philippine embassy's cunning responses. Expressing my concerns that some Australians might not believe me, I asked him whether he would like a copy of the article, and would such a bombshell be safe to put in the post?

1985

Like my family, Jun had never once questioned or criticized my actions during my twelve-day ordeal in October of 1968. It was as if he instinctively knew I would do my very best in any situation, which was good enough for him. Early in the year he wrote, "Steph, I really admire your guts for daring to tell what other women would try to cover up . . . that kind of news will be *wholeheartedly* believed here in the Philippines since *everybody* knows what kind of a sex maniac Marcos is. Now he is paying for it because Imelda is two-timing him." Jun added the spicy gossip that as far back as 1982 when George Hamilton had visited his country to promote *Love at First Bite*, Imelda had been "on with him." He finished by telling me he would like to read my exposé and that I should send it via regular mail so as not to arouse suspicion.

On 26 January Jovito Salonga and his wife dared to return to the Philippines after four years in exile. They rightly assumed that after the cold-blooded murder of Aquino, Marcos would know the world was watching and would have no alternative but to allow his arch-rival to mingle freely with opposition leaders. By late July Jun had written his response to the feature article, reiterating his belief and support in me. Despite wanting to share this exposé with his friends he had decided such action might be dangerous, for me as well as himself. "Everybody knows who ordered the killing of our beloved Ninoy Aquino and Mayor Climaco. Now Marcos is getting rattled, and once again threatening to impose Martial Law. We don't give a damn anymore, since he never lifted it in the first place. He will meet his cruel fate very soon . . ."

In late August General Fabian Ver was acquitted by a special court constructed by Marcos before being reinstated as Armed Forces Chief of Staff. This, coupled with the assassination of Aquino, acted as a significant catalyst in galvanizing the people to action. Bob Hawke, PM of Australia, to his credit blasted the Philippine government for its human rights abuses. Predictably Marcos responded by refusing to allow Australia to use the Clark Air Base. Now US President Reagan was caught between a rock and a hard place, fearful that if he withdrew his support, the Subic Naval and Clark Air Bases might also be denied to the US. And if the Marcos regime were to topple, Reagan had reason to believe the NPA with its communist links might fill the power gap.

Jun's job now required him to spend weeks away from Bel, his son Jo-Jo, and baby daughter. He agonized over this, but work was scarce in a country overwhelmed with unemployed people. The new position required him to travel throughout Mindanao by air, sea, and land to the most difficult and dangerous regions. The sea voyages were often undertaken on the dilapidated old cargo boats like the ones that had carried the Mighty Malaria Trio Rob, Claro, and me to and from Siocon, so I pictured those perilous voyages and empathized. He described having to contend with "water snakes, big waves, and the most dangerous species of all . . . the uncouth and abusive soldiers of the Armed Forces . . . on the other hand, I am also brushing elbows with the NPA (communist insurgents) and I find them very educated and gentle. However, to play safe, I just keep my mouth shut, and my eyes open."

Opposition parties were gathering momentum, and Marcos, barely able to walk and covered with bandages, must have been keenly aware that the vultures were circling, especially when in October the ever-popular Salonga was elected as President of the Liberal Party. Making one last ditch at legitimizing his rule both in the Philippines and abroad, Marcos announced he would hold a snap presidential election early in February 1986. This time, however, his enemies knew exactly what to expect—wide-spread and one-sided election fraud. They also knew they must quickly find a leader to unite them in the crusade to come. Aquino's widow Cory became the chosen one, in every way the opposite to Marcos, not only in gender but as a political novice whose ideals lay at the heart of honest democracy. After one million signatures urged her to run for the presidency, Cory agreed, soon transitioning from symbolic figurehead to practical leadership. By December the anti-Marcos brigade now had their Joan of Arc, and the campaign of all campaigns was on the march.

1986

From the outset of Cory's challenge Marcos had been scornful, declaring that she had no political experience. Delightfully parrying that, Cory conceded that he was correct. She had no experience in "cheating, lying to the public, stealing Government money, and killing political opponents." In a display of blatant hypocrisy, given that it was well-known that his wife was now holding the reins of power, Marcos sneered that a woman's place was in the bedroom. Cory simply highlighted the irony by stating, "May the best woman win." Her platform consisted of amnesty for any surrendering members of the New People's Army, ruling with advice from honest qualified people such as Salonga, and addressing problems of hunger and poverty by creating more jobs. Her modus operandi would be to restore her country's credibility and confidence in both local and foreign investors.

The Catholic clergy, headed by Cardinal Sin, promised to support Cory. Filipinos like Jun were suddenly deliriously hopeful, even though they knew that the official result in the forthcoming election would not match the real one. By 5 February the extensive Aquino campaign took place with an eight hundred thousand strong crowd forming a sea of yellow over Roxas Boulevard and Rizal Park. Two days later the voting began, and just as expected, the contrived vote favoured Marcos. However, this time the masses were not about to passively accept the result, and when Cory's campaign manager was assassinated, a crowd of no less than two million gathered in protest in downtown Manila. Cory Aquino called for nationwide civil disobedience along with a boycott of all companies owned by Marcos and his cronies. This marked the beginning of one of the greatest non-violent revolutions the world has ever seen.

Eleven days later, in the heart of downtown Manila, a yellow clad throng (including Jun) led by nuns and priests gathered in a peaceful demonstration to bring Marcos down. Behind the scenes the military split into rebels and loyalists. General Ver, ever Marcos's right-hand man, advised his president to order the remaining loyalist troops to fire on the protesters. Mercifully Marcos refused, but tear-gas was used against the crowd which not only held their ground but grew larger by the minute.

It was at this point Juan Ponce Enrile, who ever since being sacked by the president in 1983, had waited and watched for his chance to seize power, declared he was now on the side of the people. To undermine Marcos further, he publicly admitted that in 1972 he and Marcos had conspired to fake the attack on his white Mercedes to further justify the imposition of martial law. Enrile conspired with some others in the military to conduct a coup against the Marcos government, but the loyal and steadfast General Ver discovered the plot and quashed it, hours before it was due to commence.

Jun described events as happening faster than he could absorb both the triumph and the gravity, proudly stating he was "always on the street contributing a little to get back our cherished freedom." On 24 February the front page of the *Australian* featured Prime Minister Hayden calling for Marcos to step down. The headline was ominous: "Philippines on brink of War!"

As if they had heeded our PM's call, one day later the Marcoses, along with General Fabian Ver and treasures including jewels and rare paintings, fled into exile. On the same day Cory Aquino, the adored widow of Ninoy Aquino, moved into Malacañang. Jun declared, "Cory will be one of our greatest presidents. We love her so much for daring to stand up against the juggernauts of Marcos—and we won't let her down." At that moment in history the phone began to ring off the wall in my cottage. Many papers, even a TV station in Sydney, wanted to hear my story. The *Morning Show* flew me to Sydney for a one-on-one interview with a presenter who hadn't done his homework and asked very few questions. This allowed me to speak at length about the political situation of the Philippines without one mention of my secret meetings with Marcos. It wasn't until after my interview, as I was being shown around the station, that a long-standing *Morning Show* host rushed up, saying she had just learned of my personal involvement with Marcos. With a grateful smile

I replied, "And thank you for not asking me." If I could have described the lady's face, she looked like a thirsty person who had just been denied a life-saving drink.

The very next day a sympathetic and balanced article appeared in the *News*, written by journalist Diane Beer, concentrating not only upon my sensational meetings with Marcos but also my reasons for going public. "People there risked their lives for me," I had told her. "I don't want to emphasize the sleazy part, but want people to understand the politics of the country." Diane quoted me accurately in describing how Marcos had promoted violence in the Philippines in order to justify martial law and dictatorial control, and that this man "would stop at nothing to get what he wanted." And as for what I wanted, that was "for him to go without bloodshed because he did not deserve to be a martyr. I wanted him to sneak out."[13]

My cause was further supported when alongside my picture and Diane's article appeared another by an unnamed journalist from New York headed "No red carpet treatment for ex-leader." This featured Marcos's fall from grace and a photo of the deposed president, looking frail, exiting a plane in Hawaii "to a cool reception from officials." At last I could bask in sweet triumph, made sweeter by a letter from Jun in March describing the fall of the Marcos dynasty from his point of view. Clearly he felt uplifted that he had played a part in the tyrant's downfall and thanked me for my sincere concern for his family in particular, and for his country in general.

Jun would never come to know about the existence of the Marcos diaries, which were discovered shortly after the Marcoses fled from the palace but not made public until some years later. One entry shows the extent of self-delusion from this man who had faked his own war hero story and had deliberately stirred up a veritable cauldron of chaos in his country. "I often wonder what I will be remembered in history for. Scholar? Military hero . . . builder of roads, schools . . . uniter of the variant and antagonistic elements of our people . . . strong rallying point or weak tyrant?"

---

13. Dianne Beer, *News*, February 1986.

It seems from this February 1972 entry that Marcos, although certainly aware he was on the stairway to tyranny, was unsure as to whether his particular model would be seen as brutal or benign. Within the following fourteen years there would be no doubt, unleashing one of the most suppressive and ruthless regimes the Western world had ever seen. As for uniting "the variant and antagonistic elements" of his people, surely Marcos had his tongue firmly in cheek over that statement!

Shortly after the Revolution, Aquino's widow, President Cory Aquino, entrusted the recently returned exile Jovito Salonga to investigate and recover the ill-gotten wealth of Marcos and cronies. This wonderful man, whom I had welcomed on behalf of the Rotary Club of Zambo in 1968, would eventually win the Ramon Magsaysay Award for "the exemplary integrity and substance of his long public career in service to democracy and good government in the Philippines."

Jun's end of year letter was full of elation. He and his family had "celebrated Christmas under a free atmosphere for the first time since 14 long years…there were lots of fireworks welcoming Christmas . . . so we are expecting this New Year's Eve to be the loudest in Philippine history." He went on to describe the generals who had failed in their bid to take power, and "paid hacks" who occasionally turned out to support Marcos in "pocket rallies" and who were no match for Cory. "We love her and will even give our lives to protect her and our newfound democracy."

Jun's last paragraph was the icing on the cake as far as I was concerned. "1986 was a good year for me and my family. We have more plusses than minuses. We were able to build a house we could call our own . . . we have two beautiful kids, I have a good job . . . we have lots and lots of beautiful friends (special mention Stephanie), and of course, I have Bel—a very special person in MY world." There was a feeling throughout his letter of relief and safety which he had not enjoyed for a long time, and I truly believed there was no need to worry about Jun from now on.

1987

On January 22 a horrendous massacre took place on Mendiola Street, the nearest street to Malacañang Palace. Australian reporter Keith Dalton was present with a tape recorder and microphone, standing amongst the 10,000-15,000 "mostly farmers dressed in their rural work-clothes, side by side with mothers . . . and many children,"[14] demanding "justice for millions of landless peasants denied comprehensive land reform in a country where the vast bulk of the land was owned by oligarchs and corporations." When the Philippine military suddenly and brutally opened fire on the crowd, Keith describes the panic and mayhem. Those protesters who weren't lying injured or dead, stampeded to get away "as the marines with M16s and mask-wearing truncheon-wielding police"[15] pursued them.

Keith himself was one of those who fled, cowering behind a concrete pillar along with two young Filipinos, and within minutes the trio were all witness to the brazen execution by police of a man nearby. When the killers looked up they spotted the three terrified witnesses, one of them obviously a foreign reporter. It was sheer good luck that the two rogue police decided that they might not get away with killing a foreign journalist and the two men under his protection. After what seemed like an eternity they casually wandered off, "leaving the body in the middle of the street."[16]

So, how could this have happened under Cory Aquino's watch, almost within sight of the palace? Dalton answered this question via email, reassuring me that although Aquino had denounced the violence, the Mendiola massacre was a reflection of her powerlessness—in the early months of her government—"to assert power over a military machine that had for so many years grown used to doing whatever it chose to do with impunity and little or no accountability."

Within a few days of the massacre, the film meant to show off Marcos's wartime heroism was given a one-off screening in downtown

---

14. Dalton, *Reinventing Marcos*, 237.
15. Dalton, *Reinventing Marcos*, 240,
16. Dalton, *Reinventing Marcos*, 242.

Manila. Years before, *Maharlika* had been banned by Imelda, furious and jealous that her husband had been caught out having an affair with its starlet Dovie Beams. The token screening only served to remind Filipinos that their exiled tyrant had been exaggerating, if not lying, about his wartime heroism. In mid-year 1987, Cory held snap elections which Jun described as "honest and peaceful" while pointing out that Marcos's former Defense Secretary Juan Ponce Enrile, "a very arrogant and dangerous man," was campaigning to garner support for himself and therefore, indirectly, the recently ousted President Marcos.

Jun's unease that Enrile might organise a coup, this time against Cory, was well-founded. At the end of August various uprisings, stoked by Enrile, broke out simultaneously throughout the country. In one week forty-five of the NPA, twenty-five Philippine soldiers, and seven policemen were killed in the clashes. The first female president of the Philippines rightly dubbed Enrile a "National Political Turncoat," imprisoning him for a short while in Fort Aguinaldo. It was clear that from now on Corazon Aquino's success would depend upon her dubious ability to control the military.

1988

By the end of 1988 and into 1989 the Filipino people were glued to their television sets on Channel 2 to watch the Australian series *A Dangerous Life*, set in the final years of the Marcos presidency and covering the assassination of Aquino and the People Power Revolution. Jun wrote that "everybody but everybody is looking forward to view it." To him, its story represented a final victory for him and all those who had suffered and taken risks to regain democracy and free speech in the Philippines. He noted that the series was opposed by "the lone oppositionist senator Juan Ponce Enrile but he did not win. I guess he is just envious that Cory gets all the publicity. Sour grapes."

The summary aftermath . . .

The Philippines embassy had been right about one thing—my entire story did resemble a fairytale. Obstacles had been overcome and good had triumphed over bad. However, there is always a tale beyond the tale for those who dare to seek it, and perhaps it is inevitable that the aftermath will fail to end "happily ever after."

The tyrant died in exile during September 1989, yet the bad seeds he sowed have lived on. The violence and division Marcos encouraged over twenty years would not suddenly vanish with one puff of the peace pipe, nor would the bad elements within the military, despite the ongoing efforts of Cory's loyal generals to root out the rogues. The immense wealth of the Marcos family's ill-gotten gains was never fully recovered, and it remains bitter gall to the revolutionaries that Imelda, her children, and the likes of Fabian Ver continued to live in luxury while their country buckled beneath massive foreign debt.

Perhaps it was Marcos's death which spurred some of the pro-Marcos military to attempt a coup against Cory's government on 1 December 1989, taking control of Villamore Air base at 12.20 A.M. and bombing Malacañang palace at 6.30 A.M. Three days later Jun wrote describing the lightning events which took him and all other Aquino supporters by surprise. "Fortunately Cory was not hit, but she was inside the palace. Gutsy little woman, since she won't hear of suggestions for her to vacate the palace. We were apprehensive since that meant the rebels were controlling the Air Force. They were also able to bomb Camp Crame and Camp Aguinaldo, the 'heart' of the Armed Forces. So, you could just imagine the sigh of relief when the Armed Forces announced at noontime that . . . most rebel planes had been destroyed."

It was only then that Jun knew the tide had turned in Cory's favour, especially when two US phantom jets flew over Malacañang, scaring off the last rebel plane and boosting the morale of the recent revolutionaries. By 3 December, according to Jun, "the bulk of the rebel forces surrendered after a severe bombing beating they got from the Fifth Fighter Wings loyal to the govt." He added that at the time of his writing, on

4 December 1989 at his rented abode in Makati, there were still "about 200 rebel troopers who occupy the high-rise buildings in Makati for their last stand." He finished off by wishing me a happy birthday and praying that I would have "thousands more birthdays to come. Oh yes, and the merriest of Christmases and the happiest of New Years."

This was the last letter I ever received from this plucky, honest, deep-thinking, and loving person. Because Jun was a man of his word and had twice promised that "Only death will stop me writing to you" I must assume that he would have sealed up the letter and wandered out into Makati to post it, before being shot and killed by one of the die-hard rebels.

As time went on the division between Muslims and Christians in the far south widened, wealthy Westerners often kidnapped by Muslim terrorists and held until hefty ransom sums were paid by families. Thus it was for my foster father Charlie Reith in 2011, kidnapped one night from his home at Patalon. The gang of Muslims headed by Abu Sayyef had targeted the Reith family because they were prominent and wealthy. For more than two months poor Charlie, who had heart problems, was marched over rough terrain to many different hiding places in the jungle. His captors had threatened to cut off his finger if his family didn't pay the ransom of twenty million US dollars. The threats escalated to cutting his throat. His mother Susie Reith and family scrambled to raise the money, until finally the ransom could be paid and he was freed. The Philippine police claim that in a dawn raid they surprised the gang who fled, leaving Charlie unguarded. A newspaper photo shows the seventy-two-year old being lifted out by a medivac helicopter, and although he was bearded and thin and the photo grainy, I instantly recognized that wonderful grin.

On 9 September 2013 a crisis erupted in Zamboanga as a faction of the Moro National Liberation Front (MNLF) attempted to take the city. For nineteen days the town was held under siege, a place of terror and urban warfare, until government forces prevailed. However, skirmishes continued, one hundred thousand civilians were displaced, many killed, and the city's economy was hit hard. It makes me sad that my friend Ali's village, Rio Hondo near Fort Pilar where I had foolishly trespassed one afternoon in 1968, was involved in the siege.

Two years later a bomb exploded on the ferry leaving from Basilan Island, killing and maiming many people, with Abu Sayyaf once more the prime suspect. It was the same ferry I had taken several times to visit the island, once as the special guest of a Muslim youth group, which included Ali with his smile equally as wonderful as Charlie's. In his penultimate letter Jun had noted that "our beloved Zamboanga will never again be as safe as it was when you were there Stephie."

During the writing of this memoir people have asked me whether I would like to revisit the Philippines, especially Zamboanga, but as I reach my seventies I feel strongly that such recollections need to stay the way they are—as memories of another era when I as a teenager met a man before he revealed himself to be a tyrant; when I deeply loved and was loved by a guitarist called Chito before he was brutally murdered; when my friends and I frequently took off in a jeep along the coast in the moonlight, singing our hearts out or clowning around on a palm-fringed beach before it was too dangerous to venture out after sundown; when I conquered Mount Pulong Bato and swam in flooding rivers before I was too old and cautious to do so; when I enjoyed the hospitality and kindness of Christians and Muslims alike in the City of Flowers before it became the City of Tears.

Despite reaching the grand old age of ninety-eight, turncoat Juan Ponce Enrile returned to government office in 2022 as the Chief Presidential Legal Counsel in the administration of President Bongbong Marcos. This is irony at its best—the turncoat who once worked for Marcos, who then enabled the ousting of Marcos before switching to organise coups against Cory Aquino, and who in recent times was re-employed by the Marcos dynasty!

Jun's letters have been donated to the Bantayog museum, a monument and research centre in Quezon City dedicated to the martyrs and heroes of the struggle against the Marcos dictatorship. While the letters are on public display, given that the Marcos dynasty has returned to haunt and taunt all those who remember the atrocities, Jun's true name is best kept a secret until his beloved mother country enjoys true democracy and prosperity once more.

Acknowledgments

With love and gratitude to:

Maurice Linehan, my ever-supportive husband whose talent as a Graphic Designer shows itself on the front and back covers of *T&T*.

Jim McCarthy, my sharp-eyed son who improved *T&T* with a massive edit in its early ragged stages.

Noah M and May Rodriguez, inspirational Filipino colleagues.

Elizabeth (Billie) Gobolos, who used her eagle-eye to spot inconsistencies.

Glenn and Barbara Holliman, authors, friends, supporters, advisors.

Keith Dalton, former foreign correspondent, author of *Reinventing Marcos* who has assisted me greatly in enriching *T&T* with his on-the-ground experiences during martial law.

Sunbury Press, with its wonderful crew, made the publishing process easy and enjoyable.

About the Author

Steph McCarthy has been writing for the screen, stage, page and radio for more than fifty years, winning awards across the media spectrum. She has served as Script Assessor for the South Australian Film Corporation and the Australia Council. An editor and creative writing tutor, she has engaged students and adults in the creative writing process, and in more recent years  has been a guest speaker delighting groups of all ages with her biography *Tom Price – from Stonecutter to Premier*. Her autobiographical exposé of Ferdinand Marcos Sr, *The Tyrant and the Teen*, has waited for the perfect moment in history for its publication.

www.ingramcontent.com/pod-product-compliance
Lightning Source LLC
Chambersburg PA
CBHW011716220426
43662CB00017B/2391